**A must-read** for managers and others working directly or indirectly in web analytics. Here you get guidance from the organizational setup to creating value and dashboards—and ultimately producing insights for your business.

—*Peter Munk, senior digital marketing manager, LEGO Group*

*Successful Analytics* is likely to become a must-read for professional managers. It's **the next step**, explaining how to exploit analytics for business success.
—*Professor Ingemar Cox*
*Department of Computer Science, University College London*

Heads of marketing, marketing directors, and SVPs need to read this book to **understand the value** of investing in digital analytics and in the right senior manager to lead it.
—*Jessie Willson, global search marketing and analytics manager, Sony*

This book **moves beyond the details** of tools, technologies, and practicalities of analytics to address important challenges around people and process. Above all, this book focuses on moving from data and analysis into insight and business value.
—*Ashley Friedlein, president, Centaur Marketing; founder, Econsultancy*

Here's your opportunity to address the real issue of why your analytics isn't delivering the results you expected: the problem isn't technology, it's organizational. *Successful Analytics* **dives deep into the management** aspects of running your digital analytics team.
—*Stéphane Hamel, director of innovation, Cardinal Path*

Exceptionally good at explaining the important things. Full of **powerful tips** that are invaluable when you are communicating at the board level.
—*Sofie Westlake, digital marketing manager, Red Gate Software*

Guides executives through the maze of analytics-related considerations and **brings business analytics to life** with a series of case studies that should inspire you to a new level.
—*Niklas Myhr, assistant professor of marketing, Chapman University*

**Previous Books by the Author**

*Advanced Web Metrics with Google Analytics*

*Advanced Web Metrics with Google Analytics*, 2nd Edition

*Advanced Web Metrics with Google Analytics*, 3rd Edition

# SUCCESSFUL
# ANALYTICS

# Brian Clifton

# SUCCESSFUL ANALYTICS

## GAIN BUSINESS INSIGHTS BY
## MANAGING GOOGLE ANALYTICS

**Advanced Web Metrics Ltd**

*Successful Analytics: Gain Business Insights by Managing Google Analytics*
By Brian Clifton

Published by
Advanced Web Metrics Ltd
1st Floor Premier House
46 Victoria Road
Burgess Hill, West Sussex RH15 9LR
United Kingdom
www.advanced-web-metrics.com

See www.brianclifton.com for resources related to the book
or to contact the author.

ISBN: 978-1-910591-00-0

Cover: Mattias Lager, www.addkolon.se
Chapter opening illustrations: Cris Hammond, www.crishammond.com
Design and composition: Dick Margulis, www.dmargulis.com
Proofreading: Katharine Wiencke, kwiencke@verizon.net
Index: Marilyn Augst, www.prairiemoonindexing.com

First Printing, November 2014

Manufactured in the Republic of Korea

*To my family*

# About the Author

**Brian Clifton (PhD) is an** analytics advisor, author, and educator who specializes in performance optimization using Google Analytics. He is recognized internationally as a Google Analytics expert. His book *Advanced Web Metrics with Google Analytics* was issued in three editions and has sold more than 70,000 copies. It is used by students and professionals worldwide.

As Google's first head of web analytics for Europe (2005–2008), Brian built a pan-European team of specialists whose legacy was the online learning center for the Google Analytics Individual Qualification (GAIQ).

Brian is a guest lecturer at University College London and at the Stockholm School of Economics. You can hear him speak at numerous conferences around the world—particularly in Europe, where he presents on web measurement, digital marketing, content optimization, and how these can all interlink to create a successful online business strategy. Brian is currently director of data innovation at Search Integration AB.

# Contents

# Foreword

**If you have $100 to** *invest in magnificent, glorious success from your analytics efforts, invest $10 in tools and implementation and invest $90 in big brains (people!).*

I humbly postulated that ground truth as the 10/90 rule on May 19, 2006. With every passing year, I've come to believe in that rule more and more (and more and more). The reason is quite simple. Every facet of the business world is throwing off ever more data, and every facet of our personal existence (and insistence on sharing) is throwing off ever more data. Data, it turns out, is free; identifying specific actions business leaders can take based on rigorous analysis is not free.

This is why I'm so excited about Brian's book. It dispenses with the normal *omg, omg, look at how much data is there and is that not amazing, let us spend 18 months on implementation,* and gets to what it really takes to shift from data puking to recommending business actions based on data.

Here's one of my personal examples of the difference in emphasis, and what ultimately drives success. In every company, every leader wants a dashboard. "Get me a summary of the business performance. Decisions shall be made!" Analysts scurry around and an intense burst of data, manifested as tables and charts, is presented on a vanilla-scented piece of paper. Happiness? Job promotions?

Sadly, no.

It turns out that the higher you go up the chain of command, the more analytical skills go down, and the context required to make sense of the numbers on the dashboard is also dramatically reduced. Few decisions are made, and if there is a meeting to discuss this it devolves into a discussion of the data quality, missing data, colors in charts, and everything except making a business decision.

The answer? Words in English. More specifically: insights, actions, business impact.

Every dashboard in the world should include as few tables and charts as possible. It should include insights written in English (or your native language) by the analyst, followed by the recommended actions and—the most important critical must-have bit—the impact on the business if the actions are taken.

That vanilla-scented piece of paper will no longer drive one more awful discussion about the data itself; it will drive a discussion of which actions to take first. Hallelujah!!

It is incredible to realize that in the end, data by itself does nothing. It is just data. It is the $90 part—the big brains—that identifies insights, actions, and business impact that will push your company's profitability and customer delight to new, incredible, heights.

Next time you receive a dashboard, look for the balance between tables, charts, and English text, and you'll know if it will add value or waste time.

That's my little appetizer for you as you dive into Brian's wonderful book.

The entire book is awesome. It is beautifully structured, and you should go from Chapter 1 to Chapter 10 on your *we will make the most of data* voyage. But if you wanted to be a little naughty and jump around, my favorites are Chapter 8 (you can read it anytime, and you can't work on the recommendations soon enough!) and Chapter 10 (every time you find a task daunting, find hope in the success of others in the case studies).

I wish you all the very best. Carpe diem!

*Avinash Kaushik*
Digital Marketing Evangelist: Google
Author: *Web Analytics 2.0, Web Analytics: An Hour a Day*

# Preface

**This is my fourth book** on Google Analytics, but this one is different. Rather than making it a tool-specific practitioner's bible (as my *Advanced Web Metrics* series endeavored to be), I approached this book as I do my work: helping ambitious organizations make a success of their business by using data intelligently.

As I have come to realize over the years, success does not depend on tool expertise alone. The bigger issue is the organization. It needs to trust the data and have confidence in the process, structure, and people behind it—things not directly related to the tools being used. So I approached this book very much from the business point of view first, then worked backward toward the nontechnical aspects of the tool— Google Analytics. My intention is that senior managers, stakeholders, and practitioners all speak a shared language and set a common path to building a credible data-driven environment. I hope the method has worked.

As for all authors, my writing of this book was not a solo exercise. It required love, support, help, guidance, advice, friendship—even random and unrelated conversations. (You would be surprised at what can spark an idea connected with data!) The people I list here are those who have directly contributed to the book or to my thinking about applying successful analytics.

Sara Clifton's never-ending love, support, and guidance keep me on the right track and always help me to see the bigger picture of measurement, digital, and life in general.

Shelby Thayer has sanity-checked every word of my last three books, including this one. She is a great analyst, with a ton of experience at driving web measurement acceptance within a large organization, and her feedback and experiences have helped me significantly in writing a tightly focused book.

Brad Townsend is my valued technical editor. He is a smart (and modest) Googler who, as a software engineer, knows the technicalities and back end of Google Analytics like no other. David Vallejo, an expert Google Analytics implementer, developer, and all-round smart guy, helped me enormously with his technical problem-solving skills. Nothing can't be done with this guy at hand! Dave Evans expertly reviewed Chapter 7 ("Data Responsibilities") and provided insightful discussions about data privacy law. Dick Margulis is my trusted editor, who has now helped me write and structure three books and is my go-to man for navigating the tricky waters of the publishing world. His guidance and advice have been invaluable.

Avinash Kaushik has honored me (again) by writing the foreword to this book and setting the scene so enthusiastically and logically for the reader—in a way that only he can. I am lucky to count him as a friend and former colleague. He inspires me (and many others) with his advocacy and excitement for all things that can be measured.

John Wedderburn, Tobias Johansson, and the team at Search Integration (where I work) have engaged in many "quality time" meetings and open-ended discussions that have broadened and deepened my knowledge.

And last but not least, the vibrant and smart GACP community pushes back the boundaries of what can be done with Google Analytics, and importantly, what can be simplified with it.

I hope I have remembered everyone.

*Brian Clifton*
January 2015

# SUCCESSFUL
# ANALYTICS

# Introduction

"We think we want information when really we want knowledge."

—*Nate Silver, from* The Signal and the Noise

According to a recent survey of IT professionals,[1] **"55% of big data analytics projects are abandoned."** Most of the respondents said that the top two reasons the projects fail are that managers lack the right expertise in house to connect the dots around data to form appropriate insights, and that projects lack business context around data. Similarly, the "Online Measurement and Strategy Report 2013" from **Econsultancy[2] asked companies, "Do you have a company-wide strategy that ties data collection and analysis to business objectives?" Only 19% said yes**, a figure that had hardly changed during the previous five years.

I wrote this book for those managers struggling to make headway—to empower you to make informed decisions and overcome the obstacles.

My goal with this book is to get you to think in terms of *insights*—not Google Analytics data. An insight is knowledge that you can relate to. It's a story that puts you in the shoes of your visitors, so that you can understand their requirements when they come to and view your website, app, or other digital content.

A company's ability to satisfy the needs of a website visitor depends on two important factors:

- Visitor expectations, discerned from how they got to your content—what search engine, campaign ads, or social conversation drove their decision to seek you out
- User experience—how easy it was to use your content, to navigate around, find information, engage with you (contact you, purchase, subscribe, give feedback)

It is your organization's ability to manage, analyze, and improve these two factors that determines your digital success (or not). In this book I describe how insights are used to pull all of the relevant data points together to build a story of your visitors' journey and their experiences. With that knowledge you can improve these: as I show in Chapter 10, improvement can be dramatic performance gains in terms of your online visibility, revenue, or efficiency savings.

Yet Google Analytics doesn't provide insights by itself—no tool can. Producing insights requires an understanding of your business and its products, your value proposition, your website content, its engagement points and processes, and of course its marketing plan. Google Analytics provides the data (and lots of it) that enables you to assess these. However, people—not machines—build insights. This is the role of your analytics team. They sift through the noise to find the useful data, translate it into information to explain what is happening, then build stories of useful knowledge for the organization—the insights.

This book is about showing you how to do that. This book is about knowing what to focus on, what you can expect in return, the talent you need to hire, the processes you need to put in place, the pitfalls to avoid, and how much investment is required in order to make it all happen.

This is a detailed book by necessity. Building an environment where you can trust your data, understand it, and make important decisions based on it requires a deep level of immersion, not an executive summary. However, my approach throughout this book is to focus on the insight gained for the business, not the minutiae.

This book is for you if you are a manager who needs an overview of the key principles of website measurement, the capabilities of Google Analytics, and how to grow and give direction to your organization when it comes to its digital strategy. Your ultimate interest is in insights and knowledge, not more data!

In short, I aim to put you in control and provide a perspective on the entire process of building a *data-driven* environment using Google Analytics.

## REFERENCES

1    http://visual.ly/cios-big-data

2    https://econsultancy.com/reports/online-measurement-and-strategy-report

# Preparing to Measure Success

**You know measurement is important** to your success—be it for you, your organization, or your career. In many respects, Google Analytics is just a tool, like the plethora of other data tools organizations use to help them make better decisions.

But web analytics—the area, technique, and industry that Google Analytics resides in—is different. Its reach and potential are far greater than any other tool you have. Why? Because not only can it measure the engagement, transactions, and revenue from your *customers*, it can also measure your *potential customers*—where they come from, what they are looking for, and how close they come to becoming a customer before they bail out (and where on your site or mobile app this happens).

This integration of customer and potential customer data is unique to web analytics—and therefore extremely powerful. For example, the vast majority of websites have very low conversion rates—typically 3% (Figure 1.1).[1] That is, only 3 visitors out of 100 go on to become customers. While many a business analyst is tasked with optimizing for that thin sliver of a segment, there is clearly a much greater potential in understanding why the other 97% of people that expressed an interest in you (they visited your website) did not convert—and using this information to improve matters.

Google Analytics can be used to analyze both customer and non-customer behavior. All that is required is a single digital touch point during

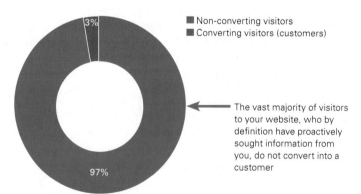

**Figure 1.1** *The vast majority of website visitors do not convert, though most businesses focus on analyzing the small number who do.*

their engagement with your organization. Usually, the touch point is a visit to your website, though with Universal Analytics (the latest enhancements to Google Analytics, described in more detail in Chapter 6), it need not be. For example, a potential customer receives an offer from you via snail mail. This contains a coupon that they take into your brick-and-mortar store to make their purchase. At the point of sale, your store sends the purchase details (product name, value, coupon code, and so forth) via the Internet to your Google Analytics account. The result is that Google Analytics can generate a report on the performance of your direct mailings and sales in your store.

The digital touch point in this example was the actual purchase. If

$a$ = number of direct mailings sent = 100,000
$b$ = number of purchases with coupon = 725

then

campaign performance = $b / a$ = 0.7%

Suppose your direct mail encourages recipients to visit your website *first* in order to obtain their coupon code. The second digital touch point is your website, and visits to it reflect the interest in your offer. Now you have a simple yet powerful set of data that can be analyzed—even if the recipient does not go on to purchase. For example, if

$a$ = number of direct mailings sent = 100,000
$b$ = number of purchases with coupon = 725
$c$ = number of campaign visitors to your website = 8,000

then

interest level = $c / a$ = 8.0%
campaign performance = $b / a$ = 0.7%
website conversion rate = $b / c$ = 9.1%

The extra data point collected in this second list ($c$) tells you that evaluating the results of a direct mailing is not as black and white as just the number of purchases: 8,000 people are actually interested in your offer; without this piece of information, it looks like only 725 people are interested. Armed with this extra data, you can now improve your direct mailing to increase that number—that is, grow the interest level. Simultaneously, you can work to improve your website landing pages to go beyond 9.1% conversion, and you can also try to increase the order value for those

### Business Intelligence Defined

All analytical tools that help your organization understand itself come under the umbrella term *business intelligence*. Google Analytics is one of these tools. For clarity, I define three particular subcategories of business intelligence.

**Customer Analytics**   The mining of existing customer data in order to discover buying patterns and demographic information. Often this information is used to compile a marketing campaign for the upsell and cross-sell of products to existing customers, as well as improve customer retention.

**Web Analytics**   The study of your website visitor's online experience in order to improve it. The vast majority of data is completely anonymous. Google Analytics has traditionally been used as a web analytics tool.

**Digital Analytics**   The evolution of web analytics to encompass all Internet-connected devices that can send a structured packet of data via HTTP, such as mobile apps, barcode scanners, checkout machines, stock taking, call center performance, or RFIDs. With its latest update, Google Analytics is now a digital analytics tool.

purchases (perhaps you can upsell and cross-sell related products). The result is that you now have a great deal more options to improve sales and measure the impact of your various efforts—so you can focus on the most profitable. Powerful numbers indeed.

## THE VALUE OF WEB ANALYTICS DATA

Consider the following exercise:

Many a business analyst is tasked with customer analytics (see sidebar, "Business Intelligence Defined"). Results can be used to compile a campaign for the upsell and cross-sell of products as well as to improve customer retention. Typical revenue increases are on the order of 1–9%.

Let's invest the same amount of energy with a web analyst for the same organization. In this case, it is to understand the pain points of your website conversion process. The information gained is then used to reduce the friction of the process and improve the conversion rate—that is, generate more customers. In my experience, typical improvements are double digits, often triple digits (Figure 1.2).

In addition, the changes made to improve the conversion process on your website are compound. For example, if you make your website 10% more efficient at converting a visitor to a customer, that improvement is not just a one-off hit—it lasts perpetually (though not quite in practice). Therefore, in twelve months' time when different visitors are coming to your site, 10% more of them will be converting than before. Additionally, a visitor who turns away in frustration because of a poor user experience is unlikely to return. But for *every* new visitor you acquire through an improved process, there is a better chance they will convert and become a long-term paying customer. The result of both of these is that your increased revenue will grow way beyond the initial uplift. Your marketing efforts just became a whole lot more efficient!

The huge potential of being able to convert more visitors into customers, or being smarter at acquiring higher-value visitors, is the great ability that web analytics brings to the table. And Google Analytics is a class-leading product in this field.

Suppose that by looking closely at how visitors interact with your website and using techniques such as sales funnel analysis, exit points, bounce rates (single-page visits), and engagement metrics, you were able to improve your online conversion rate from 3% to 4% (a 33% improvement

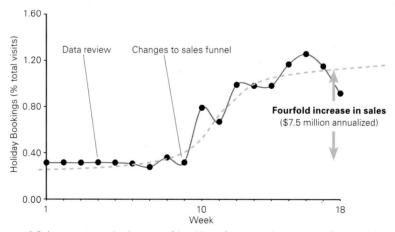

**Figure 1.2** *Improvement in the rate of bookings for a travel company after studying their web analytics data*

in the base rate). What would that mean for your bottom line? Let's look at a hypothetical example. If

> $v$ = number of visitors = 100,000
> $c$ = cost per visit = $1.00

then

> $a$ = cost of all visits = $v \times c$ = $100,000

The visitor acquisition cost is the same regardless of the conversion rate. The non-marketing profit margin, marketing costs, and revenue per conversion are also independent of the conversion rate:

> $m$ = non-marketing profit margin = 50%
> $s$ = marketing costs = $100,000
> $u$ = revenue per conversion = $75

Table 1.1 shows the results of improving the conversion rate from 3% to 4%.

The last two rows of Table 1.1 put the analysis into context: profit will rise by $37,500 and return on investment will quadruple to 50%. Note that this is achieved solely by improving the conversion rate of the site—visitor acquisition costs remain the same. This is the value that web analytics can bring to your business. As a practitioner of over 15 years, I see this potential time and time again. It's real and attainable.

## WHAT'S DIFFERENT ABOUT WEBSITE MEASUREMENT?

I often find that measuring the performance of a website is misunderstood by senior managers. That is not surprising considering that over

**Table 1.1** *The Economics of Improving Your Conversion Rate*

|  | **Before** | **After** |
| --- | :---: | :---: |
| $r$ = conversion rate | 3% | 4% |
| $C$ = conversions = $r \times v$ | 3,000 | 4,000 |
| $T$ = total revenue = $u \times C$ | $225,000 | $300,000 |
| $n$ = non-marketing costs = $(1 - m) \times T$ | $112,500 | $150,000 |
| $P$ = total profit = $T - (n + s)$ | $12,500 | $50,000 |
| $R$ = total ROI = $P / s$ | 13% | 50% |

the years the web analytics industry has struggled to define itself as it migrated from the IT department into marketing.

The principle of web analytics is straightforward:

---

**Web analytics is the study of online experience in order to improve it.**

---

However, managers who require data to guide their decisions are much more used to certainties—for example, the certainties that come from customer analytics about how much money you make, what the profit is, and how many customers you have, as well as operational analytics that tell you how many staff you have, what they cost, what your manufacturing costs are, and so forth.

By *certainties*, I am referring to hard numbers—solid numbers, where there is little or no error. If you wanted to know how much cash your company took in last month, you could simply print out your bank statement. That number is definite because it represents confirmed transactions. Your bank has done all the hard work to ensure that only valid payments are processed, transactions are legitimate, and the money sitting in your account is actually yours. Similarly, if you wanted to know the number of customers you have, you could make a query to your CRM system. That number is definite because it represents real people—the names and addresses of customers who have ordered and paid you. Your sales team has done all the hard work to ensure this is correct.

Things are very different when it comes to web analytics. This is because *all* your reported numbers are fuzzy, fluffy, hazy—in other words,

---

### Describing Digital Analytics

Throughout this book I refer to *web analytics*, as this is the main use of Google Analytics today—analyzing website performance and its impact on other sales and marketing channels. However, that platform-specific definition that has existed since the 1990s is now beginning to erode. Users connect with your brand in multiple ways, be it through a traditional web browser, a mobile app, digital TV, or any other Internet-connected device capable of sending an HTTP request. An example of the latter is tracking the performance of your in-store checkout machines, or scanning badges as people walk into your event. In other words, there are lots of possibilities. The latest version of Google Analytics is capable of all these. More in Chapter 6.

inaccurate. Unlike the traditional business analyst, the web analyst needs to take responsibility for data quality.

## Data Quality and Ownership

Data quality problems come from a variety of sources, the most common being an incomplete or poorly implemented setup: there is no bank or sales team verifying the data (your analytics team must do this, though I have found from experience this rarely happens). But even if you were able to attain a perfect setup, there are inherent inaccuracies. That's because the vast majority of collected data from your website is from anonymous visitors (the other 97%)—you have no idea who they are. Therefore, there isn't a one-to-one correlation of data to a specific person.

For example, if a visitor does not log in to your website or connect with you in some unique way, that visitor will be counted as a separate visitor to your website should they return using a different device—a tablet versus a smartphone versus a laptop. As far as your web analytics tool is concerned, this is counted as three different one-time visitors. The same effect happens if they use multiple browsers for subsequent visits, such as Internet Explorer, Chrome, or Firefox.

What about transactions?

You may feel that e-commerce data collected by your web analytics tool would fare better and be more accurate than anonymous visitor data. After all, a transaction is confirmed as completed, so you have the extra check taking place. That is true, but web analytics tools are poor at handling cancellations and returns because of what this actually correlates to. For example, a return of goods will cancel out the effectiveness of

---

### How Accurate Is Web Analytics?

Don't worry, the inaccuracy of web measurement is something you get used to. It's an error bar. However, that error bar must be continuously monitored and corrected—it is not a set-and-forget operation. The web analytics team must take ownership of data quality. This is an important differentiator between web analytics and other forms of business analytics.

Assuming you have a good implementation of Google Analytics, your error bars should be within 5% of the true number. That is actually a very small error bar compared to the estimates that traditional marketers have to work with, such as newspaper circulation figures and TV viewing figures. See Chapter 4.

the campaigns that drove the visitor to your site in the first place. But if, say, I ordered the wrong size shoes from your website and returned them, the campaigns that drove my interest in your business are still valid, and should be credited for the purchase. So it makes more sense, from a marketing evaluation viewpoint, to keep *all* transactions within your web analytics data (except of course any fraudulent, test, or obvious error transactions).

As with all data, accuracy is important. Even a perfect setup of Google Analytics will degrade over time as your website changes, the web changes, and user behavior changes. In order to trust your web analytics data and therefore have confidence in it to make important strategic decisions, you must take ownership of data quality.

A final point on accuracy is the perception by many people, even smart people, that the vast volumes of data web analytics tools collect make the data accurate. My feeling is that most people are aware of the concept of small sample sizes yielding inaccurate results. Therefore, it is tempting to think that a huge pool of data drowns out any inaccuracies. However, web analytics data is so easy to collect that this common assumption is not true. The reverse can be the case: it is all too easy to collect inaccurate data and lots of noise, drowning out the important signals.

## WHERE GOOGLE ANALYTICS FITS

Your website is in a unique position. As the first point of call for your digital presence, it is where your customers and noncustomers (potential customers, job seekers, investors, press, even competitors) go to find information on your business, products, and services. As such, web analytics is the only place where you get to see the data for *all* of these, side by side.

The side-by-side comparison of disparate data is invaluable for a senior manager. It lets you zoom out and see the bigger picture so you can use the same metrics and methodology to determine the relative success of each area—compare apples with apples, in other words. And that provides you with context—something often missing when analysts come to you with their deep-in-the-woods investigations. Context ensures you focus on the areas that have the biggest impact for your business.

That said, a single tool is not a panacea. Google Analytics (Figure 1.3) is in a unique position to connect your organization's digital activities with traditional offline marketing and your existing customers. Nonetheless,

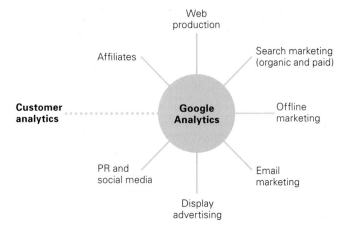

**Figure 1.3** *Google Analytics measures not only your customers' activity but also your potential customers' activity.*

those individual areas still require their own tools for day-to-day management. For analyzing and understanding the performance of these other areas, use your central analytics platform—Google Analytics—as your unified measurement tool. Otherwise you will waste a great deal of time and energy chasing numbers from different tools that in principle should match but in reality never do. When it comes to counting, there are in fact differing techniques, methodologies, and definitions for the same thing!

Google Analytics collects and reports data. It is great for telling you *what* happened and *when*, but it does not tell you *why* it happened. That is where your analysts come in. A good web analyst uses her knowledge and experience to build a hypothesis to explain the *why*. Then she hunts down other data points to either support or refute the hypothesis— potentially outside of Google Analytics. If the data is inconclusive, a test (experiment) is performed. More on this in Chapter 8.

### Data Is Not a Silo
Web analytics is different from other forms of business analytics—in terms of its potential (customer *and* potential customer data), data quality ownership (within the web analytics team), and the lack of certainty in the numbers produced (the large amount of anonymous data). But web analytics should not be treated differently as an information source within your organization from other kinds of analytics. Instead, I want to

## Why Google Analytics Is Not Customer Analytics

The dotted line between Google Analytics and customer analytics in Figure 1.3 is deliberate. I use it to emphasize two important points:

- The vast majority of web data (typically 97%) is anonymous, whereas customer analytics deals wholly with specific people and companies. Even assuming you have a separate login for your customers (thereby identifying them), not all will use this when browsing your website. They remain anonymous even though they are your customers.
- When you track your customers with Google Analytics, the performance of your website is not the same as the performance of your sales. For example, your website may be great at converting visitors into customers. However, your sales may be poor because of returns.

You can do a great deal of customer analysis using Google Analytics. But bear these two points in mind to avoid overanalyzing the wrong area.

get you to think differently about how you treat all your data within your organization.

Most often data analysis is in a silo within an organization: it is set up as a separate department to be consulted with as needed. The people working in the data department are considered nerds by their colleagues—number crunchers, bean counters, analytical rather than creative (left brain rather than right brain) thinkers. As any data nerd will tell you—and I am one myself—collecting or studying data is boring. It's what you do with the resulting knowledge that is exciting and creative!

There is nothing more demoralizing for a team of smart people who have exciting insights to share than to find that none, or very few, of their suggestions or ideas are taken on board by the organization, that no change happens as a result of what has been learned from studying the data. This happens when the data is kept in its silo and the team is reduced to being report monkeys; it's a wasted opportunity for the business and a waste of resource talent.

By integrating your data, all data (though specifically I am referring to web analytics), within your marketing, PR, sales, web development, content creation, customer retention, and other teams, you will be able to create an environment for change. On the Internet, if you are not continuously evolving, even a market leader can be dead in the water within a couple of years.

Building an environment for change using a foundation of solid data is my approach throughout this book.

## WHY GOOGLE ANALYTICS IS DIFFERENT

Two key things to be aware of about Google Analytics are its pricing model (free) and its dominant market share.

### The Free Version

In November 2005 Google launched Google Analytics for free. That event created quite a stir in the web measurement industry (I was the head of web analytics for Google Europe at the time). Legitimate questions were raised: Why is it free? What's the catch? What will Google do with this client data? Can we trust the data provided by a vendor with a vested interest—that is, where we also advertise? (See "The Delicate Questions Answered," later in this chapter.)

What became abundantly clear was that before Google Analytics, price had been a limiting factor for measurement adoption. At Google we suspected this, but not to such a great extent—within one week of launch, more accounts were opened with Google Analytics than existed in the entire web measurement industry before the launch (Figure 1.4).

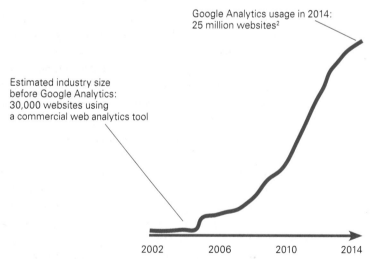

**Figure 1.4** *The schematic rise of web analytics adoption since the launch of Google Analytics in November 2005*

According to builtwith.com, Google Analytics is now found on 25 million websites.[2] Free has clearly been an important driver in that adoption. So have its strong and continuously evolving feature set, ease of use, and large user community that openly shares knowledge and best practice. Those additional benefits have resulted in Google Analytics being adopted by many enterprises as well—firms where price is not a key factor in selecting the right tool for the job (Figure 1.5).

Google Analytics is a robust and user-friendly analytics platform that millions of businesses around the world rely on (it is available and supported in 40 languages). It is also an enterprise-class product trusted by brands that include P&G, Visa, General Electric, Sony, Toyota, Twitter, and the BBC. A longer list is available at http://brianclifton.com/who-uses-ga.

**The Paid Version**
In September 2011, Google expanded its analytics offering with the launch of Google Analytics Premium—a paid version with a fixed fee of

### Google Analytics Market Share
There are two ways to estimate the level of adoption for Google Analytics:

- By viewing the public source code, or HTTP headers, of web pages. This can be automated and therefore is highly scalable. However, there is no way to determine if the tool used is the free or paid version.
- By surveying participants. This is limited by survey size and cannot be automated. Paid versus free usage can be determined.

*89% of surveyed businesses use Google Analytics*
A 2013 survey of 896 businesses (two-thirds of them from the UK) revealed that 89% are using Google for analytics (94% of agency clients). Of those using Google Analytics, 11% use the paid version, with 26% considering it.[3]

*63% of Fortune 500 companies use Google Analytics*
A 2013 study by Enor Inc. revealed that 63% of Fortune 500 companies use Google Analytics.[4]

*Half of the web uses Google Analytics*
A 2010 study by Metric Mail, who analyzed the pages of Alexa's top one million domains by searching for the Google Analytics tracking code text within pages, found Google Analytics was on 50% of the domains.[5]

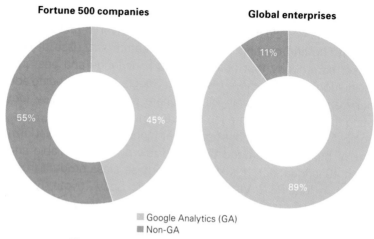

**Fortune 500 companies**

55%   45%

**Global enterprises**

11%

89%

■ Google Analytics (GA)
■ Non-GA

**Figure 1.5** *The market share of Google Analytics*[3,4]

$150,000 per year. The Premium product is specifically targeted at the enterprise market. The key differences of Premium over its free sibling are

1  More horsepower for large data volumes
2  A service level agreement (SLA)
3  Installation, training, and support included with the fee
4  Additional features suitable for the enterprise environment

The Premium product is not a different kind of Google Analytics or a replacement for the free version. Rather, it is an extension of the free product to cater to the needs of enterprise clients. If you were to log in to Premium, you would be hard pressed to notice the difference from the free version. The user interface is virtually identical.

### Why the Need for a Paid Version?

If you are an existing Google Analytics user, the main reason you would consider paying for Premium is data volume. If you regularly exceed 10 million data hits per month (roughly one million visits per month), then you need the extra horsepower of Google Analytics Premium. The free version is limited to 10 million data hits per month. This is written in the terms of service but is not restricted in the tool itself. That is, you can go over the limit and not lose data. But if you regularly exceed the limit, you can expect a call from Google politely asking you either to sample your data collection or upgrade.

If you are new to Google Analytics, item 2 may also be important to you. Large enterprises can have difficulty procuring a free product and would rather see a binding legal contract with commitments from Google with respect to data ownership and processing.

For a more detailed discussion of differences between the two products, see Chapter 2.

## The Delicate Questions Answered

While I was working for Google, I spent a considerable amount of my time addressing the concerns I alluded to earlier in the chapter. The questions are still relevant today. Here is how I explained them.

### Why Is Google Analytics Free?

The justification for a free model is this: Google is a media company; 91% of its revenue came from advertisers in 2013.[6] That is, advertisers pay to have their ads displayed next to Google search results. By the end of 2013, this was worth $50 billion per year.

So by removing any cost barrier for adopting a web measurement tool, Google was able to empower its customers with information about their advertising expenditures. The theory is that an informed advertiser is a happy advertiser. That's good for customer retention and for growing an advertiser's spend over time.

The justification for a paid model is simpler. Enterprises want face-to-face contact with their suppliers (account management), a contract to refer to if something should go wrong (SLA), more horsepower for large data sets (more than 10 million data hits per month), and features specifically relevant to them (such as BigQuery for database-type queries). See Chapter 2 for a more detailed discussion.

So there is no catch—it's a *freemium* model.

### Can Google Be Trusted?

In other words, what will Google do with our data? That's a valid question to ask of any data behemoth. In my view, this boils down to two questions:

- Who—that is, what human beings—will see my data at Google?
- What non-human processing of my data takes place for Google's benefit?

The answer to the first question—who sees the data—is a small number of support staff and maintenance engineers who need to ensure the service is running day to day. Viewing client data is managed on a strict need-to-know basis. If you require someone to view your reports, then it is you (the account administrator) that initiates this with Google. In addition, you will need to explicitly grant report access to Google within your Google Analytics account settings.

In terms of non-human processing, clearly Google wants your data. The company makes a lot of money by selling highly targeted advertising and it is data that powers the targeting. Any data set that helps it do that is valuable to Google. Such data helps it improve its products—be it improving its advertising platforms (AdWords, AdSense) or improving tools such as Google Analytics itself. Like any data-savvy organization, Google values data.

Non-human processing concerns the analysis of vast quantities of data to understand trends. When you need to make business decisions based on billions of data points collected each day, looking at individual accounts would be both time-consuming and ineffective.

My view is that you should consider Google's use of your data in the same light that your website visitors (and customers in general) consider your use of their data. Trust is a key part of the relationship. Lose it, and not only do you lose the customer but that bad experience can also become viral on the web—and a great deal more expensive for you.[7]

## Who Wouldn't Use Google Analytics?

Of course, working with Google may not suit everyone. With Google operating in so many areas now, it has quite a few competitors. If your business is in some way competing with Google, you may not wish to have your data collected and reported on by them.

Google does not build highly customized products. The secret to Google's success for all its products has been its scalability—growing to millions of accounts. If you require a highly customized data collecting and reporting platform, for example data retention beyond the 25 month limit (Google Analytics Premium has 36 months of data retention), Google Analytics is probably not right for you. That said, ensure you understand the capabilities of Google Analytics (chapters 2, 5, and 6).

Other than these two areas, I am struggling to find a reason why not to use Google Analytics. Having worked with Google products pretty much all of my professional life, and worked within the company for three years, I have seen both sides of the fence and consider myself independent (to the point of criticizing Google if I feel it justified). Recommending Google Analytics does not generate income for me. Working with great products does. I would not recommend them if I did not feel they met my high standards.

## WHAT YOU CAN ACHIEVE

As I state in the introduction, my goal with this book is to get you to think in terms of *insights*—not data. An insight is knowledge you can relate to. It's a story or, more accurately, a coherent hypothesis (there are very few certainties when it comes to understanding anonymous data). The point of insights is to put you in the shoes of your visitors, so that you can understand their needs when they come to your website and view its content.

A visitor's needs depend on two key factors:

- Their expectations, discerned from how they got to the page—what search engine, campaign ads, or social conversation drove their decision to seek you out
- Their user experience—how easy it was to use your website, to navigate around, find information, engage with you (contact you, purchase, subscribe, give feedback)

It is your organization's ability to manage, analyze, and improve these two factors that determines your website's success (or not).

Clearly a set of data points, such as how many visitors come from Google, or what percentage went on to contact you/purchase/subscribe, sheds little light on those factors. On the other hand, the purpose of insights is to pull all of the relevant data points together to build a story of your visitors' journey and their experiences.

Insights come in two forms:

- Informative insights—those that help you understand your visitors and customers better, so that you can make informed decisions
- Action insights—those that require you to take action: reward a member of your team for a job well done; move your marketing budget to a better performing channel; remove friction from your website

Google Analytics doesn't provide insights by itself—no tool can. Producing insights requires an understanding of your business and its products; your value proposition; your website's content, engagement points, and processes; and of course your marketing plan. People, not machines, build insights. That said, people are inefficient without machines (tools like Google Analytics).

Google Analytics is a great tool for collecting and processing your data—that is, building reports. And it has over 100 default reports at hand. You can multiply that by a factor of 10 if you take into account all the customization and segmentation options. With ever-decreasing costs for processing, storage, and bandwidth, reports are cheap to produce.

Google Analytics has lots of reports. It has class-leading data visualization features. You can import data, export data, query your data programmatically via its application programming interface (API), query your data with SQL (via Google's BigQuery app for very large data sets), and view demographic information about your visitors. You can animate, segment, customize, filter, and even watch your traffic performance in real time—a fascinating, almost musical experience as you watch the charts rise and fall and patterns come and go. There is more on features in Chapter 5.

The web metrics industry has for many years suffered from features wars—overcomplicating the product with tick boxes of features. That sort of worked when companies sent out RFPs to potential vendors. The RFP approach doesn't work anymore; that is the *big* change Google brought to this industry—a different approach centered around the value of data to an organization. Making Google Analytics free proved the point. And that is the point I am trying to make: improving your website comes down to understanding the two key factors I define that determine success—visitor expectations and the user experience. Google Analytics provides the data (and lots of it) that enables you to assess these.

By extracting data about visitors' expectations and their user experience, you can improve their experience. And that's what you can achieve with Google Analytics.

## SPEAKING OF MEASURING SUCCESS...

| When I hear this... | I reply with... |
| --- | --- |
| We need to see where our traffic is coming from. Tell us which channels are sending us visitors? | This is usually one of the first requests I receive when a client has a new Google Analytics setup. It's straightforward to answer, but a better request is "Show me which channels are producing my most valuable visitors." |
| Content is king on the web; search engines love it. Show me the most popular pages viewed. | A better request is "Show me the pages that our most valuable visitors viewed." |

| When I hear this... | I reply with... |
|---|---|
| If we are smart about how we set up our offline marketing campaigns, can we see if these visitors are also influenced by our online marketing efforts? | Yes, and it's not rocket science. By that I mean that a good digital marketer can own this process. It is not an IT project. |
| Can we track the following: a visitor views an online ad on their laptop, views our website, visits our store, and checks our website again via their phone. Then they go home and purchases from an affiliate. | Yes. And if the visitor made the purchase within your store, you can also track that offline conversion in Google Analytics. |
| We have other tools in our organization that overlap with Google Analytics. They track some of the same things. However, when we compare these, the numbers are different. Which one is correct? | Avoid comparisons at all costs! They are fruitless and a waste of your time. When it comes to counting, there are differing techniques, methodologies, and definitions for the same thing. Therefore, use a centralized approach (one tool), when you need to compare metrics across the board. Google Analytics is intended for that purpose. |

## CHAPTER 1 REFERENCES

1    According to the e-tailing group's 12th Annual Merchant Survey of 2013, 46% of US merchants report a purchase conversion rate between 1.0% and 2.9%. www.e-tailing.com/content/wp-content/uploads/2013/04/pressrelease _merchantsurvey2013.pdf

2    Builtwith.com lists the number of websites running Google Analytics tracking as 25,218,196 as of the week beginning 21 July 2014: http://trends.builtwith.com/analytics

3    Econsultancy. "Online Measurement and Strategy Report 2013": http://econsultancy.com/reports/online-measurement-and-strategy-report

4    Enor Inc. study of Fortune 500 adoption of Google Analytics: www.e-nor.com/blog/google-analytics /google-analytics-solidifies-lead-in-fortune-500-adoption-in-2013

5    Metric Mail study of Alexa's Top 1 million domains: http://metricmail.tumblr.com/post/904126172/google-analytics-market-share

6    Google Q4 earning results: http://investor.google.com/earnings/2013/Q4_google_earnings.html

7    A great example of a bad experience going viral is Dave Carroll's "tribute" to United Airlines, who broke his Taylor guitar. With over 13 million YouTube views, Dave authored a book about his experience of corporate indifference that changed the perception of social media. www.davecarrollmusic.com/book

# 2

# Choosing the Right Tool

**Two versions of Google Analytics** are available—the free version and Google Analytics Premium (the paid-for version). Which one is right for you? First off, let's get price out of the way. The standard free product is of course free to use, though you need to allow a budget for building a data strategy, implementation, and performing insights analysis. On the other hand, Google Analytics Premium is an annual contract, billable monthly, at a fixed cost of $150,000 per year.

Is that good value for money? For those websites with very high traffic volumes, Premium can represent great value for money when competitive tools bill by volume.With some other tools, the more data you have, the more you pay. Premium's price is fixed up to one *billion* data hits per month (approximately 100 million visitors per month). In addition, for budget planners a fixed-fee pricing model is advantageous for when your traffic can vary significantly, for example, by season: you know exactly what your analytics bill for the coming year will be.

For websites with modest volume, spending $150,000 a year on data collection and reporting can look like a big expense. Therefore, the tool needs to be clearly justified within the organization.

In the middle are websites that have the necessary budget but need guidance on selecting the right tool for the job.

All users want to make an informed decision as to which is the right tool for their organization. No one wants to spend $150,000 a year on a product they could have gotten for free. Likewise, no one wishes to advocate a free product and risk not being taken seriously by colleagues due to underestimating the significance of the task it is required for.

## THE VALUE PROPOSITION OF PREMIUM

From an analyst's point of view, the free and Premium products appear almost identical. In fact, if you were to log in to the user interface of each product, you would be hard pressed to tell the difference—either visually or by features. So why is there such a gulf in price? To answer that, consider the four cornerstones of the Premium value proposition, as shown in Figure 2.1: the contract, horsepower, features, and service.

The value proposition of Premium is not just about gaining access to extra features. Rather, Premium is tailored to the needs of the enterprise as a whole. For example, all users love the idea of free-to-use products. However, at the enterprise level, procurement departments have a hard time dealing with free. That's because many enterprises require clear

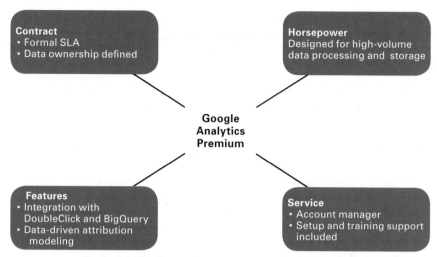

**Figure 2.1** *The Google Analytics Premium value proposition*

answers to questions such as Who is responsible for this service? Who has access to it? What if it stops working? Who owns the data? Who is our account representative? These answers need to be formalized into a legally binding document before the product can be adopted as an official business tool within the organization. That formalization process isn't available with a free product. If this describes your organization, then Google Analytics Premium is the right product for you.

### The Contract

Having a formal contract in place solidifies responsibilities and provides a direct point of contact for ensuring the service is running. And that means having an SLA in place. For Premium users, Google's standard SLA provides the following guarantees. These percentages are based on a calendar month:

- 99.9% guaranteed uptime for data collection
- 99.0% guaranteed availability of the user interface and reporting
- Data freshness guaranteed to be within 4 hours

(*Data freshness* means that the data in your reports is never more than 4 hours old.) If any of these levels is not maintained, you receive a credit against your next invoice.

As you would expect, Google provides no service-level guarantees for the free product. As any Google user knows, the reliability of Google products is extremely high and rarely an issue. In fact, I am only aware of two periods of unexpected Google Analytics outages that lasted more than a few hours since 2005. (Google is pretty good at running its networks!) That said, data freshness for the free product is delayed by the volume of data you have. Often freshness is within 4 hours, though it may be delayed by as much as 48 hours.

## Horsepower

By *horsepower*, I am referring to the software capabilities with respect to its data processing and storage. Premium has more of this available. Having more horsepower means Premium can

- Process larger amounts of data and store it for longer than the free service.
- Maintain report freshness regardless of volume.
- Avoid report sampling.

### Data Volume

Data volume only becomes an issue you need to consider if you have more than 10 million data hits per month. This is the limit set in the terms of service of the free product. That's quite a lot of data—approximately equivalent to 1 million visits to your website per month. However, popular B2C sites can have a great deal more than this. If that describes you, then you need the Premium product—or you will need to restrict the data hits you collect (see the sidebar "What Is a Data Hit?").

For Premium users, 1 billion data hits per month are included with your fixed fee. You can also purchase more—up to 20 billion data hits per month (data volumes can get very large for popular high-traffic websites). Note that the Premium limit is applied on the business entity—the Premium customer—not for each of your websites. If you have, for example, three web properties each receiving 100 million visits per month, one Premium account will cover your needs. That is, you do not require three accounts.

### Report Freshness

Report freshness becomes slower the larger the volume of data Google Analytics has to process. However, Premium guarantees this will never go above 4 hours. If you are using Google Analytics for free and have small to medium website traffic, you will see a similar time for freshness. However, the delay will increase with data volume. If your website receives

## What Is a Data Hit?

From Google's perspective, a data hit is the data sent by each user interaction on your website. The only user interaction Google Analytics collects by default is the visitor's pageview. If you receive 1 million visits to your website each month and on average each visitor views 4 pages, Google Analytics will collect 4 million data hits.

Other common data hit types include events, transactions, and social interactions. If a visitor viewed 8 pages on your site (8 pageviews), downloaded a PDF brochure (1 event), made a purchase (1 transaction of 2 items), and then clicked on your Facebook "Like" button, that would be a total of 13 data hits.

When estimating data requirements, I allow for 10 data hits per visitor. In other words, 1 million visitors per month will generate approximately 10 million data hits.

### Restricting Your Data Hits

You are required to restrict your data hits if you are regularly exceeding the 10 million data hit limit of the free Google Analytics product. If, for example, your website receives 50 million data hits per month, you need to restrict your data collection at 20% in order to remain within the terms of service for the free product.

Restricting your data collection can be a strategic decision (you simply do not collect parts of the visitor journey in the first place, such as not tracking visits to your blog area), or a setting you make within your tracking code on your pages to randomly exclude visitor sessions in your tracking. The latter is preferable as it is statistically safer.

over 1 million data hits in a single day, your reports will only be refreshed once for that day in the free version. That is, you will have no intraday processing.

### Report Sampling

Most Google Analytics reports are not sampled (free or Premium version). However, as you drill down into your data, the data associations become more complex. As with all software products, as complexity grows the performance deteriorates. To avoid this impact on the service, Google Analytics introduces sampling limits.

For the free version, sampling kicks in when the number of visitor sessions in the *analysis pot* exceeds 500,000. Typically you will see this if you have a large volume of traffic or you are viewing data over a long date range, such as year-on-year comparisons.

For Premium, the sampling limit is 20 times higher, at 10 million sessions, though this value is continually being revised upward. Reports can also be downloaded unsampled up to a limit of 100 million sessions.

## Features

There are not a great deal of feature differences between free Google Analytics and the Premium version. This is deliberate. After all, powerful features are what *all* analysts require—the direction of Premium is not about pro versus amateur features! However, a small number of enterprise-class features are tailored for the Premium product:

- Integration with DoubleClick
- Google Cloud storage and BigQuery
- 200 custom metrics and 200 custom dimensions
- Data-driven attribution modeling function

### *Integration with DoubleClick*

DoubleClick is Google's ad management software that manages display advertising—essentially banner ads. Content-rich websites that sell ad space on their pages can use DoubleClick to power the display of ads. The same product also allows advertisers and agencies to manage their campaigns. Well-known brands—enterprises—are the typical users of

---

### Sampling Explained

By sampling visitor sessions at random, Google Analytics reduces its processing load. For example, if the analysis pot you are investigating includes 2 million sessions, the free Google Analytics will sample 1 in 4 of those sessions at random to bring the pot size down within its limit. After processing the sample, Google Analytics scales the results back up by multiplying by 4. This is a standard statistical method when dealing with large volumes of data. A smaller representative subset of data is used to estimate the total values.

Although the scaled numbers are statistically accurate, problems occur if you further analyze the sampled report, such as when you drill down within your sampled data to examine conversion rates or revenue numbers. As these are an even smaller subset of the sampled data, the error bars of the scaling become significant. Sampling is discussed in further detail in Chapter 5.

---

## Google AdWords Integration

Contextual text ads that appear next to search results on Google are powered by Google AdWords. Both Google Analytics free and Premium versions integrate with AdWords, and the relevant reports are identical for both products.

online banner advertising, and DoubleClick had 18% of the US display ad market in 2013.[1]

Premium integrates with DoubleClick so that advertisers can view ad costs, impressions, and click-throughs and view-through traffic (those users that viewed your banner ad but did not click through). Because DoubleClick uses a third-party cookie to track ads displayed across the web, it is also able to gather demographic information of website visitors that see those ads. This non–personally identifiable information includes gender, age range, and interest category data—sports, tech, food and drink, travel, and so forth—and their subcategories.

The free version of Google Analytics does not integrate with DoubleClick.

### Google Cloud Storage and BigQuery

Google Cloud storage gives you the option to export your data and query it using a variant of Structured Query Language (SQL)—a standardized way to query data that is familiar to all analysts. Google's variant is called BigQuery. It's a superfast query engine for massive data sets—data sets too large for standard relational databases.[2]

The result is that BigQuery allows you to build complex, specific queries that go way beyond the capabilities of what can be achieved within a graphical user interface. The free version of Google Analytics does not integrate with Google Cloud or BigQuery.

In addition, Premium guarantees to store your data for a period of 36 months; the free version is limited to 25 months. In both cases Google has never actually deleted any data (I have reports going back to 2005). However, it reserves the right to do so if those time limits are reached.

### More Custom Metrics and Dimensions

The free version of Google Analytics has the ability to set 20 custom metrics and 20 custom dimensions. Think of these as labels assigned to your visitors during their sessions. A typical custom dimension I often use is *customer* versus *noncustomer*. The visitor is labeled as a customer if they have purchased from you. By using a cookie, the label can be set to stay with the visitor on subsequent visits. Knowing this visitor label lets you separately assess the visit behavior of your customers versus noncustomers. The behavior of these two visitor types (segments) on your site can be quite different and informative. Other potential custom dimensions include *subscriber, logged-in, commenter, engager*, and *social sharer.*

Custom metrics and dimensions also provide flexibility—for example, to integrate with your CRM system or your marketing automation system. If these tools rate or score your visitor engagements, you can pass this information back into Google Analytics as custom metric or dimension, such as *top-tier customer* (dimension), *propensity to become a customer = 58%* (metric), *noncustomer but spoke with sales rep (dimension)*, and so forth.

Premium works in exactly the same way; the difference is you get ten times as many to experiment with.

### Data-Driven Attribution Modeling

Standard attribution modeling techniques allow you to attribute the revenue you make (or value from lead generation) back to the referring websites who sent you your visitors. This is a common technique if affiliates are an important part of your marketing efforts. However, it can be applied to all your website referrers. Consider Figure 2.2.

Figure 2.2 schematically shows a visitor to your site who made 4 visits before finally converting (becoming a customer, subscriber, or lead). Without attribution modeling, all referrers are considered equal. If the referrers for this path were a Google search, followed by a social media conversation, followed by a banner ad click-through, followed by a click from your affiliate, each of those referring sites would be considered to have

---

**Metrics versus Dimensions**

Google Analytics reports consist of two different types of information—metrics and dimensions.

A metric is a number, for example, the number of visitors to your website, the number of conversions from a campaign, the amount of revenue gained, or new leads generated.

A dimension is textual information, for example, the list of your top-performing pages, the most effective campaign names, or your best-selling products.

---

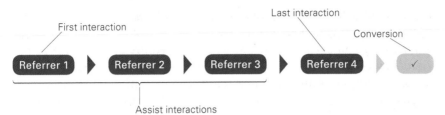

**Figure 2.2** *Anatomy of a conversion path. In this example,* path length *(number of interactions to conversion) = 4.*

an equal importance. Attribution modeling allows you to give a different weighting (a different proportion of the resulting revenue) to your referrals.

Both free and Premium have the same attribution modeling techniques to choose from—you can even customize your own. However, Premium has one extra—data-driven. With this feature, rather than your having to manually compare and choose from different models (a complex process fraught with caveats that frustrates even experienced analysts), data-driven attribution modeling does the work for you. The model *automatically* distributes credit across marketing channels. Google achieves this by using sophisticated statistical techniques to calculate what the weighting of each referral should be—based on analysis of paths that convert as well as those that do not. Attribution modeling is discussed in more detail in Chapter 6.

## Service

Historically, enterprises have struggled with web analytics. Typically they paid out a great deal of money to get the latest tool with the 10,000 or so features they were told they needed (a slight exaggeration, perhaps). Once the tool was in place, it seems no one informed them they had to regularly invest further resources to actually build a data strategy, configure the tool accordingly, investigate the data, understand it, go back and adjust the setup, further investigate, communicate to the business, and so on.

My friend and former work colleague at Google, Avinash Kaushik,[3] came to prominence around 2004 by describing this with his 10/90 rule—meaning organizations were investing 90% of their money in having the tool and only 10% in using it to make smart decisions with it. Lambasting this shortsighted approach, he evangelized passionately to reverse that ratio. (With Google launching their free web analytics tool in 2005, hiring such a smart and vocal advocate was a no-brainer.) Avinash's point is that it's what you do with your analytics tools that matters, not the tool itself.

When Premium launched in 2011 with its fixed-fee pricing model, a key element was service, including help with building a data strategy, getting the tool set up to reflect this, and training your team to understand how to use the product. It is not an unlimited supply of resource, but it will ensure you have a best-practice setup that meets the expectations of your business and that your organization gains the internal knowledge to use it. Service can be provided by Google Analytics Premium authorized resellers (www.google.com/analytics/premium/partners.html), or direct from Google itself.

As you will have guessed, no service is included with the free Google Analytics product. However, a specialist partner network exists of Google Analytics Certified Partners that can tailor a service offering around the free product (www.google.com/analytics/partners).

## DETERMINING THE SELECTION CRITERIA

The Econsultancy–Lynchpin "Online Measurement and Strategy Report 2013"[4] posed two important questions to its surveyed audience:

- For Premium users: What are the key reasons for using Google Analytics Premium?
- For non-Premium users: What is the main reason your organization doesn't use Google Analytics Premium?

The responses to these two survey questions are shown in Figures 2.3 and 2.4. The lack of importance given to the sampling of data is surprising to me—see Figure 2.3. It indicates that good governance (data ownership, an SLA, and included support) is considered more important at

---

### Google Analytics Certified Partners (GACPs)

Google has an official global network of over 200 certified Google Analytics partners, known as the GACP network (www.google.com/analytics/partners). These companies help you with service requirements such as data strategy, implementation, training, and analysis. Regardless of which product you use, you should at least seek out a GACP for advice.

Google Analytics Premium authorized resellers are a subset of the GACP network.

**Figure 2.3** *Reasons given for using Google Analytics Premium. Respondents could select up to two options.*

the enterprise level than having more processing horsepower—although maybe these Premium users do not have high traffic volumes and therefore sampling is not an issue. Whatever the situation, I predict that processing power will become a more important part of the Premium offering as data volumes grow beyond websites to mobile app usage and other Internet-connected devices, such as store checkout tills.

Figure 2.4 shows how good the free product is—nearly half of all respondents said it met their analytics needs.

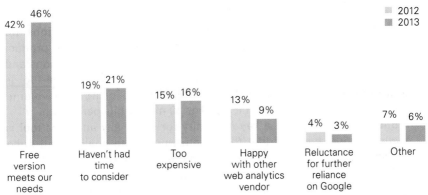

**Figure 2.4** *The main reason given for not using Google Analytics Premium. Respondents could select up to two options.*

For analytics needs, there are four types of potential Google Analytics users:

- Existing Google Analytics users currently using the free product considering the upgrade to Premium
- Existing Google Analytics users currently using the free product and not considering the upgrade to Premium
- Existing analytics users—users of another analytics vendor (or internal proprietary tool), looking to switch to using Google Analytics
- New analytics users—not using an existing analytics tool

Regardless of which type of potential user you are, the flow diagram of Figure 2.5 guides you through the key decisions you need to make. The following sections consider each of the potential user types in terms of defining the criteria to determine the right tool for the job.

**Existing Google Analytics users considering the upgrade to Premium** If you are currently using the free version of Google Analytics, you are familiar with its value proposition—it has class-leading features (see Chapter 5 for examples), it is intuitive to use and comparatively straightforward to implement, it has a large user base spanning the entire spectrum of organizational sizes, it is used globally by more than 25 million websites, it has an active community, and of course it's free. Google Analytics may not yet be an integral part of your business strategy, but it can be given the necessary investment. That investment means people. It includes training, education, hiring, even external help—and a great deal of time and energy to pull all of that together to drive insights. Even then,

### What If My Budget Is Limited?

If $150,000 per year is not available for data insights, your options are restricted to using the free version. The free version is a great product in its own right—I have used it with numerous global organizations and helped them achieve real and significant gains. Using the free tool is about managing expectations—an important one being data volume. You will need to restrict this if it exceeds 10 million hits per month.

But bear in mind that a key necessity for using any analytics tool is ensuring you have a budget for maintenance (data quality) and building insights for your organization (not reports). Therefore, if your budget is limited, use the free tool and invest in these. Without good quality insights, your data project really is dead in the water. Consult the flow diagram in Figure 2.5 for guidance.

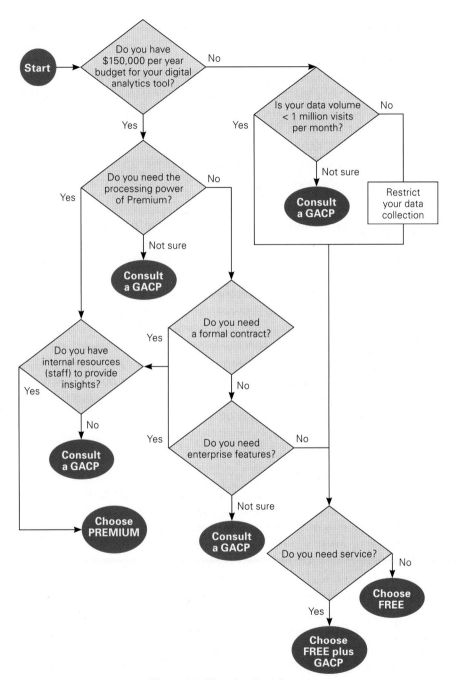

**Figure 2.5** *Choosing the right tool*

your insights need to be trusted and therefore adopted by your organization so that you can move forward. None of these depend on what tool you are using.

If this describes your situation, my advice for you is to focus on getting the most out of your existing free Google Analytics setup. For you, the only Premium criterion you should keep an eye on is your data volume. As long as you do not exceed 10 million data hits per month, you are unlikely to need Premium. Instead, invest your budget in improving your setup (data quality) and using it (gaining insights). Once you have maxed out on insights, you can circle back and consider what additional capabilities Premium can offer.

**Existing Google Analytics users not considering the upgrade to Premium** The vast majority of existing Google Analytics users will not be suitable for Premium. As shown in Figure 2.4, nearly half of all potential Premium users say that the free tool meets their needs. Usually this is because data volume is not a problem. That is, you receive fewer than 10 million data hits per month. However, at the enterprise level it is worth considering the full value proposition of Premium, as shown in Figure 2.1. If none of those are required for your organization, then great, you have just made an informed decision and saved your department $150,000 per year. However, invest that saving in building your processes—that is, ensuring the data stream is of continuous good quality—and then use it to drive insights and improvement (as described in Chapter 3).

**Existing analytics users** Many enterprises already spend $150,000, and often more, on analytics tools and processes. For these organizations, the Google Analytics value proposition is the same as for the free product—ease of setup, ease of use, class-leading data visualization, and a large user community sharing tips, tricks, and best practices. That is, you are considering switching to Premium because it is recognized as a good product (a great product in my view, packed full of innovation). If you can save budget by switching, that's a bonus. However, price is not your primary motivator. You want a tool whose vision and approach are helping you gain insights from your data—not bombarding you with features, complexity, or extra billable days of consulting.

If you are already investing Premium-size budgets in your digital analytics tools but are looking at Google Analytics as an alternative, the decision should be straightforward. All four areas of the Premium value proposition will be important to you (Figure 2.1). When comparing the price with your existing tool, make sure you factor in the service part that Premium includes. I have seen many white elephant analytics tools where the client's budget has been exhausted on license fees alone, without considering the other areas that need investment in order to make it all work. The Premium service avoids that problem.

**New analytics users**  If you are considering Google Analytics for the first time and have no legacy system in place, then getting the price right for your project will be a key initial question. Let's face it. No one wants to spend $150,000 per year on a product they could have gotten for free! It's also not about organizational size. For example, there are numerous multinational companies using the free version of Google Analytics—not because they can't afford a paid tool but because it does the job they need done.

Having an idea of what data volumes your website will generate is your first question. If you expect more than one million visitors per month, then Premium needs to be your default consideration. If you do not know what traffic volume may be generated, use your digital marketing budget as a proxy. For example, if your digital marketing budget is above $1 million per month, you are likely to generate more than 1 million visits, you are likely to be using Google's display advertising network, and you will want to dissect the results of all your marketing efforts rigorously. For any of these you should explore Premium in detail.

If neither of these applies to you, then the next question to consider is whether you have a need for a formal contract and SLA. If you are comfortable without having these in place, then you can safely start off your analytics investment with the free product. As your knowledge grows (typically over the next year or so), you can consider the value of upgrading to Premium again.

## JUSTIFYING THE BUDGET

At the enterprise level, a budget of this size can always be made available. However, justifying the idea that budget should be spent on your team and its tools is what determines if you actually get it. So how can we justify $150,000 per year on a tool, and what else do you need to allow for to make it a success?

The answers to these questions are *value* and *resources*, respectively. That is, calculate what your website is worth to your organization (its dollar

**A Painless Upgrade Process**

If you are already a free Google Analytics user, then the upgrade to Premium consists of Google flipping a switch once your contract is in place. No changes to your site or its tracking code are required, and you can view all your historical data after the switch.

value), then invest in the resources to measure and improve it (its performance and value).

## Website Value: What Is Your Site Worth?

Calculating the value of your website is straightforward when you are a transactional site. You look at the total amount of revenue collected in the relevant report. Figure 2.6 is an example taken directly from a Google Analytics report for a travel website. The value of the site is $576,000 for the month.

In addition, you have reports available where you can quickly ascertain your conversion rate, the value of each page on your website, and the value of each visitor—broken down by marketing channel and your specific campaigns. Both free and Premium versions automatically do this for you (it's a great feature of the product).

If you are a non-transactional website (the vast majority of enterprise websites are not e-commerce), then value is much harder to determine. In fact, I rarely see the calculation even attempted. However, without knowing the dollar value of your website, you are missing out on the big picture of what your website is capable of.

Monetizing your non-transactional site is critical to your success. Without it, there is a serious danger your website is just a pet project—nice to have but not treated as a serious part of the business. Hence $150K per year for a measurement tool is never going to see the light of day in your organization, and rightly so. As Jim Sterne, founder of the eMetrics Summit series[5] said, "You need to calculate the return on investment for measuring your return on investment."

Monetizing a non-commerce website is not rocket science but does require time and energy to logically think through your website's goals

| Quantity | Unique Purchases | Product Revenue | Average Price | Average QTY |
|---|---|---|---|---|
| 780 | 713 | $575,818.00 | $738.23 | 1.09 |
| % of Total: 100.00% (780) | % of Total: 100.00% (713) | % of Total: 100.00% ($575,818.00) | Site Avg: $738.23 (0.00%) | Site Avg: 1.09 (0.00%) |

**Figure 2.6** *E-commerce performance data is readily available in Google Analytics.*

and assign values to them. For example, if your website generates sales inquiry leads and you know what percentage of them result in a sale, and you also know your average order value, then you can assign a value to your website leads.

Here's an example:

- Your website receives 250,000 visitors per month.
- Your lead generation form (new sales inquiry) has an industry average conversion rate of 3.0%. That is 7,500 sales leads per month.
- Your sales team is able to convert 1 in 10 leads to a customer (750).
- Your average order value, which happens away from your website, is $1,000.

Calculating the value backwards results in your lead generator form's being worth $100 per lead. That is a total of $750,000 per month (the value of your website), or $3 per visitor.

The calculations can get a great deal more involved when you have multiple ways a visitor can become a lead—such as file downloads, newsletter subscriptions, email links, click-to-call buttons, and video demonstrations. But the calculations are no more complicated than this.

Taking this calculation a step further, not all website revenue is profit. Assuming you have a 50% profit margin, your website is generating $375,000 per month of gross profit (sales minus cost of sales).

### When Website Value Increases

Now let's suppose that with a good understanding of your digital traffic you can increase your lead generation (or e-commerce) conversion rate by a conservative 5%—that is, from 3.0% to 3.15%. Using $750,000 per

---

**Calculating Your Website Conversion Rate**

Google Analytics calculates your website conversion rate for you automatically. It is defined as

$$\frac{number\ of\ visits\ that\ convert*}{total\ number\ of\ visits}$$

\* Purchase or complete a lead generation form

If you have multiple conversion points (for example, a purchase and a lead generation form), you can select the individual conversion rates within your reports.

---

month as our benchmark, the additional improvement in the conversion rate yields an extra $37,500 per month in revenue, or $18,750 per month in gross profit. Annualized, this will pay for your Premium license with $75,000 left over to invest in insights—that is, your staff!

I consider this the tipping point. If you value your website at approximately $9–$10 million per year ($750,000 × 12), you can justify a $150,000-per-year investment in an enterprise-class web analytic tool. That is based purely on being able to deliver a 5% improvement in sales or leads, or alternatively being 5% more efficient with your current digital marketing budget. Most probably it will be a combination of both.

My purpose with this section is to provide you with guidance on how to estimate the value of your website so you can make an informed decision on whether free or Premium is the right tool for you. Of course, the real value of your data is more involved than the calculation I have presented. An extreme example of data value is Twitter—valued at $18 billion in 2013, yet its losses for the third quarter were $64.6 million.[6] Twitter's value comes from the fact that it has data (tweet patterns, geographic and biographic data) on over 250 million active users. Clearly a different type of calculation is required when your data has intrinsic value.

### Justification Rule #1—the Tipping Point

If your website is not contributing at least $10 million per year to your business, do not pay for Google Analytics Premium. Instead, invest in the resources required to get the most out of the free version.

### Resources: Do You Have Them?

If analysis of your digital data is going to be someone's full-time job—that is, working on bringing insights to the business on a day-to-day basis—then consider Premium the right tool (even more so if there is a team of people involved). On the other hand, if the investment in analysis is only part-time, say only one day per week, I recommend the free product.

Why is staffing so important?

Spending only one to two days a week analyzing your website reports will not allow you to explore the capabilities of the Premium product in any depth. You would be constantly scratching the surface without the time to go deep. Enterprise-level analysis is a full-time job for at least one person. Incidentally, this is the same for the free product, but at least it has no cost.

Of course, you could (and should) hire a consulting expert to do the deep-dive stuff for you. However, that external person or organization still needs to be integrated within your business, or they become a data silo—capable of little or no impact—in which case you need the resources to manage and integrate them properly. Chapter 8 discusses resource and team building in more detail.

**Justification Rule #2—People Are More Important than Tools**
If you cannot commit one full-time person to work with your data insights (even if you hire a third-party expert to help), do not pay for Google Analytics Premium.

## GAINING EXECUTIVE BUY-IN

Part of my goal with this book is to get you to move away from thinking about your digital performance in terms of data. That's a dichotomy for me—data of course are your building blocks and a great deal of this book (and my life!) concerns understanding its collection and quality. However, a data report is a snapshot—a status update, if you will—that allows you to see where your website is at that particular time. That is useful initially, but *insights* are where you need to get to rapidly if you want your data to help improve your business. Otherwise, your web analytics project just remains a cost to the business with no return on investment.

An insight is *knowledge*. It's not a data report. An insight tells a story of what is happening on your website and is therefore derived from your reports. It takes the form of a hypothesis—what you think is happening and why—built from cross-referencing your report data, looking for correlations, segmenting, visualizing, trending, and so on. This is followed by an action plan—what you are going to do about it. The process requires intelligent people with the propensity to change—that is, to not be afraid to take a calculated risk (based on good data) to change and experiment, with the objective of improving things and gaining knowledge. This is the role of your analyst team.

Analysts thrive on data; executives need insights.

Regardless of which product is right for your organization, you need to set aside a budget for insights—effectively a budget for building your team.

Your team could be one or more people working as a bridge between marketing, web development, app development, and sales. Or, if your organization is still in the early stages of analytics maturity, your insights team could be a third-party GACP agency. Often it is a combination of both, where in-house immediacy and business knowledge work alongside a consultancy with a breadth of digital analytics experience (see Chapter 8). That way, your data can mature into insights.

When you bring insights (not data) to the other senior decision makers of your organization, you will gain the buy-in to grow your team and invest in the tools you need. Every manager wants to base decisions on good data—I have never found resistance to the principle of measurement itself. However, providing insights, such as savings made or opportunities identified or grasped, will give you more control over the level of investment required to go further. What executive wouldn't want more of those?

## SPEAKING OF CHOOSING THE RIGHT TOOL...

| When I hear this... | I reply with... |
| --- | --- |
| We are a startup and estimate our website will be worth about $1 million a year to us. Should we be using Premium? | In terms of revenue numbers alone, my answer is no, use the free product, and invest in insights first. That is, hire someone or use a third party such as a GACP. You will see a much greater return on this than by spending your budget on a tool. Review the decision each year—upgrading is straightforward and painless. |
| We are a web portal and our free version of Google Analytics shows 90 million visits per month. Our margins are tight and we do not wish to invest in Premium. What are our options? | You are currently in breach of the Google Analytics terms of service. You need to restrict the data you send to Google by either not tracking certain interactions (for example, turn off event tracking) or sampling the data you collect (for example, only track 10% of sessions). |
| We track multiple websites around the globe, mobile apps, and point-of-sale transactions in stores. In short, this is more than 1 billion data hits per month. Can this all be tracked together so we can compare apples with apples? | Yes, any Internet-enabled device is capable of being tracked by Google Analytics (both free and Premium versions). For such high data volumes, you will need Premium. You can extend your fixed-fee contract with tiered pricing up to 20 billion data hits per month. |

| When I hear this... | I reply with... |
|---|---|
| We have the budget to either hire a digital analyst and use the free product, or use Premium—but not both. What is the best option? | Always, always hire good people ahead of investing in a tool. This does not need to be a full-time position. For example, you can pay as you go with the services of a GACP. If or when you have exhausted all the possibilities of the free version (that can take some time!), look back and consider what Premium can offer you in addition. Review Chapter 8. |
| We have a large volume of data but no internal resources to help us understand it. In short, we do not even understand how to use the free version. Hence the CEO will not invest in Premium, and we are breaking the current Google Analytics terms of service. What shall we do? | If you are still trying to come to grips with your digital measurement approach, stick with the free product and restrict your data collection to below the 10 million hits per month threshold. Invest your budget in insights—either hiring someone or using a third-party GACP, or both. When you have grown your analytics maturity sufficiently (this typically takes a year or two), revisit your tool requirements. |

## CHAPTER 2 REFERENCES

1     www.bloomberg.com/news/2013-02-28/facebook-buys-microsoft-atlas-ad-placement-tool-in-google-combat.html

2     https://developers.google.com/bigquery

3     Avinash Kaushik is probably the most popular of all web metrics gurus. As *the* Digital Marketing Evangelist at Google, he has authored two best-selling books on web analytics and founded the popular blog Occam's Razor http://google.com/+avinash. Listening to Avinash speak at conferences is well worth the money.

4     Econsultancy and Lynchpin. "Online Measurement and Strategy Report 2013": http://econsultancy.com/reports/online-measurement-and-strategy-report

5     The eMetrics Summit series: www.emetrics.org

6     http://www.bbc.co.uk/news/business-24819238

# Setting Expectations
# and Building the Process

1. INSTALLATION

2. TRAINING

3. INSIGHTS

**Although expectations and processes are** by nature specific to each organization, there is a great deal of commonality. Regardless of organization size, business sector, market (geo-location), or analytics tools used, the steps required to start off a digital measurement project—and what it takes to make it all work—are remarkably similar. It's how you achieve them that is specific to your organization.

Chapter 1 (Figure 1.3) outlines my view of the digital measurement world, using Google Analytics as your unified web measurement platform. That is a realistic ambition, though it does take time, energy, and money to achieve. Figure 3.1 shows the four required phases of implementing a digital data strategy within your organization.

Applied in order, these are

1 Installation—getting the data in by installing Google Analytics. Collecting data from your website, mobile apps, checkout tills, or any Internet-connected device that is relevant to your customers.
2 Configuration—structuring the data so it makes sense—for example, defining filters, segmentation, custom reports, or campaign tracking.

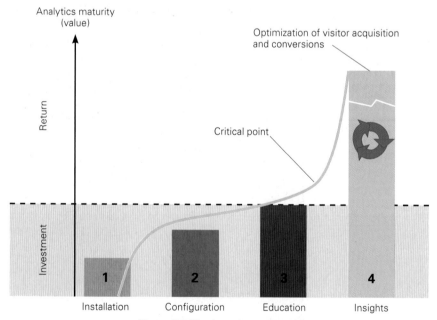

**Figure 3.1** *The four-phase process*

**3** Education—ensuring your team understands how to use Google Analytics and interpret the reports.

**4** Insights—studying the data to glean information and ultimately gain knowledge to drive informed change of your organization's digital strategy.

The vertical axis of Figure 3.1 is a representation of what your data gives back to your organization. It can be monetary value or a perceived value—that is, your organization's analytics maturity (its ability to use data effectively.[1] At the lower extreme of Figure 3.1, the data has very little value to you—it is not trusted to be used for making important decisions. Conversely, at the higher extreme the data is relied upon to drive the business forward.

The first three items (installation, configuration, education) are a cost to your organization. You need to invest in order to make them happen. Hence the value or maturity during these phases remains low but is growing rapidly. The phases must be applied in order—installation comes first—though the phases do overlap. For example, once data starts to come in, you can commence with configuring (structuring) the data—it is not necessary to complete one phase before commencing the next. However, do not change the order of the phases. For example, training people before you have structured your data is a sure way to waste valuable training days—people cannot focus on, or maintain interest in, data that makes no sense to them.

The fourth phase, insights, is where your organization needs to be in order for you to see a return on your analytics investment. That is the phase where you gain back more than you put in. This can be because your data has helped you improve your website and therefore convert a greater percentage of visitors into customers. Or it can be because your data has enabled you to better focus your marketing budgets—that is, gain more customers for the same marketing spend. Both are good news.

The change in the value of your data when you reach phase 4 can be dramatic. For example, the graph shown in Figure 1.2 shows a return that is more than 100 times greater than the total analytics investment! This critical point is reached if and when you are willing to take on board change—such as changing your website architecture or its content, or changing your marketing approach. That sounds straightforward and quite obvious. However, I have found that an organization's ability to change can be a major hurdle to moving significantly beyond the dotted "break-even" line of Figure 3.1.

### Repeating the Process

The last phase of Figure 3.1 shows a cyclical arrow. This is to indicate that all the phases (1–4) should be repeated periodically. For example, over time the data quality of your Google Analytics implementation will deteriorate. This is because of web content updates, mobile app updates, developers forgetting to add the tracking code, the tracking code no longer reflecting the actions your visitors take, technology changes, people using the web in new and different ways, and so forth. It is therefore important to continually assess all four phases of the process and adjust accordingly.

The optimal reassessment frequency depends on how often you change your digital content. I recommend reviewing quarterly, or whenever there is a significant change of content—for example, a new website design or new platform implementation (new web server or replacement content management system [CMS]). At the very least you should reassess your Google Analytics implementation and configuration on an annual basis. This review should coincide with your annual strategy and budget planning period, as it may affect those.

## WHY CHANGE IS DIFFICULT, AND HOW TO OVERCOME RESISTANCE

Unfortunately, the most common outcome for any data project is stagnation. Once the initial excitement of collecting, organizing, and reporting on the data has dissolved, nothing else really happens. Yes, there are a few tweaks made here and there and maybe an organizational change (you hire someone to look after all this new data). You will have numerous data reports to review, but essentially the digital strategy remains the same as before. You may have guessed by now, that's an attitude I am passionate about changing.

I have yet to come across a senior executive who does not believe in the principle of measurement. But senior decision makers are not analysts. They have no real interest in the data itself—such as how it is collected, how it is cleansed, what advanced filters or segmentation options were applied, or what custom reports have been built. Those are not relevant to senior decision makers (they assume that has been taken care of).

On the other hand, what hypothesis you have, the conclusions and recommendations drawn from it, and an estimate of how reliable (accurate) those are, is of great importance to the business. In short, these are your *data insights*, the information and knowledge gained from studying the data that relate to the business. Executives crave this.

Insights are what executives require in order to make informed decisions and move the business forward. Unfortunately, this is where most analytics projects go wrong—they present data instead. By only having data to discuss at the decision-making table, you limit any impact. This is because without insights, the onus of understanding is placed on non-data experts. No disrespect to the knowledge and intellect of anyone in the executive suite (many are analytical thinkers), but interpreting data is not their role—how to use information is. Therefore, any data team has to make providing insights its priority. This means learning how to tell stories with data.

---

**Analysts thrive on data; executives need insights.**

---

## The Importance of Storytelling

Communicating insights across an organization means using the data to describe a *story* that a person can directly relate to—in this case the senior decision makers of your organization. If you can communicate a compelling story with your data, you will get the executive buy-in to make the necessary changes for improvement, be it for your website, mobile apps, point-of-sales cross-sell performance, stock-keeping, event promotion—in fact, any Internet-connected device.[2]

An analytics team needs storytelling skills for two reasons:

- We are all resistant to change; one data point (or even several hundred) will not overcome this by itself.
- We all have a natural skepticism to data that does not show a direct causal effect we can relate to in our lives.

A clinical analysis of data can paint a bleak picture of underperformance. But on its own, data cannot take into account other indirect, though related, factors. It may be the case, for example, that performance is down in one area because the business focus was elsewhere at that time. Similarly, data can also give a misleading impression of success—for example, a competitor discontinuing a product at a time that coincides with your campaign launch for a similar product—in other words, luck. Hence data requires context.

Likewise, data without a context that you can relate to in your day-to-day job is just a number (the "so what?" effect). For example, the percentage of your visitors that add an item to their shopping cart—what does that number mean to you, me, or anyone else? It doesn't tell us *why* the thousands of visitors who come to your website do, or do not, do this. Without an answer (a hypothesis), the recipient of data such as "38% of our visitors add at least one item to their shopping cart" is left with a "so what?" feeling. The data is meaningless to the business.

The obvious answer to the "so what?" question is the hypothesis that 38% of visitors are ready to buy, but in reality that hypothesis is often unfounded. People visit the site to check your delivery charges, stock levels, and the final price with all the additional charges that need to be added. In fact, checking the final price turns out to be very common user behavior for visitors of travel websites and for any visitor purchasing from an overseas supplier.

Building a story is about getting your analytical points across while also addressing both these issues. It is a skill that is acquired through experience rather than formal education. I provide storytelling examples in Chapter 10.

## THE WORK PROCESS

This section focuses on building a process for website analytics. However, it is equally applicable to tracking mobile apps or any other Internet-connected process.

### Using Data to Tell a Story

An expert proponent in the art and science of using data to tell a story is Hans Rosling.[3] He is a professor of global health at Sweden's Karolinska Institute. His work focuses on dispelling common myths about the developing world. Rosling's presentations are grounded in solid statistics illustrated by the visualization software he co-developed called Trendalyzer (www.gapminder.org). This innovative and free tool brings data to life by transforming boring statistics into animated and interactive bubble charts. It makes discussing global trends crystal clear and even fun.

Trendalyzer was purchased by Google in March 2007 (after the Google founders met Rosling at a TED talk). The tool is available as a Google visualization gadget[4] and incorporated into Google Analytics—both free and paid versions—and is known as the Motion Chart feature.

Hearing Hans Rosling speak is both educational and fun. I recommend the following TED talk as a taster:

www.ted.com/talks/hans_rosling_the_good_news_of_the_decade.html

Figure 3.2 shows how each of the four phases from Figure 3.1 flow into the next and the entire process is cyclical.

In addition to the breakdown of what work each phase requires, the flow in Figure 3.2 illustrates that although the order of the process is important, one phase does not have to be completed before the next can start, so you can maintain momentum for the project. For example, phases 3 and 4 run in parallel; as you gain insights you grow knowledge, and vice versa.

The metaphor I like when I describe this process is the building and launching of a ship (phases 1 and 2), and its initial voyages (phases 3 and 4). Both processes require a significant amount of planning and investment to get the project off the ground, involve multiple people to make it happen, and produce white elephants if they are not subsequently used by people to do real-world tasks.

## Phase 1—Installation

The installation phase is where a great deal of your project's heavy lifting takes place (building the ship). Include all project *actors* and stakeholders in this phase. The actors include the analytics team and at least

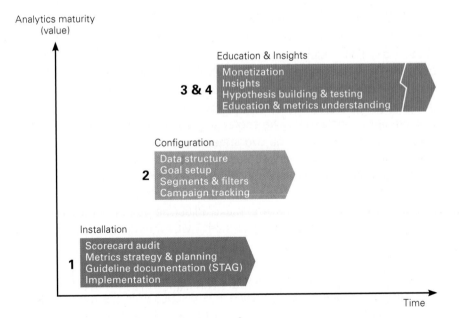

**Figure 3.2** *The four-phase process in detail, with overlapping phases*

one member of the development team that will implement the resulting tracking code on your pages. Actors should also include a member of each of the departments relevant to the project that are represented in Figure 1.3—marketing, public relations, social media, sales, affiliate management, design, and content writers.

Phase 1 includes four steps:

- Scorecard audit
- Metrics strategy and planning
- Guideline documentation
- Implementation

### Scorecard Audit

The scorecard audit is the first step. It assesses your current data situation—its completeness and its quality. If you have an implementation of Google Analytics already (getting the basic tracking code on your pages is straightforward), a scorecard audit is a 15-point checklist to highlight what you currently have set up and working correctly, as well as what is missing or not working. If you do not have Google Analytics in place, the audit is the same, though the content focuses on what needs to be tracked, rather than what is being tracked.

You can use the scorecard method to benchmark your data quality and to assess what is required for your organization to have a complete picture of its digital performance. Armed with this information, you will be able to ascertain how big a project you have taken on, and what resources, budget, and timeline are required to complete all the phases. In other words, you can set expectations. The scorecard is your blueprint for the project, and its importance cannot be overstated.

An example of a summary scorecard is shown in Figure 3.3. Note that once a Google Analytics account is opened and the standard tracking code is deployed across your pages, none of the remaining items (3–15) is tracked by default. You have to make adjustments to the tracking code, to your marketing campaigns, or to the HTML within your pages to make that happen.

Each of the listed items in Figure 3.3 is weighted according to its importance. That is, how important is it for tracking your visitor's user-journey? (How important it is for your business is discussed in the next section.) The visual presentation is shown as a traffic light system—red, yellow, green—to signify if there is a problem, or whether that item is reporting

| Scorecard Summary | | Weight | Status | Weighted Score |
|---|---|---|---|---|
| 1 | Account setup and governance | 1.0 | | 5 |
| 2 | Tracking code deployment | 1.0 | | 10 |
| 3 | AdWords data import | 1.0 | | 10 |
| 4 | Site search tracking | 1.0 | | 0 |
| 5 | File download tracking | 1.0 | | 0 |
| 6 | Outbound link tracking | 1.0 | | 0 |
| 7 | Form completion tracking | 1.0 | | 0 |
| 8 | Video tracking | N/A | – | – |
| 9 | Error page tracking | 0.5 | | 0 |
| 10 | Transaction tracking | 2.0 | | 10 |
| 11 | Event tracking (non-pageviews) | 1.0 | | 0 |
| 12 | Goal setup | 1.0 | | 0 |
| 13 | Funnel setup | 1.0 | | 0 |
| 14 | Visitor labeling | 1.0 | | 0 |
| 15 | Campaign tracking | 1.0 | | 5 |
| | **Quality score** (QS) out of 100 | | | **27.6** |

**Figure 3.3** *Sample weighted scorecard to assess your data quality and set expectations*

correctly. Obviously you will wish to see as much green as possible. The purpose is to show the status of each item but also combine these into a single weighted score for you to quickly assess your overall data quality. For the example shown, the quality score is 27.6 out of 100—that is, the implementation is only 27.6% complete. For this site, only the basics have been installed, and there is clearly a long way to go.

Producing a weighted scorecard audit is described in Chapter 4.

## Metrics Strategy and Planning

The purpose of the metrics strategy and planning step is twofold:

- For the analytics team to gain a good understanding of what metrics are required by the business
- To compare the metric requirements of the business with your current scorecard—what data is currently available and accurate

## Showing Progress

In addition to benchmarking your current analytics position, the score-card can be used as a data point itself—monitoring the progress of the first phase of the project. The scorecard is a useful illustration of what work is taking place behind the scenes in order to ensure that future analysis uses good quality data. This becomes increasingly important if your implementation timeline is long.

In some cases a best-practice implementation can take many months to complete (sometimes longer!). Having a regular score helps reassure senior executives that progress is being made, despite the fact that useful data is not yet available. When an implementation is protracted, I update the scorecard each month. If the score is not improving, an executive push may be required to ensure the necessary work is prioritized by your web development team.

To achieve these goals, the analytics team sits down with the organization's digital stakeholders with the scorecard used to manage all parties' expectations. Before this stage, the weighting for each item on the scorecard is governed by how important the analytics team considers it for tracking your visitor's user-journey. Based on the discussions with your stakeholders, you may find yourself adjusting the weightings. For example, perhaps the downloadable brochure is more valuable to the business than you first thought? Getting agreement on the weighting (importance) of each row in the scorecard of Figure 3.3 is an important achievement in this step.

Keep in mind that this is early days in your project. The purpose here is not to set a metrics strategy in stone. Rather, it is a plan to point the flexible analytics ship in the right direction and manage the expectations of what is required to achieve this. Improvements can be added at a later stage (and should be). What is being set up in this step are the solid data foundations that will support the future modifications and additions.

With the scorecard agreed to and expectations understood by all stakeholders, you can now start to plan your implementation—that is, who does what and when to make it all happen.

### Guideline Documentation—the STAG

Documentation is often neglected, but it's critically important that your installation be documented. By that, I do not mean detailing the code or the precise page and server logic required to set up your tracking. That

### Who Writes the STAG Document?

The STAG document is a technical document and hence a person with Google Analytics developer experience is required. This could be a member of your existing development team, though most likely you will employ the services of a GACP. The role of a GACP is discussed in Chapter 2, specifically with reference to Figure 2.3.

would be a tedious read and would be out of date quickly. Rather, you should describe the reasoning for the current setup and the proposed data structure in a site tracking assessment and guidelines (STAG) document. This is the document that will go to your developers to implement the Google Analytics code.

Why is a STAG document necessary?

In Google Analytics there are at least three different tracking methods available to track the same thing—pageviews, virtual pageviews, and events (for more detail on these see the appendix and Chapter 6). Which of these methods is best for your implementation will depend on many factors, most of them technical—for example, your CMS setup, web platform architecture, content structure (for example, embedded third-party content), and the complexity associated with changing any of these. In addition, each tracking method has its own data structure. Hence it is important to document which methodology is employed for each of your tracking requirements—each item in your scorecard.

For example, if each scorecard item were to be considered in isolation, a different tracking method might be proposed for one that made it difficult to compare with the others. That is a nightmare scenario that leads to comparing apples with pears, with bananas. By having a central document that outlines the tracking choices made, the reasoning behind

### The STAG—the Analyst's Reference Document

A web analyst's first question when investigating an unexpected change in traffic patterns is "How was this data collected?" Analysts need to understand whether the change is real or perhaps an unforeseen consequence of a page edit that inadvertently altered the tracking. Without first answering this fundamental question, a great deal of time and effort can be wasted going around in circles. The STAG document is therefore the first port of call for the analyst in order to understand exactly what may be causing the observed change.

the choices, and the expected data structure, you greatly simplify any future tracking developments, troubleshooting, and analysis. The STAG document ensures all those involved in your analytics project understand the soundness of what data is being collected, *without* having to read code on web pages.

A STAG document should contain approximately one page of explanation for each item in the scorecard—a total of 15 pages. Each section should be written in a self-contained manner to help the reader refer to a specific section without the need to read the entire document as a novel. It should also include screenshots and diagrams where possible, as shown in Figure 3.4.

Although code examples may be necessary within the STAG—this document is after all going to your developers—the code should be limited to the standardized tracking code snippets that can be found at http://developers.google.com/analytics/devguides/collection/.

Figure 3.5 illustrates the concise nature of a single STAG item—in this example, for the requirement to track file downloads of different types (PDF, DOC, ZIP files). A few things to note from this example:

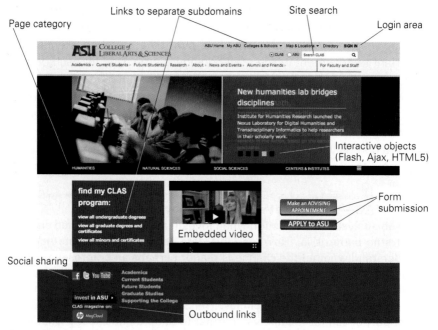

**Figure 3.4** *Sample webpage screenshot highlighting the features that require special tracking consideration*

## 5. File Download Tracking

For ALL file downloads e.g. PDF files as listed at http://www.site.com/product/shortthrow/vpl-bc825/overview, modify the onClick event handler so that an **event** is sent to Google Analytics as follows:

```
ga('send', 'event', 'Downloads', 'PDF', '$fileTitle');
```

Where $fileTitle is the PDF file title.

For example:

```
<a href="/attachment/1237486044794" onclick="ga('send', 'event',
'Downloads', 'PDF', 'VPL-SW125 Datasheet');"
name="ATTEnEU201205FPJShortThrowVPLbc825" class="button-type1" title="VPL-
bc825 Datasheet"></a>
```

In this case, $fileTitle = "VPL-bc825 Datasheet" (not the file name1237486044794)

If there are other file download types e.g. doc, xls etc., replace the string "PDF' in the code accordingly.

> A CMS technique to simplify the tracking of all file downloads (rather than finding these manually), is to define a separate HTML class attribute for your file download links. Then apply the onClick event handler to all links matching this class. Currently your PDF files have the class attribute "pdf-items box-type-1", so this may be straightforward to implement.

**Figure 3.5** *Sample STAG section specifying the requirements for file download tracking*

- The entire description of what is required is covered within half a page.
- The necessary code changes are highlighted in bold (non-bold code is the existing page HTML).
- Having outlined the data structure (using an event), I leave it to the developer to figure out how to capture the file title. The filename is meaningless in this case and cannot be changed.
- The example is for tracking PDF file downloads. I leave it to the developer to apply the same technique to other file types.
- The standardized code is shown as being manually placed within the HTML link. However, a developer will be familiar with other *listener* techniques that can automate this—for example, using a tag management system such as Google Tag Manager.[5]

The STAG item shown in Figure 3.5 conveys the data requirements and data structure clearly and concisely, while allowing the developer the freedom to figure out the best way to achieve the outcome. Ultimately, it is up to your developers to decide on the best method and what the exact code should look like (that's what you pay them for).

## *Implementation*

The implementation of tracking code is the responsibility of your development team—either internally or via your agency. It is the final step of this phase, and it should result in good, clean data being populated into your Google Analytics account. Assuming a member of the web development team has been involved throughout this phase, they should be expecting to receive the STAG document.

It is important that whoever implements the STAG realizes this is *not* a cut-and-paste operation. The developer is required to think, and time needs to be allowed for this—that is, to understand the data requirements, the thinking behind them, and the standardized code snippets presented. They then build their own version of code to go on your pages. How to deploy the code and the logic required to obtain the necessary parameters are your developer's responsibility. See the sidebar "Using a Tag Management System."

As any person familiar with a Google Analytics implementation can tell you, the required tracking code snippets are straightforward for any developer. After all, millions of blogs, hobby sites, and mom-and-pop businesses use Google Analytics around the world and certainly did not go through the detailed process I am describing in this chapter. However, at an advanced level—beyond items 1 and 2 on your scorecard—a more detailed implementation approach is required.

## Phase 2—Configuration

While phase 1 (installation) required the inclusion of all actors, phase 2 is covered by the analytics team working in conjunction with the marketing and communication teams. In phase 2 you are adjusting and fine-tuning your Google Analytics implementation. Using my shipbuilding analogy, this phase is the outfitting of the decks. The necessary work is completed either within the Google Analytics interface or during the creation of your marketing campaigns. No modification of your web pages is required (your web development team can take a break).

Phase 2 includes these four steps:

- Data structuring
- Goal setup
- Segmentation and filtering
- Campaign tracking

## Using a Tag Management System (TMS)

Think of a TMS as functioning in the same way your CMS works—except it is for managing snippets of code (tags) rather than content.

A TMS, such as Google Tag Manager,[5] works by being deployed on your pages as a *container* script. This is a JavaScript snippet—typically a dozen or so lines long. Once in place, the container allows you to insert tags (other code) into your pages via a centralized, rules-based system. The benefit is that you remove all other snippets of code and replace it with one that is edited via a separate web interface. Any additions or modifications to the tags do not require changes to your pages. Nirvana for your IT team!

If you use a TMS for your Google Analytics implementation (I strongly recommend you do), then your IT department's role can be as straightforward as deploying the TMS container on all of your pages—a one-time deployment. The analytics team then implements the STAG via the TMS web interface.

### Data Structure

Data structure affects enterprises with multiple brand-specific or product-specific websites, or a website targeting different markets. If this describes your organization, then it makes sense to have separate, stand-alone Google Analytics reports for each website or market. That way, a product manager or country manager can focus on the reports relevant to their product or country. By *standalone* I mean that your product or country managers do not wish to see data from other products or markets mixed in with their reports. For example, they will not want reports where euros are mixed with dollars, or reports including visits from different time zones if they are not relevant, as these will skew the data. By keeping reports separate for these scenarios, analysis becomes easier.

On the other hand, enterprise users also have a headquarters that requires a high-level overview of how the *entire* online channel is performing. This is when having separate report sets is laborious—you literally have to open multiple browser windows to view the same reports for each product or market. To avoid this, set up a *roll-up* report. That is, in addition to individual market or product reports, you have a single catch-all report set with data from all websites or markets aggregated. You achieve this by adding a second Google Analytics tracking code snippet to your pages. In this way, all data hits are sent to two reports sets (Figure 3.6).

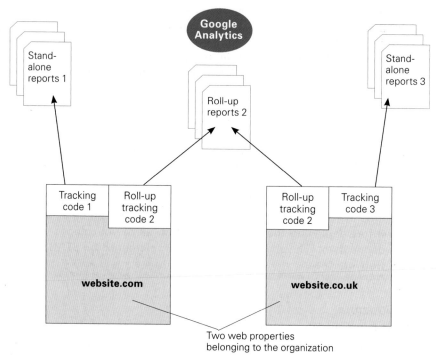

**Figure 3.6** *Using a second tracking code to simultaneously send data to multiple report sets*

Using the multi-tracker setup shown schematically in Figure 3.6, the two websites have their own data reports (report sets 1 and 3), while also sending data to a common roll-up report (set 2). The principle is straightforward, though careful consideration is required if combining currencies and media spend. For example, you will need to convert all currencies by a fixed exchange rate so that the monetary totals make sense. The exchange rate does not have to be exact, but it is important it remain fixed. Otherwise your sales performance will vary based on exchange rates and not on any improvement in your content or marketing.[6]

Which approach you take to structure your Google Analytics data depends on how your digital content is structured. It may be that your data is already aggregated and you need to figure out how to separate the data while maintaining the integrity of the visitor journey (see sidebar "Visitor Journey Integrity"). Alternatively, maybe your data is already split and you require an aggregation method.

Chapter 7 discusses geographic data structuring in more detail.

**Visitor Journey Integrity**

The common technique for separating data is to use *view filters*. These manipulate data at the hit level, not the visitor or session level. Care is required when manipulating data at the hit level. For example, the first data hit defines the start of a visitor's session and contains all the referrer information (where the visitor came from). If an applied filter removes the first data hit, you will observe odd data in your reports—such as visitors having no referrer data, or visitor sessions being restarted (duplicate counting).

## Goal Setup

Goals are the important engagements happening on your website that distinguish a genuinely interested visitor from a tire kicker. A goal is a call to action—what you want a visitor to do when they see a particular page or content within the page. An obvious goal for a transactional site is a purchase, and this should be set up so you can analyze the path on your website that leads to the sale (the sales funnel). However, this goal is black and white—visitors either purchase or not. The number of visitors who purchase from you is usually a small fraction of your total visitor volume (typically around 3% of your traffic[7,8]). So while the purchase goal is important, it is a small piece of your website's potential.

My point is that your goals become most informative when used to understand visitor interest—those engagements that help you *build* a relationship with what otherwise are anonymous visitors. Regardless of whether you have an e-commerce facility, use goals to measure visitor engagement with your brand and products. Examples of these engagements are listed in Table 3.1.

Think of goal conversions as specific measurable actions that can be applied to every visit. Up to 20 goals can be configured within Google Analytics, and your target should be that at least one goal is completed by a genuinely interested visitor. Otherwise it is fair to ask the fundamental questions: What are these visitors doing here? Is our traffic acquisition sending us poorly qualified visitors? Is our website content good enough? Is the user experience poor?

The value to your organization of each goal completion will vary. Some goals may indicate only a small interest and hence have a low value—a PDF file download, or pressing play on a demo video, for example. Others

**Table 3.1** *Goal Examples*

| Goal Type | Visitor's Action Defining the Goal |
|---|---|
| E-commerce | <ul><li>Purchase confirmation</li><li>Add-to-cart action (e-commerce site)</li><li>Got to step 3 of 4 in the purchase funnel (came very close to becoming a customer)</li><li>Transaction failed—a negative goal (one you would rather see less of)</li></ul> |
| Lead generation | Any action where personally identifiable information is passed on:<ul><li>Completed a contact request form</li><li>Clicked a mailto link</li><li>Subscribed to your newsletter</li></ul> |
| Purchase intent | <ul><li>Logged in to your site</li><li>Visited your store finder page</li><li>Clicked an outbound link to a reseller</li></ul> |
| Brand engagement | <ul><li>Logged in to your site</li><li>Downloaded a file—such as your product brochure or price list</li><li>Viewed a specific page, such as a special offer</li><li>Watched a video clip</li><li>Watched a video clip to completion (or passed a threshold of $x\%$)</li><li>Shared or commented on your content on Facebook, Twitter, Google+, LinkedIn, your blog, and so forth (social sharing)</li><li>Used a widget (such as a loan calculator)</li><li>Viewed $n$ or more product pages during a long visit (where you have set a threshold, such as $n > 10$ and time $> 5$ minutes)</li><li>Used advanced features of your internal site search facility (examples: more than one related search; using filters)</li><li>Used any content feedback or rating mechanism</li></ul> |
| Other revenue | <ul><li>Clicked on a third-party advertisement</li></ul> |

will be stronger indicators—such as watching a demo video to completion (or viewing 80% of it). Therefore, not all goals are equal.

To differentiate your goals, monetize them. That is, apply a monetary value to each goal completion. Monetizing your goals is discussed in the section on phases 3 and 4 later in this chapter.

Goals are the building blocks of key performance indicators (KPIs), which are the key metrics your organization focuses on to assess digital performance. How to establish KPIs is covered in Chapter 9.

### Segmentation and Filters
Segmentation and filters are the tools you use to group together visitors of similar behavior (segments) or cleanse your data (filters). For example,

## Defining Success—Macro and Micro Goals

Defining website goals is probably the single most important configuration step you will apply in Google Analytics, because it is how you define success. Goals are typically the reasons why your website was built in the first place. For example, was it to sell directly, to generate leads, to keep your clients or shareholders up to date, to provide centralized product updates, or to attract new staff? As you begin this exercise, you will realize that you actually have many website goals. These are your *macro* goals.

Goals don't have to include the full conversion of a visitor into a customer—that is obviously very important, but it's only part of the picture. If your only goal is to gain customers, then how will you know just how close noncustomers came to converting? You gain insight into this by using *micro* goals. These measure the building of relationships with your visitors.

a segment of visitors could be your *customers, high-value customers, subscribers, noncustomers,* or *engagers.* I use the term *engagers* to describe visitors who have done something on your site that indicates significant interest in you but who are not yet customers. Downloading your brochure can signify engagement, as can filling in a contact request form, commenting on a blog article, or socially sharing your content. You can even combine these criteria into a sequence segment—visitors who match criterion *X* and immediately match criterion *Y.*

Segmentation is the technique employed to focus your analysis on groups of visitors who have similar characteristics, rather than on the whole data pot. The purpose is to improve the signal-to-noise ratio by bubbling up data points that otherwise lie below the surface (and potentially go unnoticed). Understanding how a handful of visitor segments behave is far more practical than trying to comprehend the thousands of individual visitor patterns that exist on your site. On the Internet, with so much variability, almost everyone exhibits unique behavior. Understanding segmentation and its importance is discussed in Chapter 5.

Filters can also be used to group and segment data. However, their common use is to cleanse data. Perhaps your web page can be displayed as /Products.htm or /products.htm. To Google Analytics these are two different pages and are therefore reported separately, which is not helpful to anyone viewing the reports. By using a lowercase filter, these can be combined into a single page with all page metrics aggregated. Similarly, you may wish to remove meaningless parameters from your page URLs (such as session IDs). By removing these you make your reports easier to read and interpret.

Other things you can do with *view filters*:

- Remove visits from your own staff or agencies
- Rename obscure pages into something more memorable
- Separate visitors geographically so that you can, for example, view reports from US visitors and visitors from other countries separately
- Ensure campaign tracking is applied consistently (see next section)
- Rewrite legacy campaign tracking parameters for Google Analytics (rather than having to reconfigure existing campaign links)

### Campaign Tracking

Campaign tracking is the technique to measure the performance of your digital marketing efforts—from *all* channels. It answers questions like these: What drives visitors to our website and mobile apps? Which are the most effective drivers? How do different campaigns compare against each other? Typically your digital marketing costs are much greater than the cost to develop, build, and maintain your digital presence. Knowing the performance of your marketing and determining which campaigns produce the best results are key advantages of web analytics. You probably know that half of your marketing works. But which half? In the digital world, all marketing can be tracked. But campaign tracking does not happen by default. You therefore need a rigorous system in place to ensure it does.

I discuss the setup of campaign tracking in Chapter 6.

### Phases 3 and 4—Insights and Education

On reaching phase 3 you will be on the brink of crossing the dotted line shown in Figure 3.1. That is, your analytics project is moving from being a cost to the organization to one that generates a return. The extent of the return can be quite extraordinary. For example, according to a compilation of statistics by the Baymard Institute,[9] the average *shopping cart abandonment rate* is 67.44%. That is, of all the online visitors that have added an item to their cart, two-thirds leave without making a purchase.

Similarly, average *checkout abandonment rates* are reported at 43%.[8] That is a staggering number—43% of visitors that have completed their checkout process and are ready to pay (have their money in their hands, so to speak) bail out of the decision at the very last step. Clearly, with such significant sums of money being left on the table, any insights that can help improve conversion will have a significant dollar impact on the business. This was the basis of the work shown in Figure 1.2. In that example, the improvement resulted in a fourfold increase in revenue for the website, equivalent to $7.5 million extra per year (a significant amount for the boutique travel company concerned).

What about insights for non-transactional websites? This is where monetization comes in.

## Monetization

The purpose of monetization is to ascertain the *value* of your website and keep track of it over time. I cannot overemphasize the importance of this step. Whether you have an e-commerce facility or not, your website has value, as defined by

*total website value = e-commerce revenue + goal value*

### Cart Abandonment versus Checkout Abandonment

The *cart abandonment rate* is defined as

$$\frac{\textit{number of purchases not completed}}{\textit{number of purchase initiations}}$$

Often visitors will add an item to their shopping cart in order to check your final price, or even to obtain a price (this is common in the travel industry). Hence, the cart abandonment rate can appear to over-inflate the abandonment problem. That is, some visitors will leave the shopping area of your website for reasons not connected with their user experience.

The *checkout abandonment rate* is defined as

$$\frac{\textit{number of purchases not completed}}{\textit{number of checkout initiations}}$$

The checkout abandonment rate measures abandonment from when people are asked to make their payment—it is the penultimate step in the sales funnel and is not affected by visitors who check prices, stock levels, or delivery options. A high checkout abandonment rate is a clear indication that your visitors are experiencing problems—either technical issues (error messages or some kind of failure); a lack of confidence or trust in your ability to fulfill their order; or other reasons, such as a high shipping price or long delivery time that they were not expecting from the start of the sales process.

E-commerce revenue is tracked by the addition of specific code on your purchase confirmation page. It is the responsibility of your web development team and is a part of phase 1. On the other hand, your goals are the calls to action that the analytics team defines in phase 2 (see the section "Goal Setup," earlier in this chapter). The definition of goals takes place within the Administration area of Google Analytics. No changes to your web pages are required. In the monetization step we consider adding monetary values to your goals.

As discussed in the "Goal Setup" section (refer also to Table 3.1), the value of each goal completion will vary for your organization. Some goals—for example, the viewing of a special offers page—have zero value. They may be important for your new visitor acquisition strategy but have no tangible value. Other goals have a high value—for example, any goal that results in the visitor sending you their personal information (such as their name or email address), as this allows your sales team to contact them and work their magic. And there are goals that fall in between. Thus, not all goals are equal; you account for this by setting goal values.

Goal values are specific to your organization and therefore are not arbitrary amounts—they require some thought, though the process is straightforward. The process is the same for all your defined goals. Evaluate how often visitors who complete a certain goal go on to become customers and what that customer is worth. For example, if your sales team can close 10% of people who submit your contact request form and your average transaction is $500, you would assign $50 (10% of $500) as the goal value to your contact form request. In contrast, if only 1% of submissions result in a sale, you assign $5 to your contact form request.

Your goal values should represent a real monetary amount, though it will be approximate. Real monetary amounts are obviously preferred, so that your organization can directly relate to them. However, they can be difficult to ascertain. If this is the case for your organization, use a relative scale where the values are approximate, yet still relatable. For example, watching a demo video to completion is worth 10 times the value of a PDF download. Table 3.2 shows examples of common goal values.

By monetizing the goals on your website, you achieve two important things using Google Analytics:

- You can readily report and monitor the total value of your website over time.
- Google Analytics automatically calculates and assigns a value to *every* page viewed and *every* visitor you receive.

**Table 3.2** *Using Relative Goal Values*

| Goal Type | Example | Relative Value |
|---|---|---|
| Zero value (important touch points with your visitors, but have no tangible value to the business) | • Viewed a special offers page or other specific URL<br>• Watched a video clip (no threshold)<br>• Used a widget<br>• Viewed *n* product pages over a period of *m* minutes<br>• Used your internal site search facility and did not receive zero results | 0 |
| Low value (a strong signal of visitor engagement, though nothing to indicate sentiment) | • Downloaded a document (PDF brochure, specification sheet)<br>• Watched a video clip to *x*% completion<br>• Clicked on a third-party ad<br>• Used any anonymous content feedback or rating system | 1 |
| Medium value (a strong signal your visitors like or value your content and are likely to purchase) | • Shared socially (Like, Tweet, +1, Follow, Pin, and so forth)<br>• Visited your store finder page<br>• Clicked an outbound link to a reseller | 5 |
| High value (the ultimate engagement, allowing you to connect and talk directly with your visitors) | Provided any personal contact information, such as<br>• Form completion (contact request form)<br>• Newsletter subscription<br>• Clicking a mailto link<br>• Adding a product review<br>• Adding a blog comment | 10 |

That latter point is a great asset to focus on for analysis. It is how you identify your high-value visitors, high-value pages, and poor-performing pages. Understanding value as reported in Google Analytics is discussed in Chapter 6.

## Insights

Google Analytics is your main tool to help you understand, and therefore optimize, how visitors arrive at your website and what happens once they are there. This is what Google Analytics was designed for.

Providing insights is about providing the reasons for change. The analytics team is therefore the agent for change in your organization—change in how the digital marketing is conducted (for a better return on investment) and change in the website content or its architecture (for a better visitor experience). Getting these right determines if your website takes off successfully or remains lackluster.

Reasons for change need to be based on solid thinking to be credible—that is, analyzing good quality data and building sensible hypotheses from it (or using the data to confirm an existing hypothesis). Data insights come is two flavors:

- Deductive insights—having an existing hypothesis, you search for data to support it.
- Inductive insights—you argue backwards from a set of observations to a reasonable hypothesis.

Both approaches are valid, though I have found from experience that inductive insights are more common (I estimate 2:1).

Insights enable you to understand how to attract highly qualified leads (high-value visitors) to your website and what they do once they land on your site (convert or not). It is a powerful skill set to develop. Strongly overlapping—though separate—industries have developed around them—digital marketing and conversion rate optimization, respectively. My view is that these have separated because the sorts of people they attract—marketers on the one hand, technical people who manipulate website content and its architecture on the other hand—don't overlap much. In my view a good digital analyst needs both skill sets (see Chapter 8, "Building Your Insights Team").

### Hypothesis Building and Testing

Data is only useful if there is a hypothesis to describe what it means to the business. Otherwise, it's just noise. The converse is also true—having a hypothesis requires supporting data. You achieve this by designing experiments (tests).

For example, a hypothesis could be that your product photograph is the most important driver for a visitor on your website to convert into a customer—more important than the campaign headline or surrounding text. You can test this (provide data to support or refute the hypothesis) by showing half your visitors the original page layout and half with the image removed. At the end of the experiment you compare the conversion rates for each visitor segment. Did visitors who saw the page with the product image convert at a higher rate than those who did not? This is the basic design of A/B testing.

Taking this a step further, if the image is found to be a key component of the conversion process, you could test the effectiveness of different images. You might have 20% of your visitors see each of five alternative images. If the test data shows a significantly higher conversion rate when image 2 is shown, you know that only image 2 needs to be used on your web page for this product. You have just scientifically improved the performance of your website based on data.

Often, the conversion process is more subtle than relying on one image. Maybe there are multiple images required to tell a story to your visitors, or the product image, headline text, and surrounding descriptive text are all important and work together to procure the conversion. In this case, different combinations can be tested together. For example, you could test three product images, three headlines, and three descriptive texts (27 combinations in total). This is the basis of multivariate testing.

**Testing with Google Analytics**   There are two types of testing to consider:

- Offsite testing—experimental tests you perform with your marketing campaigns to attract visitors, such as testing different banner designs or email newsletter layouts. The experiment is conducted via a third-party vendor tool, though it is straightforward to label the visitor once they click through to your website. Google Analytics can report which test version they clicked on, and you can know which version is performing better once the visitor is on your website.

- Onsite testing—experimental tests you perform with visitors on your site, such as testing the effectiveness of different product images, descriptions, prices, and page layouts. Google Analytics includes a testing platform called *content experiments* that can conduct A/B tests. However, it is also possible to use third-party tools and integrate the results *within* Google Analytics so that reports show which version is performing better.

The Google Analytics Content Experiments platform allows you to perform simple A/B, A/B/C, etc., tests on your webpage content. It is a solid platform that can be deployed with an interesting statistical method—the multi-armed bandit model. This optional setting helps you obtain results faster than more traditional statistical methods.[10] Reducing experiment time is a key advantage of content experiments. However, in my view, a drawback of the tool is the way experiments need to be implemented on your pages. For all but simple experiments they require your web development team to reengineer how your pages are delivered. That is, versions are delivered server-side.

I find the server-side approach of content experiments is not a viable proposition for enterprise-level web development teams—it is too big of an overhead and adds a layer of complexity to running the website. As an alternative, specialist testing platforms are available that use client-side methodologies. This simplifies deployment while still integrating test results within Google Analytics.[11]

👉 *I discuss my reasoning for avoiding Google Analytics Content Experiments at* http://brianclifton.com/avoid-content-experiments

**When not to test** For data to be considered *useful* it must have a hypothesis to describe it. However, not all hypotheses require data to support them. That may sound odd, but sometimes test data is too difficult to obtain and performing an experiment is not worth the effort. For this case, expert judgment (that is, experience) can trump a lack of data. Not everything that can be tested should be tested.

If you were to test every possible combination of content elements on your site, you would be waiting beyond your lifetime for the results. The quantity of data would be overwhelming. As with all things digital, the medium moves fast. Hence, rapid incremental testing is far more effective than long-term testing (an approach that is embedded in Google's product philosophy).

Here's a real example from my days when I was working at Google, when using good judgment (experience) should have been chosen instead of hypothesis testing:

I was looking to hire. My manager in his infinite wisdom (now a senior executive who shall remain nameless) asked me why he should invest in my team. "Google Analytics is being given away for free. What more could a user want?" I explained that with more resources I could go beyond just giving away the product and actually help users make sense of the reports and so actually benefit from the product. Put simply, I wanted to help users better understand Google Analytics and hence their websites. I hypothesized that if they did, they would go on to invest more in their digital marketing. As Google dominates digital marketing, this would ultimately drive more revenue to the business, right?

"Prove it. Prove that there is a link between increased digital advertising spend and Google Analytics usage."

I spent the next two years attempting to show a correlation by testing—comparing the digital ad spend of clients with and without Google Analytics. Intuitively most people would agree with my hypothesis. So far I have not met anyone who disagrees. However, it was incredibly difficult to show any correlation. At that time, circa 2006, all things digital were growing at an exponential rate. Take into account seasonality, new advertising features from Google, changes in the competitor landscape, other tracking technologies, the growth of smartphones, social media, and more; and I was never going to succeed in building a solid data foundation for my hypothesis. The issues were too complex and the causality too easy to doubt.

My point with this story is to emphasize that testing different alternatives, just because it's possible to do so, does not mean it is a worthwhile exercise. In fact, it can be costly to your organization—I spent two years going around in circles and missing other important opportunities, such as gaining support from other stakeholders who could have invested in my team.

**When to test**   To decide if testing is required, first conduct your analysis and build your hypothesis (or vice versa) about the visitor behavior on your website. This is the most important step of any experimental setup. Your default position should be to test only if and when it is required.

Before considering if a test is required, ensure that best-practice user experience principles are applied to your website's content and structure. Do not skip this process. Conducting a test experiment can take weeks, and sometimes months. Fixing user experience issues is usually quicker, easier to scale (improvements can be applied to all your pages via templates), and negates the need to test. For example, you do not need to test what is obviously broken.

In other words, experiment by testing the important questions that matter to your business. Here are some examples.

### Testing for marketing (offsite testing)
- Different banner designs—for example, static versus animated
- Different email newsletter layouts and designs
- Different call-to-action texts

### Testing for design and persuasion (onsite testing)
- Different value proposition statements or special offers

**Fix the User Experience First**

Web developers make things work, web designers provide the creative flair, and digital marketers bring in the traffic. However, it never ceases to amaze me how little attention is given to the user experience.

For example, it's not always obvious that call-to-action buttons are just that, a call to action. Often such buttons are graphics. From a visitor's perspective, these appear to be a part of the design aesthetic. They do not look like a clickable button, and therefore suffer from *banner blindness*. The buttons are ignored—considered ads by your visitors, rather than important calls to action.

In addition, the result of clicking the button—what happens next— should be completely obvious to the visitor. The principle is called "Don't make me think." This approach is explored in the book of the same name by Steve Krug.[12]

- Different trust factors, such as logos, certifications
- Different call-to-action texts

**Testing for usability (onsite testing)**
- Revised content layout, such as shorter forms, compacted checkout process, reduced scrolling
- Simplified navigation, such as fewer clicks to destination, better site search results
- Comparing text links versus buttons versus images

*Education and Metrics Understanding*

From the start of phase 3, I recommend education running in parallel with your project. The more you democratize your data—that is, make it available throughout your organization—the more buy-in you will gain for your recommended changes. My view is that data should never be treated as a silo—it is too valuable to the organization. And having the wisdom of the crowd is an asset to be appreciated.

However, with data democratization comes an overhead—questions: What does this number mean? How can I use this number? Can you pull the same number but segmented by *y*? These questions will come through, first as a trickle, later as a torrent. After all, information is empowerment—people make better decisions with more information. So wanting more is a natural human behavior.

**Create power users** Rather than drowning your team in the work of answering all questions, educate your interested parties so they can self-serve. Raise their level of metrics understanding so that they can view the reports in Google Analytics themselves and answer their own questions. For example, in an organization with multiple regional or country-specific offices, train one suitable person from each to serve the data needs of that office. That person should be involved with the digital marketing team and be numerate and digitally savvy. They become the bridge between the data-intensive analytics team that is focused on the central digital strategy and the local office that has different day-to-day needs. These are your Google Analytics *power users.*

Power users are your data advocates. Once trained, they know the Google Analytics product well enough to self-serve, which means they absorb the more basic reporting questions on your behalf. They will understand the direction of the analytics team, yet they are embedded within their own business unit. That's a great combination—it means your power users can guide data expectations locally and escalate to the central team when appropriate. See Figure 3.7.

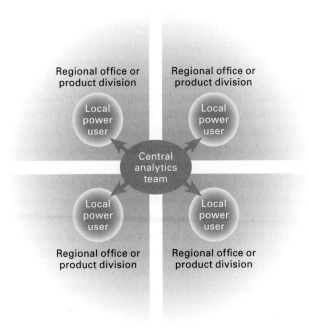

**Figure 3.7** *Democratizing the data using Google Analytics power users*

Keep in regular contact with your power users—I recommend a conference call for general updates and Q&A every two weeks. Provide continuous formal training to enhance their skill set—preferably once per year. With an engaged and effective power user network in place, you will probably find they are your next team hires. Good analytics people are not easy to find.

Building an analytics team and utilizing Google Analytics power users is discussed further in Chapter 8.

## HOW LONG WILL THIS TAKE?

How long will it take to move from ground zero to the stage where insights are produced? In Figure 3.2, a realistic time frame is to allow one quarter for each step. That is, by Q3 you should be in a position to start gaining real insights for your organization. Of course, that is an estimate that can vary greatly. However, I recently looked at over 50 client engagements, and this time frame remains a good estimate.

**Factors that alter your timeline**   Of the four phases shown in Figure 3.2, the one that requires the most heavy lifting is phase 1—installation. Once this is completed, the remaining phases can go quickly. A basic installation—items 1 and 2 in the scorecard shown in Figure 3.3—is something that can be achieved in a matter of hours for a good web developer. It can be even less if what you have is a single website domain without an e-commerce facility. However, tracking multiple websites, subdomains, e-commerce facilities, mobile apps, non-web devices (checkout tills, barcode scanners), and all the other items listed on the scorecard requires a good deal of thought and planning in order to get the implementation right.

Beyond these, timing depends on the resources and priority you can allocate to the project, the platform your content is hosted on (some CMS systems can be painful to work with if they have not been set up with tracking in mind), and who performs the implementation. The time dependence of the last variable (who) is surprising. I initially expected organizations with an internal web development team would respond the quickest. However, it turns out that organizations that employ a third-party web development agency are more agile—that is, faster to implement—on average.

Why would an outsourced third party be faster at implementation? For a third-party web development agency, there is a finite time they can allow for the project's completion—the longer it takes, the less profit they make. On the other hand, internal web development teams tend to suffer from a number of issues that result in the analytics implementation taking longer—internal politics, lack of tracking prioritization, lack of interest (tracking is not what they do or want to do), and lack of ownership. They view tracking as a function of marketing.

Bring the web development team on board as a key stakeholder from the beginning of the project. Their role does not end when phase 1 is completed. They are needed to implement tests as well as any resulting changes you require. It is a long-term relationship that requires good communication between both parties.

## BUDGET—WHAT DOES IT COST?

How much should you budget for web analytics? This question can be interpreted in two ways:

- What do other users spend on their web analytics?
- What should *we* invest in web analytics?

To answer the first question, review Figure 3.8, taken from Econsultancy's "Online Measurement and Strategy Report 2013."[13] The amount spent on web analytics covers the costs for internal staffing, technology

**Figure 3.8** *How much do users spend on web analytics each year?*

Source: Ecoconsultancy

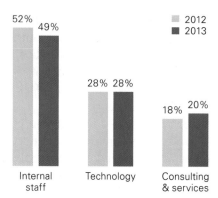

**Figure 3.9** *The areas web analytics users spend their budget on*

Source: Ecoconsultancy

(tools and implementation), and the use of third-party consulting services. See Figure 3.9 for the expenditure split.

Figure 3.8 shows that more than half of the survey respondents spent less than a total of £10,000 per year (approximately $15,000) on their web analytics. With the free version of Google Analytics, this is expected. My reasoning is that users consider a free tool as not worthy of much investment. Conversely, if the exact same tool has a high license cost, I predict that more expenditure will be committed to ensure it is used effectively—psychologically, no manager wants to have their purchase viewed as a white elephant.

To answer the second question, if you take your data seriously then you need to invest in your web analytics. The free version of Google Analytics is very powerful and suitable for most organizations. However, you still require internal resources (trained staff), technology (ensuring a continuous supply of good quality data), and consulting services (third-party expertise) if you wish to make informed, strategic decisions based on the data. Getting the mix right is discussed in Chapter 8.

Almost every organization I have encountered initially underestimated the value of data—in terms of both the value of it to their organization and what it costs to achieve an integrated approach. Wherever you place yourself on Figure 3.8, consider moving two places to the right. That is, if you initially anticipated spending £10,000–£25,000 ($15,000–$40,000) per year on your web analytics, consider a more realistic amount to be £50,000–£100,000 ($75,000–$150,000)—if you wish to achieve what I set out in this book, that is.

## Why a GACP Is Important

Google Analytics Certified Partners are companies that specialize in defining and measuring success using Google Analytics (and possibly other complementary tools). Every organization is unique in its metrics strategy, so having an *internal* day-to-day resource within your organization is a key requirement. However, an external GACP resource ensures you apply best-practice principles from the start. That's important, as poor or unreliable data cannot be corrected for later—it has to be discarded.

When it comes to insights, experience counts. A good GACP will work with numerous organizations across a broad spectrum of industries. That lateral thinking is a great asset when it comes to hypothesis building and testing.

Google Analytics Premium may also be the right tool for you (see Chapter 2 for making an informed decision on this). If so, the price tag for the product is $150,000 per year.

## SPEAKING OF EXPECTATIONS AND PROCESSES...

| When I hear this... | I reply with... |
| --- | --- |
| We want to have all this set up by the end of the quarter. | Be realistic with your requirements. If you have a single website domain, with no subdomains, and no e-commerce facility or other complex tracking requirements, then you can build solid data foundations within three months. However, avoid skipping the processes described in this chapter. They are required for good reasons. |
| As a global company we have multiple country websites, subdomains, and a network of resellers we supply leads to. Our site is aimed at new purchasers, existing customers, investors, and job seekers. We wish to measure and understand all of these areas. What resources should we be considering (budget and staffing)? | This varies in the same way the cost of building your website varies. However, the following is a guide based on my own experience.<br>**Staffing**  Three to four full-time staff, one at senior manager level.<br>In addition, build a network of power users to support country offices or specific departments (see Chapter 8).<br>**Technology**  Consider Google Analytics Premium as the potential tool for your organization (see Chapter 2).<br>**Consultancy services**  Leverage the experience of experts in Google Analytics. Hire a GACP to support you.[14] |

| When I hear this... | I reply with... |
| --- | --- |
| Continuing the above: Who should be our stakeholders for this project? | Your marketing and web development teams are key stakeholders; the project will fail without them. Beyond this, consider any senior manager who has an interest in the digital channel and can contribute budget or resources to the project. Making a contribution to the required investment is a great way to qualify your stakeholders. |
| We have a junior marketer who can be our internal resource on this project. She can spare one day per week on Google Analytics. | Other than for a small business, this is not enough resources for an organization to make use of their data beyond traffic volume numbers. It will result in data stagnation—repetitive report generation without insight. At the enterprise level, allow a minimum of one full-time person for your internal resource and use the services of a GACP to support you.[14] See Chapter 8. |

## CHAPTER 3 REFERENCES

1     Analytics maturity models aim to assess an organization's ability to use data in order to move their business forward. A champion of the online model (OAMM) is Stéphane Hamel of Cardinal Path:
      www.cardinalpath.com/services/online-analytics-maturity-model.

2     Google Analytics refers to its ability to track any Internet-connected device as Universal Analytics. More on this in Chapter 6.

3     Professor Hans Rosling is one of my very few modern-day heroes:
      http://en.wikipedia.org/wiki/Hans_Rosling.

4     The Motion Chart feature for Google Analytics explained:
      https://developers.google.com/chart/interactive/docs/gallery/motionchart

5     The Google Tag Manager (GTM) is a tool to add and manage page tags such as Google Analytics. It uses a centralized web interface to minimize the IT overhead of tracking: www.google.com/tagmanager.

6     This article from me discusses why and how to implement a fixed exchange rate method when combining multiple currencies into Google Analytics:
      http://brianclifton.com/multi-currency-support.

7     According to the e-tailing group's 12th Annual Merchant Survey of 2013, 46% of US merchants report a purchase conversion rate between 1.0% and 2.9%:
      www.e-tailing.com/content/wp-content/uploads/2013/04/pressrelease_merchantsurvey2013.pdf.

8     MarketLive Performance Index, Volume 24, Q1 2014 (PDF download):
      www.marketlive.com/how-we-think/commerce-strategies.html

9     Baymard Institute compiled 22 different studies containing statistics on e-commerce shopping cart abandonment rates (2006–13):
      http://baymard.com/lists/cart-abandonment-rate.

10    An excellent article from Steven L. Scott describes the principles behind the multi-armed bandit model: **https://support.google.com/analytics/answer/2844870**.

11    Specialist client-side testing platforms that integrate with Google Analytics include Optimizely and Visual Website Optimizer.

12    *Don't Make Me Think* is the title of the excellent book by Steve Krug. His simplicity of approach when explaining user experience and website usability was groundbreaking when first published.

13    Econsultancy and Lynchpin. "Online Measurement and Strategy Report 2013": **http://econsultancy.com/reports/online-measurement-and-strategy-report**

14    Google has an official global network of over 200 certified Google Analytics partners, known as the GACP network: **www.google.com/analytics/partners**.

# Assessing Your Data Quality

**A major hurdle that prevents** analytics data being taken seriously within an organization—by that I am referring to using web data to drive strategic thinking—is the perception that you are looking at noisy, irrelevant, or inaccurate data. A default Google Analytics installation answers only basic questions about your website. That's because without a best-practice setup, all Google Analytics can tell you is the basics: How many visitors came to our site? What pages did they look at? How long did they stay?

Answers to those fundamental questions—and there are many of them—can be incredibly powerful. They allow you to understand how your website performs through the eyes of your visitors. However, from a business point of view, non–data experts in your organization are left with the feeling of "So what?": So what if visitors stay on our website for 3 minutes and this has increased by 10% over the past 12 months? What does this mean to the business and what should I do with this information?

To the business, such basic metrics are irrelevant. To get past this stage you need to drill down into your data and answer the *business* questions your stakeholders are asking. Drilling down into your data means defining ever-smaller segment sizes. As you do this, the error bars inherent with web analytics get larger (irrespective of the tool used). Without a solid confidence in your data, you can just end up looking at noise or, worse still, similar data points from different reports providing a conflicting story. The analytics project will stagnate.

To minimize the noise and inaccuracy and maintain relevancy, you need to keep on top of your data quality. The process to do this is a health check audit of your data quality. In this chapter I show you how to perform such an audit—without the need to look at code.

## DATA QUALITY HEALTH CHECK

To assess your Google Analytics data quality, create a health check audit report. Use this report to examine and summarize aspects of your setup, weight them according to importance, and provide a single numeric representation of the quality of your data—your Google Analytics quality score (*QS*).

The health check audit report provides a succinct summary that captures the information most relevant to the analytics team. It articulates what is working correctly, what is missing from your current data setup, and where the problem areas are; and it lets you focus on which areas

## Error Bars and How to Minimize Them

As with all data sets, web analytics has its error bars.

- Setup errors—for example, incorrect filter logic applied, or typos in the tracking code. You minimize these with regular health check audits, as discussed in this chapter.

- Incorrect deployment, such as the tracking code missing from certain pages. No tracking code deployed results in no data being collected. You minimize this with regular site scans to determine your tracking code coverage, as discussed in this chapter.

- Visitors using multiple devices, such as desktop, laptop, tablet, and mobile phone. Unless your visitors routinely authenticate—log in to your website—no analytics tool can associate the same visitor across multiple devices. The only way to minimize this is to provide real value for visitors to log in—for example, applying a discount code on your pricing, providing an exclusive members-only area, or providing access to an account representative or a dedicated support area.

- Deletion of cookies. Visitors always have the right to block or delete the Google Analytics tracking cookies. If so, either data will not be collected (visitor blocked your cookie), or your visitor count is over-inflated (visitor deleted your cookie).

  Until the Edward Snowden affair, the deletion of cookies by users was considered relatively low—around 14% per month[1]—and consistent. However, this may now change. You can minimize the problem by having a clear, easy-to-read, and accessible privacy policy on your website. This is not a trivial matter—most are overly long and full of legal jargon there to protect the business rather than the visitor. Getting this right is a key aspect of building trust in your brand. See Chapter 7.

- Visitors who research online but prefer to purchase at a physical store. This has traditionally been a problem for web analytics tools, as the most important part of the digital trail is lost when the visitor goes offline. However, with Google Analytics' new protocol (Universal Analytics), this can be overcome. See Chapter 6.

- Differing processing time frames. A classic example is when payment details received late on a Friday night are processed by your transaction system on a Monday morning. However, Google Analytics will show this as revenue collected at the time of purchase (late on Friday night). There is not a lot that can be done to minimize this other than to allow for it when trying to reconcile numbers.

to prioritize to meet the organization's data requirements. Figure 4.1 is an example of a first-page summary of the audit report. It's aimed at senior managers in order to get an at-a-glance understanding of the current data quality status.

In Figure 4.1, first focus on the overall $QS$—the number in the last row. In this example the $QS$ = 13.8. This ranges on a scale from 0 to 100, where 100 represents a best-practice setup for your organization. The data quality in the example is not credible for analysis.

The first priority therefore is to achieve a critical value—a score above which you can perform basic analysis in confidence, which means that the information obtained is based on solid and reliable data. The exact

**Scorecard Summary**
January 2014: 112,000 visitors, 157,000 visits
*Time on site* = 3:08; *pages per visit* = 3.75; *bounce rate* = 45%;
AdWords spend = not linked to Google Analytics
Operational since March 2011

| | | Weight | Status | Weighted Score |
|---|---|---|---|---|
| 1 | Account setup and governance | 1.0 | | 5 |
| 2 | Tracking code deployment | 1.0 | | 10 |
| 3 | AdWords data import | 1.0 | | 0 |
| 4 | Site search tracking | 1.0 | | 0 |
| 5 | File download tracking | 1.0 | | 0 |
| 6 | Outbound link tracking | 1.0 | | 0 |
| 7 | Form completion tracking | 1.0 | | 0 |
| 8 | Video tracking | N/A | – | – |
| 9 | Error page tracking | 0.5 | | 0 |
| 10 | Transaction tracking | 2.0 | | 0 |
| 11 | Event tracking (non-pageviews) | 1.0 | | 0 |
| 12 | Goal setup | 1.0 | | 0 |
| 13 | Funnel setup | 1.0 | | 0 |
| 14 | Visitor labeling | 1.0 | | 0 |
| 15 | Campaign tracking | 1.0 | | 5 |
| | **Quality score** ($QS$) out of 100 | | | **13.8** |

**Figure 4.1** *Sample health check audit summary. Ideally, your quality score would be 100, a 100% complete best-practice implementation of Google Analytics. While that should be the long-term aim, obtain a score of at least 50 before you attempt any in-depth analysis of your data.*

## Be Transparent with Your Quality Score

As your organization will be making key strategic decisions based on your data, you will want to be able to provide your *QS* to back it up. Your *QS* is *the* key metric that shows how reliable your data is. You should monitor it regularly—see the section "Monitoring Your Quality Score" later in this chapter.

critical score varies by organization. However, to simplify the process I use the following general rule: Until you achieve a *QS* of 50, don't try to do any analysis. A value below 50 leaves too many holes and caveats in the data.

When you can demonstrate a high score—for example, *QS* > 80—you and your peers will have the confidence in the data that you need to base strategic decisions on it.

Once you understand your quality score, look at the overall scorecard summary. The table summarizes the 15 key items that make up a best-practice implementation by showing the weight (importance), its status (red, yellow, green), and the weighted score for each (weight × status). Clearly you want to have many greens in the Status column and be able to explain the yellow and red items in the report's supporting pages.

Table 4.1 shows the values associated with the status colors.

The weight for each of the 15 items in Figure 4.1 is a relative measure of the importance of tracking that particular item, with 0 representing no importance and 1.0 representing the highest importance. A weight of 2.0 is reserved for transaction tracking, because of its special importance. For each non-green item in Figure 4.1, consider its weight. This is your priority list for work to be done to improve your *QS*.

Page 1 of the audit report (the scorecard summary) is the most important part of the report—as a manager, your focus is on this page. The

**Table 4.1** *Scorecard Status Values*

| Status Color | | Explanation | Status Value |
|---|---|---|---|
| Green | | Working as expected. No action required. | 10 |
| Yellow | | Partially working, or not working in an optimal way. Action required. | 5 |
| Red | | Not working or not implemented. Action required. | 1 |

---

**Balanced Scorecard Approach**

You may be familiar with the balanced scorecard (BSC) approach—a strategy performance management technique developed in the 1990s and used by managers to keep track of activities within their control.[2] The health check audit report is based on the BSC technique.

---

remaining pages of the report explain why items receive a yellow or red status value.

◆ *You can download the full example audit report from* http://brianclifton.com/example-audit.

## BUILDING YOUR HEALTH CHECK SCORECARD

The health check audit report is built by the analytics team and is typically four to five pages long (including the summary page shown in Figure 4.1). Most, but not all, of the table items will be applicable to you. Mark others as "not applicable" rather than removing them from the table. For example, video tracking (row 8 in Figure 4.1) is not applicable to this fictitious client website. I explicitly state this in order to indicate that video tracking has been investigated and considered not applicable. If that item were missing, it would raise the question, "Have we considered everything?" For large sites with thousands of pages, the precise content and features can easily be forgotten. Therefore, it is good practice to make a formal assessment.

Following the scorecard summary page, the supporting pages expand on why each item received the score it has in bullet point form. For items that receive a green status, no further detail is required. Therefore, the report focuses on the yellow and red tracking items. The information presented should be concise and succinct—that is, in note form. The intention is to help point the person responsible for the specific tracking item in the right direction. Each item should be no more detailed than the following example:

Item 5: File download tracking

- A google.com search reveals we have 5,000 PDF files located in the search engine's index (they can be found by Google).
- However, no file download tracking is in place.

An alternative could be the following:

- A google.com search reveals we have 5,000 PDF files, 200 ZIP files and 100 XLS documents located in the search engine's index (they can be found by Google).
- However, only PDF files are currently tracked, and a meaningful file-name is not reported.

In both examples, the justification for tracking is stated followed by the current tracking situation.

## Weighting Your Scores

As described in Chapter 3, the weighting of items to track is a balance of two considerations:

- Is the activity an important part of the visitor's journey?
- How important is the activity to the business?

The weighting is relative, on a scale from 0 to 1.0, with 1.0 indicating the most important level. There is one exception to this rule—if you have an e-commerce website, weight transaction tracking is 2.0. That is, if you are collecting revenue directly on your website, it is super important to get this tracked correctly in Google Analytics.

For the range of weights, I use five possible values: 0.0, 0.25, 0.5, 0.75, 1.0 (and 2.0 for transactions only):

0.0   Not required. This could be, for example, clicking on images within a carousel. (Why websites bother with carousel images is a mystery to me. The user experience is very poor.)

0.25  Nice-to-know metrics, but the business is not asking for these at present. Examples include clicks on certain links, such as outbound links, or widget usage.

0.5   Somewhat important to know, but not a business priority at present. For example, error messages. These are important if you are launching a new website or rolling out a redesign. But for day-to-day operations, errors are dealt with by the web development team and are usually logged separately to Google Analytics.

0.75  Important metrics though not top priority. For example, these could be social sharing of content while the business is still figuring out its social strategy.

1.0   A key part of the visitor's journey and an important engagement for the business. For example, any action that results in a visitor providing their personal information to you, such as a lead generation form submission.

2.0   Vital metrics. Generally used for transaction tracking only.

The analytics team is responsible for producing the scorecard report. My approach is for the team to make the initial assessment of the weights for each tracking item. They answer the first question: Is the activity an important part of the visitor's journey? This sets the stage for the rest of the organization to understand what your website visitors experience.

The document then becomes the basis for further discussions with your stakeholders—the rest of the business that has invested in the analytics project. The follow-up discussion assesses the second question: How important is the activity to the business? The purpose is to fine-tune and finalize the importance of each weighting. This is a straightforward process and should be accomplished within one or two meetings.

### Calculating Your Quality Score

The weighted score is the last table column of Figure 4.1. The calculation is the weight of the item multiplied by its status value (taken from Table 4.1):

$$weighted\ score = weight \times status\ value$$

A few examples using Figure 4.1, illustrate how straightforward this is:

Item 1, Account setup and governance: The weighted score is $1.0 \times 5 = 5$.
Item 2, Tracking code deployment: The weighted score is $1.0 \times 10 = 10$.
Item 3, AdWords data import: The weighted score is $1.0 \times 0 = 0$.

Your *QS* is calculated as the sum of your weighted scores divided by the total of the weights representing a perfect score:

$$QS = \frac{sum\ of\ weighted\ scores}{sum\ of\ weights \times status\ value\ for\ green}$$

Again, this is straightforward. The *sum of weights × status value for green* is the sum of weights multiplied by 10. Using the example in Figure 4.1, this is $14.5 \times 10 = 145.0$. Therefore, $QS = 20 / 145 = 13.8$.

### SCORECARD ITEMS—WHAT TO ASSESS

For each row of Figure 4.1, what needs to be checked, why, and how? Most of this process concerns asking questions about what data is present in your reports, or what settings are configured in your Google Analytics account.

There is no specific order for the items to assess, and this is deliberate. Starting with having a Google Analytics account and deploying the tracking code across your pages (items 1 and 2) makes sense. However, the remaining items are not ranked by importance. This is because when viewing data and tracking code, it is easy for even expert eyes to glaze over. What determines if the tracking works correctly or not can be subtle. The random ordering of items in the scorecard forces the assessor to crosscheck reference points and is therefore a self-check for such subtleties.

For this reason, I recommend that only one person be responsible for the status assessment. They should be comfortable with HTML, JavaScript, and the architecture of your websites. This person should be on the analytics team, not someone from IT.

## Aren't These Tracked by Default?

Regardless of how a visitor arrives at your website, as long as you have deployed your tracking code, Google Analytics will track by default the visit, the visitor (the same visitor may make several visits), and the pages viewed by your visitors. That is a simple yet powerful data set that allows more than 100 visually rich reports to be automatically built for you. These show

- The time and date visitors arrive, and from which countries and cities—accurate to approximately a 25-mile (40 km) radius.
- The number of times they have come: are they a first-time visitor or a repeat visitor, and if so, how many times did they come before?
- What drove them to visit you: which search engine did they use, which social website or other website was involved in bringing you your visitors?
- The content visitors view: which pages are popular, how much time is spent on each page and on your entire website?

However, counting how many visits, where the vistors came from, and what pages they looked at is still a small piece of the data pie. It tells you almost nothing about engagement—whether your visitors achieve anything worthwhile to them, or how close they get to becoming a customer or repeat customer. It tells you nothing about your visitor value—that is, are you receiving high-value visitors or low-value ones? And it tells you nothing about which pages are important to your visitors—the pages that are most influential or persuasive—versus pages that just waste your visitors' time.

## Check in Real Time

The real-time reports of Google Analytics are a subset of reports that show you what's happening on your site—*as it happens*. Visit data is processed within a few seconds of the visitor's arriving on your site. Here is an example.

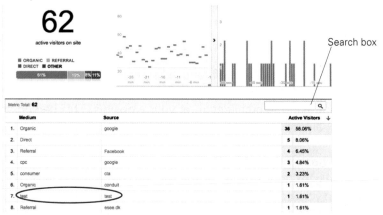

Search box

*A real-time report showing an up-to-the-second view of where visitors are coming from*

I use real-time reports to test what data is being reported on. The technique is to show real-time data for only your *own* visit—that, is while you are auditing your website. In this way you can see what data is being sent to Google Analytics (if any) that corresponds to your action.

Open two browser windows—one for your Google Analytics real-time reporting, one for your website. To isolate yourself from all other visitor traffic, visit your website with the addition of two extra campaign tracking parameters in the URL. For example, www.example.com?utm _source=test&utm_medium=test will be displayed in your real-time reports, as shown in table row 7 above. If you do not see the test row in your table, use the search box. By clicking on *test* in the Medium column (row 7), you can automatically segment your data in Google Analytics. That is, you isolate just that visitor traffic. As this URL is unique to you, it corresponds to your actions.

Now you can navigate the real-time reports and only view your own data. In your other browser window, click around your website viewing different pages. Assuming you have the basic Google Analytics tracking code in place, you will see the page URLs you have clicked on appear in the real-time content report.

Determining whether an action is tracked at all and how is the basis for many of my tracking tests within the scorecard.

Items 3 through 15 of the scorecard cover the collection of data points required to get a more informative picture of your visitors' experiences.

## 1. Account Setup
The first row of the scorecard summary table, Google Analytics Account Setup, concerns your Google Analytics account governance and includes the following three areas:

### Account Structure
Google Analytics is not a relational database. You cannot simply throw data into a big pot and then figure out the data relationships later. How you collect your data determines its structure. You can manipulate your data structure within your account setup using filters.

**What to assess:**
- Are you excluding visits from your own staff? These visits could represent a significant proportion of your total traffic, and they are not from your target audience. If tracking your own staff visits is important, create a separate report set for them.
- Are you excluding visits from your third-party agencies?
- Is there a backup report set to protect you if something should go wrong with your data?
- Is there a testing report set allowing you to experiment with changes before applying them to the main data set?
- Are any content filters applied and, if so, are they valid and working?
- Is the number of report sets (referred to as *views* in Google Analytics) reasonable and manageable for your organization?
- What other filters are present that are manipulating the data?

**Where to check:**   In order to make your assessment, you need admin access to your Google Analytics account. Within the Administration area (Figure 4.2a), check what views are available and what filters (Figure 4.2b) are being applied to your data.

### People and Access
Who has access to your data? This includes people both in your organization and in external third parties (agencies, consultancies, developers, partners, resellers, affiliates, and so forth). Similarly, who has the right to change the setup? As is the case with your bank account, your data is confidential and should only be viewable by authorized people.

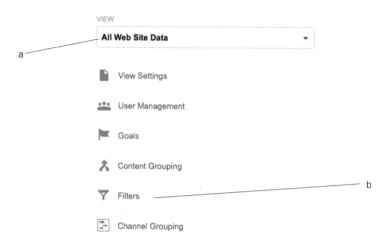

**Figure 4.2** *The Google Analytics Administration area for a report set: (a) assessing different report sets (views); (b) assessing applied filters*

**What to assess:**
- How many people have access to your data?
- What level of access do people have? View-only access, or full admin rights to change anything?
- How many admin users are there? This should be limited to a very small subset of users who have experience with Google Analytics administration and take full responsibility for their actions. The total number of account administrators should be as small as possible, and the requirement of being an administrator should be justified for each individual. As a rule of thumb, I red-flag any account with more than ten administrators.

**Where to check:**   To make your assessment, you need admin access to your Google Analytics account. Within the Administration area shown in Figure 4.2, select the User Management menu item and review the people listed and their associated permission levels.

### Content and Information
Documenting your setup (building a health check audit report is part of this), and understanding what type of data is being collected, is an important part of good governance. For example, Google Analytics has some restrictions on the type of data and volume of data you can

send it. These are covered in its terms of service (US version here: www.google.com/analytics/terms/us.html[3]).

**What to assess:**

- What is the volume of data being sent to Google Analytics? This includes all pageview, event, and transaction data. The free version of Google Analytics is limited to 10 million data hits per month. For Premium users, the standard limit is 1 billion data hits per month.
- Is personally identifiable information (PII) being collected? This is a red flag. No PII can be reported in Google Analytics. If it is, you risk your account being closed down. (*Note:* I am specifically referring to the collection of PII by Google Analytics. Collecting visitor PII in your contact database is fine, so long as this is done with the consent of your visitors.)
- Is there any documentation explaining the data collection methodologies employed? That is, has a scorecard audit been delivered previously, and does an implementation guidelines document exist (see Chapter 3)?
- Is there a suitable privacy statement on your website explaining how your organization collects and processes visitor data?

**Where to check:** To assess your total data volume, access your reports and enter the Behavior section (Figure 4.3). The overview report (a) lists your pageview volume for the past 30 days—the default date window. Add this number to the total number of events tracked, obtained from the Events ⇨ Overview report (b). This number should be less than 10 million

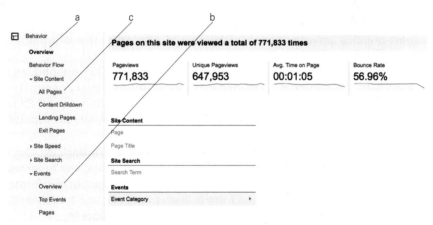

**Figure 4.3** *The Google Behavior report area: (a) pageviews; (b) events; (c) page content*

for a 30-day period in order to stay within the free Google Analytics terms of service. If not, consider the options discussed in Chapter 2 for this scenario.

PII can end up in your Google Analytics reports a number of different ways—for example, via transaction tracking, custom dimensions (known in older versions of Google Analytics as custom variables), event tracking, and pageview tracking. Any method of collecting PII breaks the Google Analytics terms of service. If someone has consciously made the decision to track PII in your Google Analytics account, then your situation is pretty dire. You must close the offending web property and all report sets for it, delete it (losing all previous data), and start again without collecting PII.

Even without making a conscious decision to track PII, it is possible to inadvertently collect it using Google Analytics—see the sidebar "How PII Gets into URLs." To assess this, review your Site Content ⇨ All Pages report (Figure 4.3c). This report contains a list of all page URLs viewed by your visitors. Conduct a table search for any possible PII collected in the visited URLs. Typically this is for potential field names such as "name," "email," or "address." Searching for the email @ symbol is also a good way to bubble up any potential email addresses captured.

If PII is present in your reports, you must close the offending web property, delete it, and start again without collecting PII.

---

### How PII Gets into URLs

If you collect personal information via a web form, ensure your developers use the POST method for form submission. This ensures the information contained in the form is not visible in your page URLs (for best-practice privacy reasons, you should also send the information encrypted via https).

If form submission data is not transmitted via the POST method, any form field information is appended to the page URL as a query parameter. The page URL is what Google Analytics tracks by default. Hence if PII is present in your URLs, this will appear in your Google Analytics reports. An example URL could be

/form/subscribed.php?name=Brian%20Clifton&email=brian@brianclifton.com

Apart from bad practice, losing the trust of your visitors, and breaking the Google Analytics terms of service, passing around personal information on the Internet in clear text form is likely to get you into trouble with the data protection authorities of the countries you operate in.

See Chapter 7 for a detailed discussion about PII and privacy.

## 2. Tracking Code Deployment

The Google Analytics tracking code (GATC) is the JavaScript snippet of code (typically a dozen or so lines) that you paste into the header area of all your pages. Without this tracking code present, no data collection can take place. In addition, a patchy deployment of the GATC—that is, some pages tracked, some not—leads to unexpected results, often the double counting of visitors.

**What to assess:**
- Is the tracking code working—that is, collecting data?
- Is cross-domain tracking required and implemented? This is when a visitor traverses more than one website that you own. This can be a subdomain (www.example.com ⇨ blog.example.com) or a full domain change (www.product-site.com ⇨ www.support-site.com).
- What version of the tracking code is running? Since the launch of Google Analytics, there have been three versions of the tracking code. The latest, launched in late 2013, is named analytics.js. It is commonly referred to as Universal Analytics.
- How is the tracking code placed on your pages—using code snippets or via a TMS? If a TMS, which vendor and who is responsible for it?
- What proportion of your website pages can be tracked? Your target is 100%. That is, at the very least your GATC should be deployed on *all* of your public-facing website pages. After all, if your organization has gone to the trouble to produce content, you should be tracking it. Otherwise, consider culling the page.

**Where to check:** Checking the GATC is the most technical part of the health check audit. To perform the check, you could manually review your web page HTML source code on a sample of pages. However, that is a laborious task and is prone to human error. Instead, there are a number of tools that can simplify the task and that offer ways to automatically detect errors and issues for you.

**Google Analytics Debugger—official Google Chrome extension** Loads the debug version of the GATC for all websites you browse. It prints useful information to the developer console that can tell you when your analytics tracking code is set up incorrectly. It provides a detailed breakdown of each tracking beacon sent to Google Analytics. Free to use. (I use this daily!)
https://chrome.google.com/webstore/search/google-analytics-debugger

**Google Tag Assistant—official Google Chrome extension**  Helps to troubleshoot the installation of various Google tracking codes on your website—verifying you have installed beacons correctly as you navigate pages. It reports which beacons are present, reports errors found, and suggests implementation improvements. Free to use.
https://chrome.google.com/webstore/search-extensions/tag-assistant-by-google

**Analytics Debugger—third-party website service**  Can scan and debug your website implementation (and uniquely your mobile apps) for numerous tracking beacons, including Google Analytics. In addition, it can monitor for tracking code changes and provides *interactive* debugging—showing you what data is sent as you interact with your pages. Freemium tool. www.analytics-debugger.com/brianclifton

**Web Analytics Solution Profiler (WASP)—third-party Chrome extension**  Enables you to test and debug your website tracking beacons from virtually any tracking tool on the market. It provides a visualization of scripts and tag dependencies based on an auto-detecting algorithm. Freemium tool. www.webanalyticssolutionprofiler.com

**Tag Inspector—third-party website service**  Intelligent crawler to scan your website. Hierarchy views give you a complete picture of your tracking beacons—whether in the source code of your page, within a tag management system, or piggybacking off another tag. Freemium tool.
http://taginspector.com/brianclifton

### 3. AdWords Data

AdWords, Google's advertising platform, has its own separate reporting interface. However, this only allows you to see visitor click-throughs to your website—the number of clicks on your ads, not all the things visitors do once they arrive on your website. Clearly, there is an advantage to following the visitor's journey.

Doing so requires linking your Google Analytics account and your AdWords account. Once this is done, not only will you be able to view the full visitor journey (from ad click-through to engagement to conversion) but you can also import your AdWords cost and impression data into your Google Analytics reports.

**What to assess:**
- Can Google Analytics identify your AdWords visitors?
- Is your AdWords cost and impression data being imported?

- If you use more than one AdWords account, do your payment currencies—the currencies you pay for your ads—match? To avoid confusing the performance of your campaigns, you will want to avoid mixing AdWords currencies within one set of reports.

**Where to check:** All visitors who click through from your AdWords ad will have an extra parameter (*gclid*) appended to your landing page URLs, for example, www.example.com/product/?gclid=Q76WERbcTYuAWw. Therefore, the first check is to do a search on Google that displays your ad, click on it, and inspect the URL of your landing page. If the gclid parameter is not present, Google Analytics will not identify it as an AdWords visit. Instead, it will regard the visit as coming from Google organic search (free search)—a very different system! If you notice this problem, contact the person responsible for your AdWords advertising and ensure your AdWords account is linked to your Google Analytics account.[4]

Assuming the gclid parameter is present on your landing pages, check the AdWords section of your Google Analytics reports for cost and impression data (Figure 4.4). If these are present, then both the reporting of AdWords visitors and the concomitant cost and impression data imports are working. If not, contact the person responsible for your AdWords advertising and ask about the linking of your AdWords and Google Analytics accounts.[4]

## 4. Site Search Tracking

*Site search* is the terminology used to describe your website's internal search engine. For any website with even a moderate number of pages, site search is a critical part of your visitors' website experience. A good

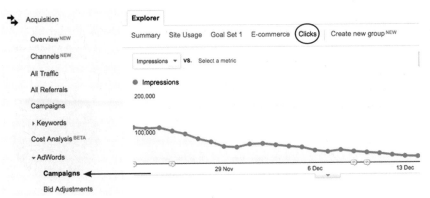

**Figure 4.4** *Checking AdWords data*

site search facility can make the difference between a visitor having an efficient, enjoyable experience and a painful one that can cost you business.

The queries (search terms) your visitors enter are a great visitor feedback mechanism. Your visitors are telling you exactly what they are looking for, in their own language and using their own terminology. Analyzing query terms can prove insightful when it comes to understanding how your visitors think about your products.

**What to assess:**

- Can Google Analytics detect usage of your internal site search facility?
- If this usage is tracked, are the keywords a visitor uses reported?
- Are keywords categorized into sensible groupings? For example, product search, support search, store locator search.
- Are you tracking zero search results—instances when your site search facility returns no results back to the user?

**Where to check:** Site search usage has its own dedicated set of reports within Google Analytics (Figure 4.5). Review these reports. Tracking zero results is particularly insightful. Typically a separate site search category is used for this. Therefore, check for its presence.

## 5. File Download Tracking

By definition, a file download is not an HTML file, and therefore this cannot receive a GATC within it. Therefore, the technique for tracking these is to trigger a Google Analytics tracking call when a visitor clicks on a download link.

**Figure 4.5** *Checking your site search data*

**What to assess:**
- Are file downloads being reported?
- Are reports clear on what file has been downloaded? Do they make sense to your marketing team, or is a lookup table required?
- Can you differentiate file types—PDF, DOC, ZIP, and so on?

**Where to check:**   There are two ways to track a file download—either as a *virtual pageview* or as an *event* (see the appendix). As a quick assessment, check your real-time reports while browsing your website. Click on a file download link and view both the content and events reports within the real-time section. This will reveal if any tracking of file downloads is in place and, if so, what method is being used.

Regardless of the method used, file downloads should be categorized in a logical manner—for example, a category name of *pdf*, *downloads*, or *files* (event tracking), or */downloads/pdf* (virtual pageview tracking). The exact naming is not important—as long as it is logical to the report user. For good account governance, ensure you document your specific setup before assigning a status value of green for this item.

## 6. Outbound Link Tracking
Outbound links are links on your website that send a visitor away to another website. This can be a completely different, though relevant, destination— such as to a reseller or partner website. The link could also send a visitor to another web property that you own—for example, a link leaving your product website could take the visitor to your support website.

As a click on an outbound link is taking the visitor away from your website, that action is not tracked in Google Analytics by default. Therefore, the technique is to trigger a Google Analytics tracking call when a visitor clicks on an outbound link.

**What to assess:**
- Are click-throughs on outbound links tracked?
- If so, how are they tracked?
- Can you differentiate your different types of outbound links—to websites you own, to resellers, and so forth?

**Where to check:**   As with tracking file downloads, outbound links can be tracked as a virtual pageview or an event. Therefore, detecting whether these are reported is the same process. Check your real-time reports while browsing your website. Click on an outbound link and view both the content and events reports within the real-time section. This will reveal if any tracking of outbound links is in place and, if so, what method is being used.

Regardless of the method used, outbound links should be categorized in a logical manner—for example, a category name of *outbound*, *links*, or *resellers* (event tracking), or */external/site-name* (virtual pageview tracking). The exact naming is not important—as long as it is logical to the report user. For good account governance, ensure you document the setup used for outbound link tracking before assigning a status value of green for this item.

## 7. Form Completion Tracking

When a visitor submits a contact request form, or any other type of form (subscription sign-up, registration), is the submission tracked correctly?

### What to assess:
- Is it possible to differentiate between a form view and a form submission?
- Does Google Analytics collect any PII?

**Where to check:**  In most cases, you will want your forms and form submissions tracked as pageviews. That is, the visitor sees the initial form page, and if they submit their details they then view a thank you or confirmation page. Try this yourself on your own site. If the URL does not change when you submit your form, you will not be able to ascertain how many submissions were made or calculate your form conversion rates.

The best way to verify this is within your real-time reports. While browsing your website, view your form, submit it, then check both the content and events reports within the real-time section to see if any pageview or event data is sent. If you have numerous forms on your website, ensure a logical naming structure is employed—either as a virtual pageview path or as an event category.

While checking if form views and submissions are tracked in Google Analytics, review if any PII is captured. This was discussed earlier in this section for item 1 of the scorecard, Account Setup. Doing so again here is a good secondary check. After all, collecting PII breaks the Google Analytics terms of service and means you will have to close and delete *all* previously collected data for a web property.

## 8. Video Tracking

Moving beyond film and animations, video is gaining popularity as a method to demonstrate products, provide how-to guides, troubleshoot problems, and record time-sensitive events, such as conference presentations. If you have embedded video on your website, you will want to know if people are watching the content and to what extent.

**What to assess:**

- Is Google Analytics tracking whether visitors play an embedded video?
- Is Google Analytics tracking whether visitors play an embedded video and view $x$% of it? For example, 50% is a good sign of engagement.
- Is Google Analytics tracking whether visitors played an embedded video to completion? Clearly, watching to the end is an indication of a very strong engagement.

**Where to check:** In most cases, you will want your video interaction tracked as an event—an interaction within a page. Therefore, check for this in your real-time reports while browsing your website. Click on an embedded video file to start the play. At the same, time view your events reports within the real-time section. This will reveal if any tracking of video interaction is in place. At a minimum, you should see an event reported for the start of the video play. Other desirable metrics include *played to completion* and *played x%* (for example, *played 50%*).

If tracking is in place, ensure a logical naming structure is employed, so you can easily identify what video was watched and view it separately from other types of events. As there are numerous ways to define a visitor's engagement with a video, document your setup before assigning a status value of green for this item.

## 9. Error Page Tracking

Generally, error pages are tracked by default. If you have deployed the tracking code to your page templates, an error page such as "page not found" will also be tracked. The problem is that the default tracking behavior results in the error being tracked as a regular pageview, with no indication it is actually an error.

**What to assess:**

- If the visitor has encountered an error with your site, is the error information sent to Google Analytics?

**Where to check:**　Check this in your real-time reports by viewing an obvious error page. For example, enter the following URL into your browser: www.example.com/product-mytest (replacing example.com).

When viewing the content report shown in your real-time section, you will most likely see /product-mytest showing as a valid pageview. If so, you will notice there is nothing to indicate that this page is in fact generated by an error (a 404 page). This should be corrected by using a virtual pageview call to Google Analytics instead. If you have this in place, you will see something similar to /error 404/product-mytest in your Real-Time ⇨ Content reports. The exact naming convention is not important as long as it is clear to the report user that the pageview is generated by an error.

Alternatively, check your page titles within the content section of your reports. If page titles contain information that a page URL is in fact an error, you can use this instead to group and highlight all URLs that are generating errors to your visitors. Document which setup (if any) you have in place for identifying errors before assigning a status value of green for this item.

## 10. Transaction Tracking

Transactions by their nature have many moving parts. From a technical viewpoint, tracking a transaction can be quite difficult. Cross-domain tracking is often required for a visitor to complete their purchase—tracking a visitor from www.example.com to shop.example.com, or www.example.com to www.payment-gateway.com and back to www.example.com.

In addition, there are numerous ways a product can be purchased: the initial purchase; modifying the purchase at a later date (paying more); changing the delivery details at a later date (not paying more). Which of these should be tracked as a transaction requires careful consideration. Generally I recommend only the initial purchase be tracked, as this is the only action that directly relates to the performance of your website—its marketing, its content, and its usability.

## What to assess:

- Are transactions tracked on your site correctly? That is, do the numbers correlate with your back-end system that processes the orders?
- Is cross-domain tracking implemented and correct?
- Are multiple currencies taken into account? For example, combining USD with EUR with GBP is not desirable.

**Where to check:** Real-time tracking of transactions is not currently available in Google Analytics. Therefore, you will need to check the standard reports for these—Conversions ⇨ E-commerce reports (Figure 4.6).

As an initial sanity check, select five or so products from your product performance report and review the quantity purchased, unique purchases, and product revenue numbers. Do these match your company system that processes orders? The match is unlikely to be exact for a variety of reasons: order errors, returns, time differences when an order is received versus when it is processed, and so forth. As a rule of thumb I accept an error of up to 5%. If the errors are larger than this, then there is likely a problem. Perhaps different currencies are being mixed or there is a technical error with the implementation?

To shed more light on this, conduct several different test transactions yourself—transactions where you know exactly what you bought, the quantities, and their costs. On completion of your purchase, the transaction ID of your order, displayed to the purchaser, can also be found in the E-commerce ⇨ Transaction report. Within this report, click on your transaction ID and view your specific order for correctness.

## 11. Event Tracking

Events are in-page actions that visitors complete that do not result in a pageview. That is, they are not tracked by default in Google Analytics.

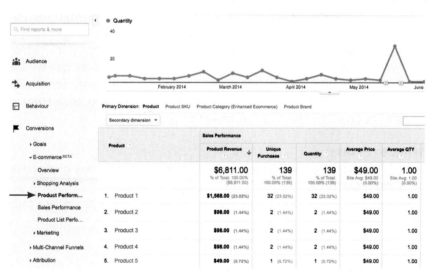

**Figure 4.6** *Example of a transaction report*

Some of these you will have already covered in items 5, 6, and 8. Other potential events include clicks on internal advertisements; rotating through a carousel of images; moving around a long page of content using HTML bookmarks; clicking on a click-to-call button; adding, removing, or modifying a shopping cart item; and interacting with widgets, such as a loan calculator.

**What to assess:**

- A key assessment to be made is whether any event tracking is required at all. Not every non-pageview click a visitor makes has to be tracked—that would generate a large amount of noise. Carefully assess what has to be tracked. For example, I have found little purpose in tracking carousel images, other than to show that no one is interested in them!

**Where to check:**   Check your event tracking reports (Figure 4.3b) to see what data is being collected and decide if it is valuable to your organization. If these events are required, ensure that what they define and what triggers them is documented before assigning a status value of green for this item.

## 12. Goal Setup

A *goal* is a key engagement point that indicates some kind of success— the success of converting an anonymous visitor into something more. An obvious goal is the conversion to a customer (purchase). However, in most scenarios it is the strengthening of the visitor relationship—either anonymously or for an existing customer. For example, these can be the download of a PDF catalog; submission of a contact request form; subscription to a newsletter; using your store finder; sharing your content socially; or adding a review or comment to your site.

**What to assess:**

- Check your conversion reports to establish whether any goals have been set.
- If so, do these reflect the goals of the business—that is, are they relevant?
- Have your goals been monetized?

**Where to check:**   If your Conversions ⇨ Goals ⇨ Overview report contains any data, then you have at least some goals configured (Figure 4.7).

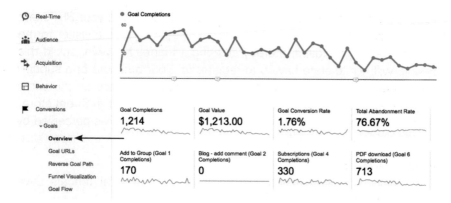

**Figure 4.7** *Sample goal conversion overview report*

Otherwise, you will see a message with words to the effect "This report requires goals to be enabled for the view." If data is present in this report, review the relevancy to your business. Are the goals tangible indicators of success? Before assigning a status value of green for this item, ensure an implementation document is available explaining what goals are defined and what triggers them.

If you know what goals *should* be defined in your reports, you can verify that these are working by monitoring your real-time reports. Visit your website and complete a goal conversion yourself; then view the Conversions report shown in your real-time section.

☛ *Goals are synonymous with KPIs. For more details, see Chapter 9.*

## 13. Funnel Setup

A funnel is a well-defined sequence of steps that a visitor goes through to achieve a goal (as in item 12). In this context, *well-defined* means that the visitor must go through the sequence of steps in order to reach the goal. A classic example is a checkout process: the visitor must go through certain steps in order for a successful transaction to take place. The steps may consist of add to cart ⇨ enter delivery details ⇨ pay ⇨ receipt page. The receipt page is the goal in this scenario (the confirmed purchase), and the preceding steps are the sales funnel. You define these steps in Google Analytics so that you can visualize shopping cart abandonment rates, pain points, and so forth.

Non-transactional sites also have funnels. A contact request (or subscription) form is always a two-step funnel—the initial viewing of the form followed by its successful submission. However, not all goals have an associated funnel. Typically a visitor can easily download your PDF litera-ture without a funnel process. You could of course force a visitor to reg-ister for your downloads, thereby creating a funnel. However, avoid this. People will not tolerate having to register for your brochure or a support document—something all users expect without hindrance (in the same way people will not accept hindrance walking into your Main Street store). Registration should only be used for high-value content, as perceived by your visitors, not by your business.

**What to assess:**
- Check your conversion reports to see if any goal funnels have been set.
- Check whether the data drop-off through the funnel appears sensible.

**Where to check:** If your Conversions ⇨ Goals ⇨ Funnel Visualization report contains any data, then you have at least some funnels configured (Figure 4.8). Otherwise, you will see a message with words to the effect "This report requires goals to be enabled for the view." If data is present in this report, review the relevancy to your business.

### 14. Visitor Labeling

*Visitor labels* are labels Google Analytics can attach to your visitors' activ-ity. The Google Analytics terminology is *custom dimensions* and *custom metrics*. However, I prefer the nontechnical term *label* to describe these. (Before the Universal Analytics update of 2013, these were referred to as *custom variables*).

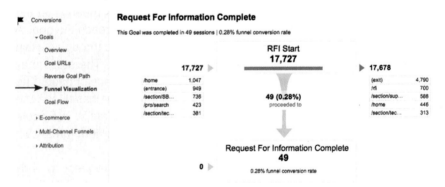

**Figure 4.8** *Example of a funnel visualization report*

There are multiple ways to use labeling. The most obvious use is to distinguish between a "customer" and a "noncustomer." A visitor may have purchased from you only once but may have visited your site many times. The same technique can be used for a "subscriber," a "contactor," or any other visitor who can be identified as engaged or interested. It is a powerful method to use for segmentation.

**What to assess:**

- Check your reports for visitor labels in use (*custom dimensions* or *custom variables*).
- If in use, do they reflect high-value actions on your site—such as becoming a customer?

**Where to check:** If you are using the latest Universal Analytics tracking code, check whether any custom dimensions have been configured; review your web property Administration section, as shown in Figure 4.9. In this example, there is one *custom dimension* defined, "AVP remembered."

If you are not using Universal Analytics (see scorecard item 2), custom variables can be viewed in your Audience ⇨ Custom ⇨ Custom Variables report. There are five slots available for custom variables. Check all five keys for data.

Regardless of which tracking code deployment you have in place, a good implementation document is required in order to understand what your labels are defining and what triggers them. Ensure this is in place before assigning a status value of green for this item.

**Figure 4.9** *Viewing visitor labels for a Universal Analytics deployment*

## 15. Campaign Tracking

Are your campaigns being tracked? If you are running paid search advertising (such as AdWords), banner ads, email marketing, social media marketing, affiliate marketing, even offline marketing, you will want to know which specific ads and which specific campaigns are working for you. To track these you must modify your landing page URLs by adding parameters to them. This is called *campaign tracking* and is described in Chapter 6.

Setting up campaign tracking is straightforward. However, for reports to make sense they must be implemented and done in a methodical way. *Note:* Tracking AdWords visitors is covered in scorecard item 3.

**What to assess:**
- Aside from AdWords, are other campaigns tracked?
- If so, are campaigns logically named and relevant to your marketing communications department?
- Are campaigns correctly grouped by channel?

**Where to check:** Your acquisition section contains two key reports for checking your campaign tracking. From the All Traffic report, select the primary dimension of *medium* and review the data table as shown in Figure 4.10. The four rows shown, representing the mediums *none*, *organic*, *cpc* (AdWords), and *referral*, are the default channels that Google Analytics detects. If you only have these four mediums present in this report, then campaign tracking is not set up. Optimally, the number of different mediums tracked should be around ten. More than that can indicate an issue with your setup, such as the misalignment of campaign tracking naming terms.

Review your Acquisition ⇨ Campaigns report. This lists all your campaign names, including any from AdWords. Are these logically named, and is your marketing team able to understand them at a glance?

For campaign tracking, Google Analytics reports WYSIWYG—what you see is what you get. Anyone (even outside your organization) can create URLs to your website with campaign tracking parameters appended to them. If they are gibberish, contain typos, or are simply wrong, they will show up in your reports as written. Document how your campaign tracking is defined so that reports can be understood and filtered if necessary. Ensure this documentation is in place before assigning a status value of green for this item.

**Figure 4.10** *Sample mediums report showing which channels are sending traffic*

## Default Referrers in Google Analytics

As long as the tracking code is deployed across all of your pages, Google Analytics tracks *all* visitors to your website by default, regardless of where they came from. However, unless you tell it otherwise, Google Analytics can only assign a visitor to one of three* channels and none of these contains campaign-specific details:

- Organic—a visitor who has conducted a search engine query and clicked through to your website via a non-paid listing (that is, not an ad)
- Referral—a visitor who has found a link to your website on another website and clicked through (an affiliate site, partner site, trade association listing, or the like)
- Direct—a visitor who has typed your web address directly into their browser because they remembered it (or used their existing browser bookmark)

Clearly, only reporting three channels is limiting. The fix is to deploy campaign tracking, which enables you to track unlimited campaigns in any way you wish.

---

\* There is a special fourth case for social network visits that Google Analytics will automatically assign—visits from Facebook, Twitter, Google+, and similar sites. However, campaign information for these social sites remains unavailable unless campaign tracking is deployed.

An important consideration when tracking social visitors is that at least half will come via a mobile app,[6,7] not via a standard web browser. Such referrals cannot be detected by Google Analytics or any other tracking tool. This means the name of the social site (Facebook, Twitter, LinkedIn, Google+, and so forth) cannot be detected. However, this can also be overcome by the use of campaign tracking.

## MONITORING YOUR QUALITY SCORE

Your Google Analytics quality score is an important metric in itself—your data health check that is part of any analysis. For example, if there is a sudden unexpected change in visitors clicking on a marketing campaign, the analyst team will first refer to the overall quality score and the score-card detail that comes with it to assess the validity of the sudden change: is the campaign in question tracked correctly?

Determining your quality score is not a one-time, set-and-forget process. Data quality can and does degrade over time. There are many reasons, but it comes down to the rapidly evolving medium of the web. Commercial websites are in a constant flux. New content is created; existing content is updated; marketing techniques evolve; new technology and new ways of presenting information come to the fore. Your business is also evolving, with new and updated products, staff changes, events, PR, policy changes, new services. After a year, if you compare your website before and after, a great deal will have changed, even if the look and feel remain the same.

This constant flux of change affects your data quality—for the worse. Tracking codes can go missing, errors get introduced, new tracking methods don't follow the original blueprint, and so forth. For large organizations, different departments working closely together at the start of the data project can drift away from the central approach and focus on their own silos. This can affect the data for all your Google Analytics users. For all of these reasons, it is important to regularly audit your Google Analytics implementation with a scorecard review.

How often should you audit?

This will depend on how much flux your website is in. To keep things manageable, I recommend at most once per month and at least once per year. Going through the audit process may sound painful, but after your initial scorecard audit, updates usually happen as part of the regular analysis of reports. That is, as part of their ongoing analysis, the analysis team will be constantly validating data. Anything found missing should be reported and the quality score adjusted for that period. The fix can then be prioritized for your next website update.

Figure 4.11 is a dashboard approach I use for monitoring a website's Google Analytics quality score over time. It shows how much confidence the analytics team has in the current data set and in which direction the quality score is heading.

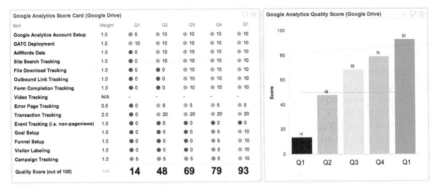

**Figure 4.11** *Google Analytics quality score tracked over time*

## SPEAKING OF DATA QUALITY...

| When I hear this... | I reply with... |
| --- | --- |
| Our stats reports in Facebook.com show much greater numbers than what Google Analytics reports. Which is right? | Unless campaign tracking has been used on your landing page links (the links on Facebook that point back to your website), visitors from Facebook will be significantly undercounted by Google Analytics. This is because mobile app users will not be correctly tracked. In addition, campaign tracking parameters are required to report campaign-specific information. |
| Who should be assigned to building and maintaining our Google Analytics scorecard? | The responsibility for this should lie with the analytics team working in conjunction with the web development team. Typically the person conducting the scorecard audit is an analyst—a person expert in Google Analytics and comfortable viewing HTML source code and JavaScript. |
| Who should be assigned to building and maintaining our campaign tracking? | This should be owned and maintained by your *internal* marketing team. Even though you may use external agencies to place ads and build marketing campaigns for you, the tracking should be centrally coordinated within your organization. This ensures a consistency of tracking across the broad spectrum of marketing activities—both digital and non-digital. |
| Our quality score varies each month— sometimes as high as 90, sometimes as low as 70. Should we be concerned? | Your quality score will vary over time due to the natural flux of all things digital. However, ensure your team understands why there is variance and try to minimize it. Learn from past changes. Also be transparent with your score items so that other teams don't waste time on analysis that may be flawed or lose trust in the reporting method. Even a negative change may be viewed in a positive light if you are transparent and can explain it. |

## CHAPTER 4 REFERENCES

1    Empirical studies using real data for cookie deletion rates are notoriously difficult to conduct. Most reports are survey-based studies, which I have concluded are inaccurate (in my experience, survey respondents exaggerate their vigilance when it comes to sensitive subjects such as privacy). However, a detailed empirical study was conducted by Paul Strupp and Garrett Clark in 2009 (both formerly of Sun Microsystems). The original article is no longer available, but the Internet Archive does contain a copy: https://web.archive.org/web/20090828151603 /http://blogs.sun.com/pstrupp/entry/cookie_retention_rates.

2    The balanced scorecard approach is defined at http://en.wikipedia.org/wiki/Balanced_scorecard.

3    The Google Analytics terms of service vary by country. Ensure that you view the correct version relevant to you by selecting the Terms of Service link at the bottom of your Google Analytics reports.

4    Step-by-step instructions for linking AdWords with Google Analytics: https://support.google.com/analytics/answer/1033961

5    In July 2014, according to a compilation of statistics by Statistic Brain, 60% of tweets came from third-party applications: www.statisticbrain.com/twitter-statistics.

6    From Facebook's quarterly earnings slides (Q2 2013), 71% of Facebook users access the site via a mobile device: http://www.cnet.com/news/facebook-earnings-by-the-numbers-819m -mobile-users/.

# Jumpstart Guide
# to Key Features

**This chapter is a quick overview** of report features so you can see how to use Google Analytics to drive your business forward. This is not an anatomy of the user interface or an endless roll of report screenshots. By the end of this chapter, you should have the confidence and interest level to investigate further. I use Chapter 10 to illustrate how some of these features are used to provide real-world insights.

## REPORTS OVERVIEW—WHAT'S AVAILABLE

While this book focuses on the significance of the available reports from a website owner's point of view, the new Universal Analytics protocol allows you to collect data from anything connected to the Internet ("the Internet of things"[1]), so these reports can be applied in other ways. The significance of Universal Analytics is discussed in Chapter 6.

Figure 5.1 shows the Audience Overview report. This is the initial report that is loaded when you log in to Google Analytics.

The navigation menu to the left is consistent throughout the interface and is your focal point for finding information. Most of the menu items contain multiple submenus that expand as you click them. Google Analytics has over 100 reports available by default. Don't worry—I am not going through all of these! Chapter 4 contains numerous screenshots if you wish to get a feel for the general report layouts and design.

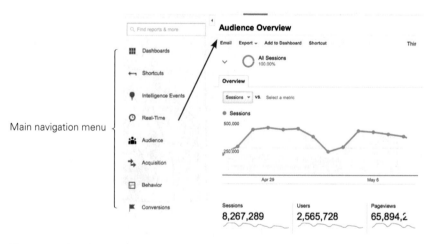

**Figure 5.1** *The initial report—Audience Overview—shown when you log in to Google Analytics*

## Custom Reports

On top of the 100+ standard reports described here, you can also build custom reports that combine the data in ways that suit your organization better.

**Dashboards** "Show me an overview of performance."

A dashboard is a custom report that you build from pieces of other reports. A dashboard lets you view disparate chunks of information, alongside each other. For example, you might want a mini-chart displaying the number of visitor engagements plotted over time, shown alongside a table of your top-performing pages. This will allow you to assess which pages are driving engagements.

The dashboard area is useful for collecting an overview of information from different reports without the need to drill down into the separate reports themselves. You can create multiple dashboards.

**Shortcuts** "Take me to that report we examined last week."

A shortcut is a link, created by you, that takes you directly to a *specific* report configuration. For example, if you have previously investigated a report—perhaps drilled down several layers and applied a detailed segment and a filter—you preserve that specific configuration when you create a shortcut for it. The shortcut link is a helpful one-click access to that report. It means you avoid the need to apply the same settings next time you wish to view the same report.

**Intelligence Events** "Has anything changed significantly?"

Google Analytics performs some clever predictive analytics by monitoring your data patterns. For example, if it detects that data patterns change significantly, an alert is created in your reports to highlight this for you. Google Analytics determines what constitutes a significant change based on your past performance. Custom alerts can also be created and emailed to you if they trigger.

This is powerful stuff, because rather than analysts having to check each day for significant change in data patterns that can be buried deep in your reports (if traffic to your website drops by 20% compared to this day last week, say, or if product purchases are significantly higher this month than last month) they (and other people) can be alerted automatically—a great second pair of eyes for the digital analytics team that works 24/7 on your behalf.

**Real-Time** "Show me what's happening right now."

As the name suggests, real-time reports are updated in real time—usually within 4 seconds (an amazing engineering feat by Google). These reports are a great way to explore the dynamics of your website and test new campaigns, pages, or website features.

Real-time reports are powerful for tracking anything that is time-sensitive, such as when you unveil a new product, launch a large advertising campaign (at half-time during a football match, perhaps), or have an important PR announcement to make.

To allow for rapid updates, real-time reports are abridged versions of the full reports. That said, they are a comprehensive suite of reports showing traffic volumes; where visitors come from (geo-location); the referral source (the campaigns and other websites providing your traffic); what content is being viewed; in-page events your visitors trigger; and the conversions generated (sales, leads, engagement).

**Audience** "Who are our visitors?"

The default report loaded when you log in to your Google Analytics account comes from this section. The Audience section is a collection of reports that inform you about your visitors without the use of any personal information: where they are located—accurate to within a 25-mile radius (40 km); their demographics (gender, age group, interest group); whether they are new or returning visitors; how long they stay and the number of pages viewed; visitor frequency and recency (how often and how recently they visit); what devices are used—Windows versus Mac, mobile, tablet, or desktop. Here, mobile and tablet reports can get very specific—right down to make and model of the phone used by your visitors.

---

### Avoid Real-Time Fixation

Shelby Thayer,[2] a good friend and analytics expert, said, "I have a love–hate relationship with real-time reports. I wish our team were the only ones that knew they existed!"

Her reasoning is that real-time reports are useful for specific things—such as testing and launching a new campaign, page, site, or product. However, beyond this they are eye candy. The issue is that because the charts and numbers update as you watch them, you become fixated. Real-time reports are addictive—a great deal of time can be wasted being mesmerized by the ebb and flow of your traffic. Use them judiciously.

**Acquisition**  "Where do our visitors come from?"

Acquisition reports tell you how visitors arrive at your site—which channels and what specific campaigns are driving visitors to you, and how these differentiate when it comes to engagement with your brand and purchasing. For example, if you run a Spring Sale campaign, you can compare its performance across multiple channels. Alternatively, for a given channel, what campaigns are successful?

Campaign information shown in your reports can get very detailed if required. They can show the performance of a particular banner ad (animated versus static); different keywords used by visitors clicking through from your AdWords ads; the success of a specific email sent versus its follow-up—even which link was clicked on within an email; and so forth.

Social interactions are also recorded here—visitors sharing your content via buttons such as Tweet, Like, Pin, or Google+, and conversations that happen away from your website on a particular social network.[3]

**Behavior**  "What do our visitors do?"

The behavior report set provides information on what your audience does on your website, such as the content (pages) they view; page load

---

### Offline Campaign Tracking

With a little know-how, your acquisition reports can also compare the performance of your offline marketing initiatives. There are numerous ways to approach this, with varying degrees of accuracy.

One technique is to use a vanity URL, such as example.com/springsale. This URL is then used in your *offline* advertising only, not published anywhere online (including your own site). In other words, the only way a visitor can be aware of the campaign page is to have seen the vanity URL via your offline campaign.

For *online* marketing efforts of the same campaign, use a separate URL, such as example.com/products/sale/spring. The URL is different and functional—it does not need to be as "attractive" as the URL used for your offline message because online visitors follow links, not the underlying syntax. Using this method, visitors resulting from online and offline marketing campaigns can be differentiated.

If you adopt the vanity URL method, it is a good idea to also run a paid search campaign in parallel. This is because some visitors will forget the full URL but may remember the product advertised or the buzzwords used. Target these words in your paid search advertising to ensure these visitors also find you.[4]

times they experience; whether they use your internal site search tool (and what keywords they use); whether they click on actions within a page (events that are not pageviews); what ads are clicked on; and so forth. Also reported in this section is the performance of any A/B testing you are conducting (displaying different versions of your content to different visitors).

**Conversions** "What are the important things visitors do?"

Conversion reports, which tell you about visitors who convert into leads or customers, are probably the most important report set for your organization. They highlight the metrics that you define as constituting success—the significant engagements that go beyond traffic levels and pageviews. These include detailed reports for e-commerce and engagements (goals). To complement these, Google Analytics includes two sophisticated reports—multi-channel (Figures 5.2 and 5.3) and attribution modeling.

Multi-channel reports show what overlaps exist in your marketing campaigns that are driving conversions, such as how many campaigns your visitors touched before they converted, which campaigns were involved, and what order your customers clicked on them.

Attribution modeling lets you experiment with assigning monetary values to each of your overlapping campaigns. Let's illustrate this with a

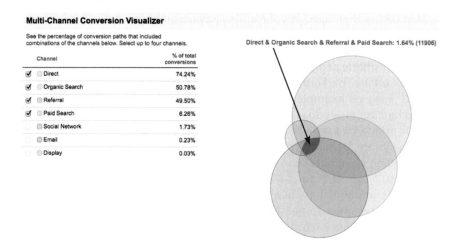

**Figure 5.2** *Multi-channel overlap report*

**Figure 5.3** *Multi-channel path report*

simple example. Suppose a visitor comes to your site on two separate occasions—a click from an organic search engine followed by a click-through from a referral (partner website)—as shown in row 10 of Figure 5.3. During their second visit they convert—either as an e-commerce transaction or as a new lead. How much credit should be given to your organic versus partner marketing efforts? Attribution modeling allows you to experiment with obtaining the best fit.

Attribution modeling is discussed further in Chapter 6.

### Metrics versus Dimensions

Google Analytics reports consist of two different types of information—metrics and dimensions.[5]

A metric is a number—for example, the number of visitors to your website, the number of conversions from a campaign, the amount of revenue gained, or new leads generated.

A dimension is textual information—for example, the list of your top-performing pages, the most effective campaign names, your best-selling products, and so on.

## UNDERSTANDING SEGMENTATION AND ITS IMPORTANCE

Apart from collecting good quality data in the first place (your installation), deciding how to segment your data is the bread and butter of the digital analytics team. Google Analytics has some powerful features that help with this.

Segmentation is the grouping together of similar visitor behaviors to facilitate understanding. Without segmentation, your website reports are a large pot of data containing a mix of visitor types who have different objectives, expectations, and desires for their website visit. As shown in Figure 5.4, visitor types include

- New customers—people who sign up or purchase for the first time.
- Existing customers—people who need support or who are ready to make a subsequent purchase. They may be potential advocates of your brand, or they may be detractors.
- Prospects—information gatherers who may one day become customers. These can be subdivided by their engagement type—for example, prospects who have subscribed to your newsletter, downloaded your catalog, or submitted a request for information form—or classified as high-, medium-, or low-value prospects. The

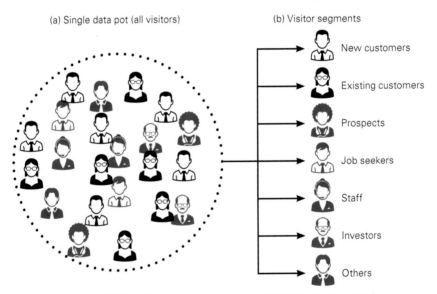

**Figure 5.4** *Website visitor types: (a) unsegmented; (b) segmented*

**Using Segments**

Segments do not alter or manipulate your data. They simply group it based on a set of rules you define. You can apply or remove a segment in your reports with one click.

A segment is applicable to all your reports (as per Figure 5.1). As you navigate through Google Analytics, the same segment—and even multiple selected segments—remain in place.

---

segmentation techniques for subdividing this group are currently a hot business trend called *marketing automation*.

- Job seekers—from the shop floor to the next potential CEO.
- Staff—people using your website content to facilitate sales and customer service.
- Investors—people who want to know how the business is doing—the vision, the direction, and its execution.
- Others—generally visitors you do not want, such as automated bots (authorized and non-authorized website monitors); spammers; visitors arriving by mistake; or simply visitors of little interest to your organization.

With a single pot of data (Figure 5.4a), very little insight can be gained. Inevitably you will draw conclusions from an average of averages. And when the population is characterized by very different visitor types, the middle ground represents nothing in the real world.

On the other hand, Figure 5.4b represents seven different types of behavior, allowing you to study them separately. At the very least, ensure you can separate your existing customers from your prospects.

**The Power of Segmentation**

Consider the needs of your marketing stakeholder who wishes to know how successfully her well-thought-out campaign is creating interest. The purpose is to increase traffic to the website. Therefore, a simple calculation to determine performance during a particular time period is

$$campaign\ performance = \frac{number\ of\ visitors\ arriving\ via\ the\ campaign}{total\ number\ of\ visits}$$

If there were 1,000 visits via the campaign in an overall visit count of 100,000, the campaign provided only 1% of traffic. That could be construed as a failure considering the investment made, and the campaign might be abandoned.

Now consider Figure 5.5. What if half of the total traffic to the site is from existing customers? And a further half of the remaining visits are from staff, with 10,000 visits from a combination of investors, job seekers, and people not relevant to the business? Now the campaign performance is calculated as a 6.7% improvement in *relevant traffic*—clearly a very different story from what the initial calculation showed. Abandoning this campaign now may be considered a significant lost opportunity. This is the power of segmentation.

👉 *Forgetting to exclude existing customers when calculating campaign performance is a common mistake. I see it often. The reason is usually that the existing customer segment is not tracked effectively.*

### Identifying Segment Signals
In an ideal world, the digital analytics team will be able to segment all of the website traffic based on the visitor types shown in Figure 5.4. Doing so requires that website *signals* be available to identify the visitor's segment. Signals are specific actions that are unique to a segment. For example, new customers are those signing up, subscribing, or purchasing for the first time—usually an easy segment to define, as these visitors take clear actions (signals) on your website to identify themselves. Of course, you will need to track these actions.

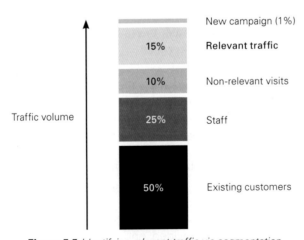

**Figure 5.5** *Identifying relevant traffic via segmentation*

Beyond the new customer segment, things become harder to classify. For example, if only your existing customers have access to a login area of your website, anyone using that facility can be labeled and segmented as an existing customer. So far, so good, as there is a clear signal (action) for this. However, that does assume existing customers will actually use your login facility in significant numbers. Perhaps the majority prefer to make their purchase at a real-world store, or the value proposition of having a login with you is not strong enough—so existing customers do not create one.

What if no login area exists for current customers?

For these situations, it may be possible to combine other website signals to identify the existing customer segment. Ask the question, "Why would existing customers come back to our website?" If it is to keep informed about product developments, consider setting up a subscription-based newsletter just for existing customers. That way, your customers are informed and won't need to visit your website! However, by embedding "read more" links into your emails, you can track any subsequent click-throughs—solving the identification issue for this segment. Once you have identified it, cookie the segment information of your visitors so that any subsequent visits that do not originate from your subscription emails are also identified correctly.

To facilitate segment identification, the digital analytics team will often need to request changes to the website content, or its architecture, in order to create the signal. Having the web development team on board as a key stakeholder of the analytics project is clearly an advantage.

Similarly, job seekers and investors will view specific areas of your site—assuming such areas exist and are well targeted to your audience. In other words, only people who are job seekers or investors are likely to view that content. Again, the architecture and design of your website may mean that assumption is not valid. To solidify it, discuss potential changes with your web development team so there are clear data signals from these segments. Although job seekers and investors may not be valuable to your sales and marketing stakeholders, it is still important to be able to identify this group of visitors—so that you can exclude them to improve the accuracy of calculations for your other segments (as per Figure 5.5).

☞ *A consequence of adding, or improving, visitor segment signals on your website is improved website usability. Having a much clearer user experience is something that will always stand you in good stead with your visitors.*

## Prebuilt and Custom Segments

A number of segment signals in your data are collected by default, such as visitors from mobile devices versus tablets versus desktops (three segments); purchasers versus non-purchasers; people who have visited your site more than once versus single visits; visitors arriving via paid search advertising versus non-paid; visitors who bounce away from your website (single page, no interactions) versus those that stay and browse around. These are all prebuilt segments that you apply to your reports with the click of a mouse—you do not need to identify the segments yourself, as Google Analytics does this for you. The prebuilt segment list is shown in Figure 5.6.

Despite the power and ease of use of the built-in segments, things become very interesting when you build custom segments specific to your business. Table 5.1 lists some examples.

The Type column of Table 5.1 has two components:

**Condition or sequence match**   This defines the logic used to match the segment definition. For example, a condition where *medium = email* will match all visits that come via email click-throughs. Multiple conditions can be used with AND or OR logic. For example, *medium = email* OR *medium = organic* will match visitors that arrive from either email click-throughs or organic search engines.

A sequence segment is defined in the same way—using conditions. The difference is that for a sequence segment, conditions must be matched *in order*. For example, where *medium = email* followed by *event = customer*, a visitor arrives via an email click-through and subsequently becomes a customer. Visitors who arrive via an email click-through and do not become customers are excluded, as are customers who arrived another way. Another example could be when *event = watched demo video* followed by *event = subscribe*. This would help you understand

| | | | |
|---|---|---|---|
| All Sessions | Bounced Sessions | Converters | Direct Traffic |
| Made a Purchase | Mobile and Tablet Traffic | Mobile Traffic | Multi-session Users |
| New Users | Non-bounce Sessions | Non-Converters | Organic Traffic |
| Paid Traffic | Performed Site Search | Referral Traffic | Returning Users |
| Search Traffic | Sessions with Conversions | Sessions with Transactions | Single Session Users |
| Tablet and Desktop Traffic | Tablet Traffic | | |

**Figure 5.6** *The prebuilt segments of Google Analytics*

**Table 5.1** *Examples of Custom Segments*

| Segment Name | Type | Description |
|---|---|---|
| Remove outliers | Condition match; visit-based | Excludes anyone viewing fewer than three pages, or less than 30 seconds, or more than 10 minutes |
| Loyal visitors | Condition match; user-based | Includes only visitors who have come to your website on at least three occasions |
| Big spenders | Condition match; visit-based | Visitors who have purchased with a transaction value of greater than $1,000 |
| High-value customers | Condition match; user-based | Visitors who have purchased a total transaction value of greater than $5,000 over the course of multiple visits |
| Visits from affiliates | Condition match; visit-based | Includes only referral visitors from affiliates |
| Cohort subscrip-tions in May | Condition match; user-based | For visitors who first arrived in May, includes only those who went on to subscribe (in any subsequent visit) |
| Campaign conversion | Sequence match; user-based | For visitors landing on a specific campaign page, includes only those who went on to become a cus-tomer (in any subsequent visit) |

whether your investment in video production is driving your business forward with subscriptions.

**Visit- or user-based**   If a segment is defined as visit-based, it means the conditions must be matched during the same visit (session). *User-based segment* means the same visit or subsequent return visits. This is a very powerful way to define your segments. The caveat is that your users must use the same device and browser combination on their repeat visits for this to work (cookies are device- and browser-specific).

If multi-device usage is common for your website, you can overcome the loss of tracking cookies by implementing the user ID tracking feature of your known visitors.[6]

## UNDERSTANDING VISITOR FLOW

Visitor flow is a visualization technique aimed at understanding how your visitors flow around your website. An example is shown in Figure 5.7.

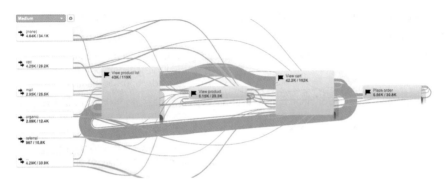

**Figure 5.7** *Sample flow visualization report*

You will see this report type in several places—the Audience, Behavior, and Conversions report sections. Essentially, they all attempt to do the same thing—help you understand how visitors move around your website.

What is clever about the flow reports, and the reason I highlight them in this chapter, is that this is *not* path analysis. Google Analytics is not trying to show you every path variation your visitors can take. Few visitors share common paths, so there is no value in analyzing these (assuming analyst time is a premium for you and you value the sanity of your digital analytics team). What Google realized early in its product development is that visitors essentially take random walks through website content until they find what they are looking for. Hence the grouping of *similar* paths is what flow visualizations do.

Google Analytics will automatically group what it considers to be similar paths. However, you can also customize this (referred to as Content Grouping) and apply your own segments—for example, "show the flow of customers only around the sections of my site." In my view, the data visualization of this technique is industry leading.

☞ *A recent extension to flow visualization reports is the addition of events (non-pageview user actions such as using loan calculator widgets). That is, the same method can be used to visualize page and event flow.*

## UNDERSTANDING VALUE

Monetization plays a fundamental role in analysis. Apart from putting a monetary value on what your website is worth—interesting to both transactional and non-transactional websites—if you monetize a process on your website, Google Analytics automatically provides a wealth of additional information.

Monetization allows you to

- Differentiate your most valuable visitors from others. This can be those who purchase the most, comment the most, share the most, download the most, and so forth.
- Identify what content is the most valuable to your visitors. For example, what leads them to become high-value visitors?
- Identify poor-performing pages. These are not necessarily your least popular pages, as conversely pages with low traffic levels may be your most valuable.
- Identify your most valuable campaigns—again, not just what is the most popular at generating traffic; rather, what is most valuable to your business.

There are two ways to monetize your website—using goal values or having a transactional website. The setup of these is discussed in Chapter 3. With your website monetized, reports auto-populate with page and session (visit) values. See Figures 5.8 and 5.9.

## What Does Page Value Mean?

Page value measures the value of a page to your organization in monetary terms—whether you have an e-commerce facility or not. Essentially, it

**Figure 5.8** *Sample report showing page values*

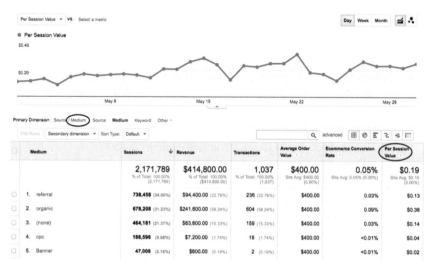

**Figure 5.9** *Sample report showing per session values*

is a way for you to prioritize the importance of your pages. For example, for testing new campaigns or special offers, you will want to start by first looking at pages with the highest page value, as they will have the greatest impact.

To illustrate how this works, consider the following e-commerce example of four visitors who take different paths on your website. A transaction happens on page D and for the simplicity of explanation I fix the revenue at $100:

Visitor 1: page B ⇨ page C ⇨ page B ⇨ **page D**
Visitor 2: page B ⇨ page E ⇨ page B ⇨ **page D**
Visitor 3: page A ⇨ page B ⇨ page C ⇨ page B ⇨ page C ⇨ page E ⇨ page F ⇨ **page D** ⇨ page G
Visitor 4: page B ⇨ page C ⇨ page B ⇨ page F

To calculate the page value of each page visited, Google Analytics allocates $100 to the transaction page (page D) and to each unique page in the path that *precedes* the transaction. Pages viewed after a transaction are ignored. Each page value is then divided by the number of unique times it is viewed by all visitors. The results are shown in Table 5.2.

Consider page A—this page only occurs once and it happens before a transaction (for visitor 3). Therefore, page A is assigned the revenue from visitor 3. The calculation of its page value is simply 100 / 1 = $100.

**Table 5.2** *Calculating Page Values*

| Page | Revenue / Unique Pageviews | Page Value |
|------|---------------------------|------------|
| A | $100 / 1 | $100 |
| B | $300 / 4 | $75 |
| C | $200 / 3 | $67 |
| D | $300 / 3 | $100 |
| E | $200 / 2 | $100 |
| F | $100 / 2 | $50 |
| G | $0 / 1 | $0 |

Page B occurs eight times in the visitor paths. However, multiple views of the same page in a single path are ignored for the calculation. Hence the number of unique pageviews is 4. As three of these occur before a purchase (for visitors 1, 2, and 3), page B is allocated the revenue three times. The page value of page B is therefore 300 / 4 = $75.

The calculation proceeds in the same way for all the other pages. As you can see, a particular page value is dependent on how many visitors view it on their way to a transaction *and* the value of the transaction (I use a fixed value of $100 to keep it simple). Page value is therefore a great way to determine the important content on your website.

Because page value is so powerful at highlighting your most valuable pages, I consider it a KPI that can be applied to both transactional and non-transactional websites. For a non-transactional website, your goal values are used for the calculation instead of transaction revenue. See Chapter 9 for details on defining KPIs.

☞ *Page values are independent of order. Before a conversion, it does not matter if page A comes before page B (or vice versa) for visitor 3.*

## What Does Session Value Mean?

Compared to calculating page values, determining the value of a visit (session) is quite straightforward:

$$per\ session\ value = \frac{total\ revenue}{number\ of\ sessions}$$

where *revenue* can be either your e-commerce revenue or goal value. Hence you can view these numbers in either your e-commerce reports or goal conversion reports.

Per session values are interesting when you compare where your visitors come from—as shown in Figure 5.9. Organic visitors are much more valuable than any other channel (at $0.36 per session, nine times more valuable than AdWords visitors). But bear in mind that per session values are based on attributing revenue to the current referral source of the visit. Any previous visits by the same user that did not convert into a purchase are not taken into account.

☞ *A per session value is a good first-guess approximation as to the value of different marketing channels to your organization. A more thorough understanding of value from different traffic sources is obtained from attribution modeling, though this is more complex to set up. Attribution modeling is discussed in Chapter 6.*

## INTEGRATING WITH OTHER DATA

Google Analytics integrates with a number of other Google products, namely AdWords, AdSense, Google Webmaster Tools, Google Sites, and YouTube. The integrations are usually very straightforward—typically a checkbox and the adding of your Google Analytics account ID—for the data to flow in to your Google Analytics reports.

A particularly strong integration is with AdWords, with a two-way relationship:

- AdWords can import your Google Analytics goal setup. This allows you to use conversion rates (rather than click-through rates) within your AdWords account as the basis for your optimization.
- Google Analytics can import AdWords data (impression, click, cost, and creative information). This allows you to view the complete visitor journey of your AdWords visits within your reports, and measure your return on investment—what money you make from your advertising.

Google Analytics can also integrate with your back office systems, such as your CRM system, using its User ID feature. Essentially, if your visitor authenticates with your internal CRM system that allocates a unique ID value (typically a customer ID), this value can override the anonymous cookie ID Google Analytics uses for visitor tracking.[6]

Implementing user ID tracking means you are tracking real people—as opposed to anonymous cookies used by the default tracking option.

These are not quite the same thing, and therefore user ID tracking provides two important benefits to your digital analytics team:

- Improved accuracy—a user ID provides more accuracy than a cookie, as it is unique to the user. It is not degraded by visitors using multiple devices or multiple browsers to access your site (cookies are device- and browser-dependent).
- Multi-device usage—analyze how your visitors use multiple devices (or browsers) to consume your content. For example, research shows 45% of people who research via mobile go on to purchase via desktop or tablet.[7]

The key for taking advantage of User ID is having your visitors identify themselves in some way. Typically this is via a login or authentication facility. In turn, this requires you to encourage your users to create an account in the first instance and for them to actually use it for each visit. For it to work in practice, there must be a real value-added benefit for the user to do so.

Amazon is a great example of the always logged in approach. However, few other organizations have been able to replicate such a strong consumer engagement to be permanently logged in.

☞ *A potential workaround for user login is to have your known visitors click on a customized link within an email generated by your CRM system, such as a newsletter where each link contains the user ID for the specific recipient.*

## IMPORTING DATA INTO GOOGLE ANALYTICS

As I discuss throughout this book, Google Analytics is moving away from being a great visualization and insights tool for web data to being a great visualization and insights tool for *all* your business data. This evolution of the product is called Universal Analytics, and it launched in 2013. A key part of being able to provide insights beyond web data is for organizations to be able to upload their own complementary data sets.

For example, if your internal systems calculate a lifetime value for each customer and keep track of their contract renewal date, you can upload this information into Google Analytics so that it is reported alongside other relevant data. Then, within your Google Analytics reports you can see if there is an increase in web activity from customers who are close to their renewal date and investigate what factors drive an increase in lifetime value.

You can import seven different data types into Google Analytics, as shown in Figure 5.10. All of these are straightforward to implement—you create a comma-separated value (CSV) file with the first row defining the column names, such as Transaction ID and Product Name for refunds. Then upload the file from your computer. The upload is immediate, with file processing taking a little longer, dependent on file size (it may take up to 24 hours for processing).

## Why might you use data upload?

Clearly there are lots of use cases for this functionality and some are quite obvious from the descriptions in Figure 5.10. Here are three:

**Product data upload**   You have an e-commerce site and your product names change. You want your new product names to be reflected in your historical Google Analytics reports. Uploading a file containing the product SKU (a unique item ID) and new product names allows you to overwrite the old product names in your historical reports.

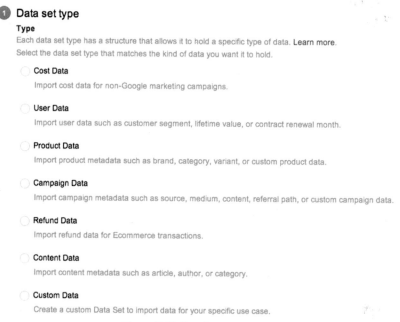

**Figure 5.10** *Data import types*

Similarly, if for some reason it is difficult for you to rename products on your website, you can also use this technique to rename them en masse for future reports—that is, for future transactions.

**Campaign data upload** Rather than placing your campaign details in your URLs to populate reports with useful campaign information, you can use a simplified code. For example, sending a visitor to *example.com ?utm_id=101* labels the visitor as coming from a specific campaign. In order to have human-readable campaign details in your reports, upload a file with the descriptions. For example, for *utm_id=101*, substitute *source = customer_db*; *medium = email*; *campaign name = renewal_message*.

This method not only hides your potentially sensitive campaign information from competitors, but it also greatly simplifies the task of campaign tracking—reducing errors and inconsistencies. It is particularly useful if you have distributed marketing teams.

**Refund data upload** Processing e-commerce refunds is an obvious need for a business. However, some thought should go into this before applying it to your Google Analytics reports. Take the following example: I purchase shoes from your online store and change my mind when they are delivered (wrong size, wrong color, just not my style). Whatever the reason for my refund, the marketing campaigns that led me to your website and to purchase are still valid. Removing this transaction from your reports will underestimate the value of your marketing efforts. For this scenario, my advice is to keep such transactions in place.

However, there are times when removing a transaction is required, such as when an obvious mistake has been made (wrong item purchased), during site testing, or in the case of fraudulent transactions. To do this,

---

### What Happens If I Upload a Mistake?

If you find you have made a mistake in your upload file—added a typo, for example—you can upload again to overwrite and correct it. If you later decide you wish to revert to your original data set prior to the upload, simply remove the uploaded file.

☛ *File upload sizes are currently limited to 1 GB per file. If you have a 10 GB product database to upload, split this into 10 files of 1 GB each. There is no limit as to the number of files you can upload.*

upload a CSV file containing the transaction IDs to be refunded. Partial refunds can also be applied.[8]

## SCALING WITH AUTOMATION

The Google Analytics user interface is powerful and intuitive to use. However, it does not scale well when you are managing a large number of websites or users, or when the standard reports require constant customization to meet your needs. This is where automation fits in.

Google has a tradition of providing access to its systems and data via application programming interfaces (APIs). Essentially, if you need non-human access to your Google Analytics reports, the APIs provide the route. APIs enable developers to query Google Analytics and build applications around your data. They do this by means of scripts that automate processes for you so that they can scale. Such scripts can be used, for example, for the management of multiple users or a bespoke query of your data.

Google's approach is to simplify API access and therefore make it available to everyone—though developer knowledge is required. The APIs have proven so successful that an industry of full-blown third-party applications has also evolved to do this for you. If you prefer the ready-made approach, browse the apps by Google Analytics Technology Providers at www.google.com/analytics/apps/search/apps.

If you prefer a more hands-on approach and have the resources available (a web developer on hand), there are numerous specific APIs available.[9] These fall into four groups:

**Reporting APIs**   These allow you to query any part of your collected data, for any date range, including your real-time reports. Data can be accessed and saved into a spreadsheet or database, for example. This method is extremely powerful for building your own dashboard, or when you wish to combine Google Analytics data with other data sources for further manipulation and display—such as your sales data, call center data, marketing plan, or social media activity. Most third-party tools for Google Analytics use the reporting APIs.

**Provisioning APIs**   These allow you to create new accounts, properties, views (report sets), and new users. This is very useful if you are an Internet service provider or hosting company, where you may have thousands of accounts and users to set up—a laborious task if you were to use the user interface. An example is automatically setting up and pre-configuring a Google Analytics account when a new customer signs up.

**Management APIs** This is a collection of APIs allowing the automatic management of your Google Analytics configuration. Create or edit data filters en masse; change user permissions; bulk connect AdWords accounts, and so forth. Management APIs are aimed at large organizations with multiple websites, multiple Google Analytics accounts, or a large number of users requiring data access.

**Embed API** This is an API to create and embed a dashboard of your Google Analytics data on a third-party website—this could be your intranet site, for example. The Embed API allows you to build custom Google Analytics visualizations and layouts to meet your stakeholder needs.

## UNDERSTANDING REPORT SAMPLING

Sampling is a standard statistical approach when dealing with large volumes of data. In business and medical research, sampling is widely used for gathering information about a large population—for example, clinical trials of new drugs, predicting the result of an election, or manufacturing quality control. These all rely on the use of random samples as a method to estimate characteristics of the whole population.

The vast majority of Google Analytics reports you are likely to view are *not* sampled—regardless of data quantity. These are the 100+ default reports that you have access to when you log in. They are precalculated aggregates and always contain the complete data set. However, if you apply segments, add secondary dimensions, or build your own custom reports, Google Analytics has to go back and reprocess your raw data tables as an ad hoc request. This is when sampling can occur, applied in order to make efficient use of Google's processing capacity.

The purpose of sampling is to ensure your reports are loaded quickly and you are not waiting for long periods of time while the data is reprocessed. The sampling thresholds are shown in Table 5.3 for both Google Analytics free and Premium (paid-for).

When the thresholds of Table 5.3 are reached, Google Analytics takes a random sample of your data at the visit level (only whole visits included[10]), uses this sample to perform its calculations, then scales the numbers back up to represent the total in the created report. For example, if the total pot of data in your custom report includes 5 million visits, a random

**Table 5.3** *Google Analytics Sampling Thresholds*

|  | Google Analytics Free | Google Analytics Premium |
|---|---|---|
| Sampling threshold (visits) | 500,000 | 10 million* |

\* This number is constantly increasing as Google allocates more resources to Premium processing.

sample rate of 10% is used for the sample calculations, which are subsequently multiplied by ten in the displayed report to estimate the totals. If you were using Premium, this report would not trigger sampling.

To indicate that a report is generated from sampled data, Google Analytics displays a notification box at the top right of the report screen, as shown in Figure 5.11. Although it doesn't say so explicitly, this means sampling has taken place (20.72% of sessions sampled).

## Pitfalls of Sampling

Sampling is a great way to obtain estimates of characteristics for the whole population. However, if you are looking for estimates of a much smaller subpopulation of the total, error bars can become very large. It is the needle in a haystack problem. With only a handful of needles in the haystack, there is a strong possibility of taking a sample of hay containing no needles at all (or very few). When Google Analytics scales the sampled number back up, the totals arrived at for the estimated count of needles can be way off—even meaningless.

### Data Collection Is Never Sampled

Google Analytics does not sample your data at the point of collection or processing. The only exception to that rule is if you break the terms of service (ToS). This states you can use Google Analytics for free for up to 10 million data hits per month (approximately 1 million visits per month). If your site regularly receives more than that, you need to upgrade to the paid-for Premium product, or throttle the data flow you send to Google— that is, sample your own data collection. If you fail to do that, Google reserves the right to do that for you.

☞ *As a rule of thumb, if your site receives less than 100,000 visits per month, it is unlikely you will come across report sampling.*

**Figure 5.11** *Report sampling notification*

Here's a real-world example:

Your conversion rate on average is 1% for global visitors, but for your particular analysis you are interested only in US visitors from Arizona—this accounts for approximately 1% of all traffic. You apply a segment to obtain this for the month of May. As you have a total of 5 million visits in your data set, sampling is invoked at a sample rate of 10%.

For the sampled size of 500,000 visits, you are looking for only 50 conversions (1% of 1%). Importantly, that comes with an assumption that all conversions are equally distributed throughout your data. However, maybe most of your conversions happened on one particular day—random sampling cannot take this into account. Nor can it take account of a smaller fraction of users making multiple conversions. Hence, it is entirely feasible for the sample taken to only include 25 conversions. That is 50% less than the true value.

## Avoiding Sampling

Sampling can be avoided by analyzing multiple smaller sets of data that are not sampled, then summing these metrics to get the totals. For example, rather than using data for the whole month of May, split it into 31 single days to avoid the sampling thresholds, then sum. This is a perfectly valid technique for certain metrics, and there are a number of API tools that provide this feature.[9]

However, be aware that summing in this way only works for visit (session)-based metrics and dimensions, such as number of visits, time on site, bounce rate, number of pageviews, goal completions, transactions, referral sources, device used, and so forth. It does not work for any metric or dimension that is user-based, metrics such as number of unique visitors; demographic information (age, gender); behavior information (new versus returning visitors, frequency and recency metrics); multi-device usage; or attribution modeling. The important point is that users are not additive—sessions are.

Consider report sampling as a sign of success—that is, you are receiving so many qualified visitors that reporting all their activity becomes a time-consuming and resource-intensive process. If you discover that sampling is a constant thorn in your analysis, consider investing in the paid-for Premium version of Google Analytics (discussed in Chapter 2).

☛ *The API automation required to avoid sampling means the extraction of data outside of Google Analytics. Report visualizations such as visitor flow and multi-channel funnels are not available for the extracted data set.*

## SPEAKING OF FEATURES...

| When I hear this... | I reply with... |
| --- | --- |
| We need to compare reports from 15 regional web properties side by side. What's the best approach for this? | This is something Google Analytics cannot provide for within its user interface. Therefore, build your own dashboard to do this with the Embed API,[11] or use a third-party tool with Google Analytics connectivity built in.[12] The latter gives you the added benefit of combining with other non–Google Analytics data sources. |
| We wish to integrate Google Analytics with our CRM and set the unique reference key as the username—that is, match up usernames in our CRM with usernames in Google Analytics. Can this be done? | Yes and no.<br><br>  The integration is entirely possible using theUser ID feature of Google Analytics.[6] However, this must be done in an anonymous way—such as using your CRM customer ID to overwrite the Google Analytics cookie ID. No personal information can be sent to Google Analytics, as this is a violation of the ToS. |
| We have a sampling issue but cannot afford the upgrade to Premium (yet!). Is there a legitimate alternative? | It is perfectly acceptable to split your data into small subsets to avoid the sampling thresholds and then sum these to obtain the results for unsampled data. This is an API technique you can build yourself, or there are third-party tools available.[9] |

## CHAPTER 5 REFERENCES

1   The term *Internet of things* was proposed by Kevin Ashton in 1999: http://en.wikipedia.org/wiki/Internet_of_Things.

2   Shelby Thayer, Director of Web Strategy, User Experience, and CRM. Penn State University: www.linkedin.com/in/shelbythayer

3   Conversations that happen away from your website are shown within Google Analytics if the social network used by your visitors is participating in Google Analytics' social data hub initiative. Unfortunately, that does not include Facebook or Twitter: https://developers.google.com/analytics/devguides/socialdata/.

4   I have written a detailed white paper specifically about tracking offline marketing. Download from http://brianclifton.com/tracking-offline.

5     Understanding metrics and dimensions:
https://support.google.com/analytics/answer/1033861

6     Tracking your authenticated users anonymously with a unique user ID is described
at https://developers.google.com/analytics/devguides/collection/analyticsjs
/user-id.

7     Custom Nielsen study, commissioned by Google (2013)—Mobile Path to Purchase: www.thinkwithgoogle.com/research-studies/mobile-path-to
-purchase-5-key-findings.html

8     Importing refund data is covered at
https://support.google.com/analytics/answer/6014861?ref_topic=6015090.

9     The full list of available APIs is found at
https://developers.google.com/analytics/devguides/reporting.

10    Google describes report sampling in detail at http://code.google.com/apis
/analytics/docs/concepts/gaConceptsSampling.html.

11    The Embed API allows you to build your own dashboard with Google Analytics
data: https://developers.google.com/analytics/devguides/reporting/embed/
v1/.

12    Tableau (www.tableausoftware.com) and Klipfolio (www.klipfolio.com) are two
well-respected data dashboard tools that integrate with Google Analytics as well
as other data sources.

# 6

# Jumpstart Guide to Key Tracking Methods

**By understanding the key tracking** methods available within Google Analytics, you will be able to direct your teams to cater for current data needs, and you will be better able to contribute to the discussion and planning of your organization's *future* data needs. That is, you will become proactive in proposing innovative ways to measure success—helping the business make smart decisions based on data.

To be innovative, you need a nontechnical understanding of how Google Analytics works, its key tracking methods, the principles of attribution, and what it's possible to do with your data *outside* of Google Analytics.

## HOW GOOGLE ANALYTICS WORKS—AN OVERVIEW

Although in the early days (circa 2005), the Google Analytics pricing of free was a strong motivator for adoption by many a small business, it rapidly became clear to many analytical experts that its real allure is its ability to be both a broad brush and a scalpel for helping you understand your website. In addition, because of its implementation simplicity, it is also incredibly flexible.

Even with its groundbreaking setup simplicity and its intuitive user inter-face, Google Analytics is a complex product. It aims to simplify compli-cated processes and visitor journeys by hiding the technicalities behind them. That of course is a good thing and I deliberately avoid any code in this book—you don't need it! However, if this subject matter is new to you, take your time understanding the concepts described in this chapter. Your knowledge gained will stand you in good stead for your career—being comfortable with data in the digital world is becoming an expected skill, rather than an optional extra.

### Google Analytics for Websites
Google Analytics is known in the measurement industry as a *page-tag* solution. That means it uses a snippet of code (the tag) placed on your

---

### Not Just Web Page Tracking
As with this entire book, my focus is on the tracking of website visitors. This is what Google Analytics is mainly used for today. However, there are also Google Analytics tools available to track how your mobile apps are used—both on Android[1] and iOS.[2] In addition, Google Analytics is now moving into an area referred to as Universal Analytics—a central platform to track anything that can communicate with the Internet—from barcode scanners to turnstiles.

---

pages to collect and transmit visitor information to Google servers. For Google Analytics, the snippet of code is approximately a dozen lines of JavaScript and is called the GATC. By this method, all data collection, processing, maintenance, and program upgrades are managed by Google as a hosted service—software as a service (SaaS). The process and data flow are illustrated in Figure 6.1.

The operational process for the latest tracking code, released in 2013,[3] is described as follows (note that previous versions of the tracking code work in a similar, though not identical, way):

1  Nothing happens until a visitor arrives at your website. This can be via many different routes, including search engines, social networks, email marketing, and referral links. Whatever the route, when the visitor views one of your pages containing the GATC, an automatic request is made for the file at www.google-analytics.com/analytics.js. This is the Google Analytics master script that is downloaded only once during a visitor session. It contains all the code required for tracking. Further requests for it will be retrieved from the visitor's browser cache.

   The JavaScript download occurs asynchronously. That means it doesn't interfere with the rest of the page completing its download. If there is a delay for analytics.js, or the file does not download, the

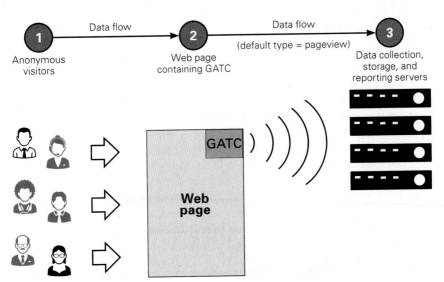

**Figure 6.1** *Schematic diagram of how Google Analytics works*

browser continues as normal—there is no impact on user experience, though data collection may be affected.

With analytics.js in place, anonymous visit and visitor data are collected, and a first-party cookie is created. The cookie contains a unique visitor ID plus some meta information regarding the version number and the domain where the GATC is placed.

2  For each pageview, the GATC sends this information to Google data collection servers via a formatted URL of the form https://www.google-analytics.com/collect?v=1&tid=UA-XXXX-Y&cid=555&t=pageview&dp=%2Fhome-page. The transmission of data takes a fraction of a second.

Although a pageview is the default hit type captured by the GATC, other hit types can be sent by communicating with the analytics.js file via JavaScript commands, such as tracking in-page events, transactions, or labeling visitors.

3  At regular intervals, Google processes the collected data and updates your Google Analytics reports. Because of the huge quantity of data involved (Google Analytics is used on more than 20 million websites worldwide), reports are typically displayed 3–4 hours in arrears. This may be longer if you have a high-traffic website, though it should not be more than 24 hours.

## Data Freshness

As described in Chapter 5, Google Analytics has a set of real-time reports where current activity is displayed with a delay of typically 4 seconds. This is an impressive subset of your data, though not every report within Google Analytics can be updated so quickly.

To compare your activity for different date ranges or different visitor segments, you will review the standard Google Analytics reports. How fresh this data is—in other words, how up-to-date your reports are—depends on a number of factors. The most relevant is the volume of data you send to the Google Analytics collection servers.

For most websites, your data is likely to be 3–4 hours in arrears. This may be significantly less if your site receives fewer than 10,000 visits per day. If your site receives more than 200,000 visits per day and you use the free version of Google Analytics, your reports are processed once every 24 hours.[4] For Premium users, freshness is guaranteed at under 4 hours—regardless of data volume. Chapter 2 details the difference between free and Premium Google Analytics.

## Tags, Beacons, and Bugs

A *page tag* (for example, the GATC) is an object embedded in a web page that is invisible to the user but allows checking that a user has viewed the page. Alternative names are *web beacon, tracking bug*, and *tag*.

The page-tag methodology that Google Analytics uses is not unique in the industry. In fact, the technique has been around since the late 1990s, and the majority of web analytics vendors employ the same technique for data collection (though each vendor has its own particular tweaks and patents for their tool).

By design, Google Analytics uses the same analytics.js tracking code for all visitors and for all website owners. That means it is cached by a very large proportion of web users—a major advantage of having an adoption base of millions of websites. If a visitor to your website has previously visited another website that also runs analytics.js, the file does not need to be downloaded at all—it will already be cached. Even if analytics.js is not cached, the typical file size is 33 KB. That takes around 200–300 milliseconds (less than one-third of a second) to download on a 10 Mbps Internet connection. The result is that Google Analytics has a minimal impact on your page loading times.

As you have probably realized from the description of Figure 6.1, if a visitor blocks the execution of JavaScript or blocks the setting of first-party cookies, or if you forgot to add the GATC to your page, or your web server does not allow the GATC to execute (that is, it's behind a firewall), Google Analytics will not function and no data will be collected. Once data is lost, you cannot go back and reprocess it, so regular audits of your GATC deployment should be part of your implementation plan—as described in Chapter 4.

## Universal Analytics for Everything

In 2013 Google launched their latest update to the GATC, called Universal Analytics. Their stated goal is to take web analytics to another level, moving away from being simply a website measurement tool, to becoming the central data platform for providing insights for an *entire* organization's activities. This could include, for example, online marketing, offline marketing, traditional e-commerce tracking, in-store sales (physical in-person sales), telephone orders, event participation, and many other possibilities that smart people around the world are currently experimenting with.

☞ *Universal Analytics is not a separate product or tracking method. It is the same GATC code described for tracking websites, and this is likely to remain its most common use. I separate the different uses here only for the purpose of clarity.*

Because analytics.js uses a standardized low-level protocol to send data hits to Google Analytics data collection servers, developers can program any Internet-connected device to send raw user interaction data directly to Google Analytics servers. The beauty of this method is its simplicity—broadcasting a formatted URL is straightforward for a developer.

As a simple example, suppose a visitor can print out a coupon for use in your Main Street store (or have it emailed to them). If the barcode for the coupon includes the Google Analytics visitor ID, then the offline conversion can be tied back to the website visitor.

Now imagine you run an event such as a conference, concert, or sports game. Visitors to your event use their barcoded ticket to access your venue. If you connect your barcode scanners to the Internet, each user can be tracked by Google Analytics as they enter and exit the venue (anonymously, of course). This is powerful stuff. You can take advantage of Google Analytics real-time reports to quickly and efficiently assess the flow of visitors to your venue.

Perhaps your event visitors also use their ticket at local merchandise stores for a special discount while the event is running. Using the same barcode scanning technique, local stores can send data to Google Analytics and provide detailed reports of the purchases made and the revenue transacted. If you manage a stadium, concert hall, or conference venue, Google Analytics can provide you with a host of performance information in an easy-to-visualize, standardized format. Tax-free shopping at airports is another example, as cashiers already check boarding cards for purchases.

You can apply this same technique to garage ticketing, premise turnstiles, electronic key fobs (your car), remote controls (your TV or music system), and security tags—in fact, anything that can be programmed to send a formatted URL over the Internet. The Olympics, World Cup, and Super Bowl are prime examples for using this type of technique to capture and display *big data*. However, any event, large or small, is suitable. For example, I have used this technique at a conference and displayed the real-time data of visitors entering the event to the audience while I was speaking. Others have tracked home appliance usage in this way—just for fun.[5] Essentially, any user-centric data is a potential good fit for Google Analytics.

Imagine the power of Universal Analytics if you run a shopping mall, supermarket, or retail store. In a relatively straightforward way (this is not rocket science), you can tie online and offline marketing to store visits, store purchases, emails, telephone calls, even your garage usage! You can integrate this data with your CRM system (via an anonymous visitor ID in Google Analytics). That way, all your online *and* offline data can be tied to a specific customer. This is potential nirvana for a digital marketer—and also any senior manager who needs data to make informed decisions.

Offline, online, and specific customer data (CRM) can all be combined into a unified data collection and reporting platform—namely, Google Analytics. Figure 6.2 shows components of offline data, with online data simplified to a single node, labeled *Google Analytics* (the constituents for online data are shown in Figure 1.3 of Chapter 1). A customer or potential customer may touch any number of these. My point is that they can and should be tracked if they are of value to your business.

**Figure 6.2** *Using Universal Analytics to combine online, offline, and CRM data*

### Universal Analytics and Data Privacy Concerns

The potential for making strategic business decisions using Universal Analytics is enormous and very exciting. My only niggling concern is privacy. With so much "anonymous" data being collected around the individual, the visitor becomes increasingly more identifiable. That is, a process of triangulating anonymous data points can lead to identifying who a person is.

A now famous example of this is the 2006 AOL search query release. This intentional data release was made public and intended for research purposes. However, users could be identified indirectly by the query terms they entered into the search engine. It is a classic example of how the power of data can be underestimated by its owners.[6]

I discuss your responsibilities with respect to data collection in Chapter 7.

## TRACKING METHODS

When it comes to tracking a visitor's interaction with your website, or whatever you use Google Analytics data collection for, there are three main techniques available to you:

- Track the interaction as a pageview—the default tracking method for websites.
- Track the interaction as a virtual pageview—Google Analytics considers the data hit sent as the equivalent of a pageview.
- Track the interaction as an event—any interaction that you would not consider a pageview, such as a visitor clicking on a file download link.

Pageview, virtual pageview, and event tracking cover the vast majority of tracking requirements. However, there are other tracking options available and special tracking considerations to be aware of. See the section "Significant Others."

### Pageviews

As shown in Figure 6.1, the default behavior when the standard GATC is deployed on your web pages is for Google Analytics to capture a pageview—the path, page name, and page title—that is loaded in your visitor's web browser. This, coupled with the anonymous visitor information—such as

## Reducing the Noise

Because collecting pageview data is so easy, you may find yourself overwhelmed with information, and you may exceed the data volume limits of your account (for the free version of Google Analytics this is 10 million data hits per month). There are two ways you can reduce the volume of pageview data:

- Place your GATC only on pages that you wish to track.
- Set a sampling rate to statistically sample your visitors and their pageviews.

The first method is perfectly valid, though it does raise a question: If you don't wish to track it, what is the point of having the content in the first place? In other words, if the content is present on your website and you wish to keep it, surely you will want to measure its performance? Therefore, I recommend the sampling technique as the better way to reduce data volume. It is a simple online setting added to your GATC.[7]

what site or campaign brought the visitor to you, the date and time of the visit, the location of the visitor, whether they have come before or not—is a powerful data set that forms the basis of your initial analysis.

Apart from deploying the GATC on your pages, the exact same tracking code on every page, nothing else is required for this to work. The ease of obtaining data by this method is a key advantage of using it. Therefore, tracking pageviews should be your default approach unless there is a specific reason for doing something else.

## Virtual Pageviews

As the name suggests, a virtual pageview is analogous to a standard pageview, except that *you* define the path, filename, and page title sent to Google Analytics. This can be useful in two ways:

1 Renaming existing pages—if your website has meaningless page names that make no sense to anyone reading your reports, you can rename these at the point of data collection.

2 Faking new pages—if a standard pageview is not tracked by default for the visitor's action, you can create one.

Consider the following standard pageviews captured by Google Analytics from the visitor's browser for a fictional leather store:

```
/section-1/sectionA/productID54?sku=123
/section-2/sectionB/productID86?sku=456
```

To anyone reading your reports, these pageviews are meaningless. They convey no information to the reader as to what content is being viewed by visitors; you would need a lookup table to translate what the *section*, *productID*, and *sku* values refer to. With some simple changes to the GATC,[8] these can be renamed into something much more readable in your reports.

Consider these alternative virtual pageviews for the same content:

```
/shoes/female/high heeled boot?size=38&color=black
/jackets/male/sports?size=large&color=brown
```

A report containing these virtual (renamed) pageviews is much more informative than the ones captured by default. The same method can also be applied to modify the page title. A smart web developer will be able to automate this process—renaming of default paths and filenames into more readable virtual paths and virtual filenames.

To illustrate faking new pages, consider an information request form on your website, with a pageview of

```
/contact/form-1.php
```

I often discover that content management systems do not modify the pageview when visitors submit the form. That is, the URL does not change in their browser when they have completed their action. This is obviously a problem for Google Analytics—it cannot differentiate between a form *view* and a form *submission*. However, such a submission is an important engagement that has a great deal of value to your organization—it is how anonymous visitors identify themselves (gold dust!). To overcome this problem, use a virtual (fake) pageview. For example, when the form is submitted, send one of the following virtual pageviews to Google Analytics:

```
/contact/form-1.php?submit=success
/contact/form-1.php?submit=fail
```

Having these additional pageviews allows Google Analytics to calculate your form conversion and failure rate. This tells you how good your website is at soliciting a contact from potential new customers.

More examples of using virtual pageviews to improve and enhance your Google Analytics reporting are discussed in Chapter 4.

## Events

Pageviews (both real and virtual) are for recording how a visitor navigates your content. Events are best for recording how users interact with that content.

An event is an interaction on your website that is not considered a pageview. For example, links to file downloads, outbound links, and interactions with embedded video are not tracked by default because they do not load a webpage. Hence, it makes sense to categorize such interactions differently. This is what event tracking is for. Other examples of event tracking are discussed in Chapter 4. As events are not tracked by default in Google Analytics, they require a modification to the GATC on your pages in order to take effect.[9]

## Significant Others

In addition to the pageviews and events described above, there are other data types that can be set or sent to Google Analytics that you should be aware of.[10]

**Transactions, promotions, and purchase items** If you have an e-commerce facility, you can capture the transaction and purchased product detail in Google Analytics. In addition, you can track the performance of product impressions—specific listings such as category lists, related products, and search results—and internal promotions such as special offers, featured products, and coupon code usage.

**Social interactions** You can measure the number of times users click on social buttons (such as a Facebook "Like" or a Twitter "Tweet") embedded in your web pages. Think of these as a special type of event tracking.

**Labels** Labels are called *custom dimensions* in Google Analytics (*custom variables* in legacy tracking code). Labels can be applied at the visitor, visit (session), or pageview level. Examples include labeling a visitor as a *customer* because they have transacted with you before (on- or offline); labeling a visit as *high-value* because the visitor has engaged with your website (added a comment, subscribed, or completed a survey, for

## Virtual Pageviews versus Event Tracking

Given the choice of two different tracking methods, what circumstances make it appropriate to use a virtual pageview, and what circumstances make it more appropriate to use an event?

Using virtual pageviews to capture actions such as form submissions or outbound links obviously inflates your pageview count. However, if the action you are tracking can be considered analogous to viewing a page of content, then a virtual pageview is valid. In my opinion, this is the case for readable content such as the thank you page of a form submission and the click on an outbound link (a page on a different website). That is, from a visitor's perspective the file format is irrelevant—it is simply content to them, in the same way your other HTML pages are content.

Use event tracking when the action being tracked is not related to a pageview. For example, the downloading of a ZIP or EXE file, the playing of an embedded video, adding an item to a shopping cart, or the interaction with an in-page widget, such as a loan calculator.

### What About Readable File Downloads—PDF, DOC, ...?

For this scenario there is an overlap in potential tracking methods—a PDF file is both a file download and readable content. Therefore, both virtual pageview and event tracking methods are valid. If all PDF files on your website are of a similar value to you *and* your visitors (for example, product brochures, user manuals, price lists), I recommend the hypothesis that a PDF file is readable content and should be tracked as virtual pageviews. On the other hand, if the value of your PDF files varies widely (for example, you also produce high-value industry reports for your members), consider event tracking as a better match. This provides more categorization and monetization options for you.

example); and labeling a pageview because it has special significance to the visitor journey (grouping content by author, for example).

**App view** In mobile app tracking, *app view* is synonymous with a web *pageview*.

**Cross-domain tracking** This is not a data hit in itself. Rather, it's a modification of your GATC to allow visitors to move between your domains as if these are a single website. This is an important modification, as it affects your count of visits and how Google Analytics attributes credit to your marketing campaigns. As this is a special case, I discuss it in more detail in the next section.

## CROSS-DOMAIN TRACKING

Cross-domain tracking applies if you own web properties where the visitor can move between different domain names—that is, where you deliberately provide links for your visitors to do this (not including sub-domains). For this scenario, it is critical for cross-domain tracking to be implemented correctly, as your reports will be meaningless otherwise. The implementation is straightforward, but understanding the reasoning behind it requires a little thought.

Consider the schematic of Figure 6.3. This shows a single *new* visitor moving between two web properties that you own (domain A and domain B). In this scenario, the visitor starts their session on domain A, follows a link to domain B, then follows a link back to domain A. In this example, the visitor is agnostic to the domain displaying your content—in fact, they probably do not notice it (it is not relevant). This scenario often arises if you have product-specific websites under the same brand, or a third-party payment gateway processing transactions for you.

Table 6.1 shows how the visitor journey depicted in Figure 6.3 would be counted with and without cross-domain tracking implemented.

The data produced when cross-domain tracking is enabled is what you wish to see in your reports—it is the correct representation of the visitor journey. When cross-domain tracking is not enabled, the number of

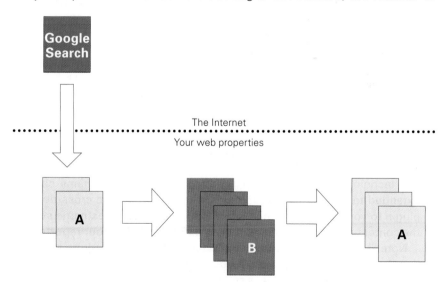

**Figure 6.3** *Tracking a visitor's path across domains*

**Table 6.1** *Cross-Domain Tracking*

|  | Cross-Domain Tracking Enabled | Cross-Domain Tracking Not Enabled |
| --- | --- | --- |
| Visitors | 1 new visitor | 2 (1 new domain A, 1 new domain B) |
| Sessions | 1 | 2 |
| Pageviews | 9 total<br>Domain A: 5<br>Domain B: 4 | 9 total<br>Domain A: 5<br>Domain B: 4 |
| Referral attribution | Google | Google (for domain A); domain A (for domain B) |

visitors and visits is over-counted and the results are both confusing and wrong. You obtain the correct numbers in three steps.

**Step 1** Track your domains as if part of a single website. Use the same GATC for both domains. This is achieved by modifying your GATC using the Google Analytics cross-domain plugin.[11] The plugin ensures visitor data is passed across domain boundaries. The modification is straightforward and automates the entire process for you.

**Step 2** Use a view filter to insert the hostname of each domain into your reports. For example, convert a pageview for /directory1/filename-123/ into www.domainA.com/directory1/filename-123/ and likewise for pages viewed on domainB.com. With all pages now tracked as a single website, labeling pageviews like this lets you differentiate them in your content reports.

**Step 3** Add both domains to the Referral Exclusion List in the Administration area of your Google Analytics account. This prevents navigations between domains from starting a new referral campaign.[11]

---

### Multi-Domain Tracking

The technique shown for tracking visits across two domains can be extended to any number of domains you own: apply the cross-domain plugin to your GATC first; then use a filter to insert the hostname so that the content viewed for each domain is differentiated in your reports.

Note that tracking users across subdomains does not require any additional configuration. However, if you wish to treat subdomains as separate websites, then a change is required.

---

By applying these steps, you solve the counting and attribution issues and still maintain the ability to view domain-specific performance in your reports.

## CAMPAIGN TRACKING

Showing how effective your marketing campaigns are is probably the most important feature set of Google Analytics. It's also a great strength of the product and a key reason why Google acquired Urchin Software (the original developers of Google Analytics) in the first place.[12]

As long as you have a working GATC on your pages, all visitors to your site are tracked—regardless of how they got there. However, being able to understand what drives visitors to your website can have a dramatic impact on your marketing return on investment. This is what campaign tracking is all about. By adding parameters to your campaign landing page URLs, you enable Google Analytics to log and differentiate your campaigns. This is a function of your marketing, not your website. That is, your marketing team is responsible for this.

With campaign tracking in place, you can distinguish which specific campaign from which specific referral source is providing traffic and customers (often, broad campaigns that drive the most traffic are the least qualified). Taking this a step further, if you monetize your website, you can differentiate your high-, medium-, and low-value campaigns based on the strength of their engagement with your content.

Consider this example: A first-time (new) visitor comes to your website and then returns a further three times—four visits in total. No campaign tracking is in place.

**Day 1** The new visitor arrives via a Google organic search (clicked on your free listing) and browses a handful of your content pages. *Referrer = Google organic.*

**Day 2** The same visitor returns via a click on your animated banner advertisement on the MagazineAd.com website (they liked your time-limited special offer). While on your website, they subscribe to your newsletter. *Referrer = MagazineAd.com.*

**Day 3** The same visitor returns again after receiving your initial welcome email and clicks on a link within it that advertises the original special offer.

They check the offer details but are not ready to commit. They leave your website. *Referrer = Welcome email.*

**Day 6** A few days later you send a follow-up email with a different special offer. The visitor clicks on the link within your email and visits your site. This offer meets their needs, and they go on to become a new customer with you. *Referrer = Follow-up email.*

All four visits are tracked in Google Analytics by default. However, only the first two referral sources will show in your reports—Google organic and MagazineAd.com. The two email visits will show no information to indicate the visitor came from your email efforts. This is because email messages are not websites, and therefore they cannot be identified as a referral source (they are reported as "none" in Google Analytics)*. As a consequence of this, the last *visible* campaign is credited for the conversion of the visitor into a customer (MagazineAd.com). Even then, if you are running multiple campaigns on MagazineAd.com or you change your campaign message, you will not be able to determine which specific campaign is working.

All this is overcome by using campaign tracking.

**The Two Approaches**
Campaign tracking relies on extra parameters being added to your landing page URLs. For example, if you are sending an email campaign focusing on two products, the links within that email would point to two landing pages of the form:

    www.example.com/productA/
    www.example.com/productB/

By adding parameters to these URLs, you can tell Google Analytics exactly which specific email and which specific link your visitors are clicking on.

You can set up campaign tracking using either of two approaches.

- The *explicit* approach uses name–value pairs visible to your site visitor.
- The *implicit* approach uses a non-obvious name–value pair that points to a list of values in a central database.

---

\* With the prevalence of webmail, some visitors can be detected as coming via email. However, campaign-specific detail, such as which email or which offer within an email of multiple offers, is not available without campaign tracking parameters.

*Explicit Values*

Two of your landing page URLs might look like this:

> www.example.com/productA/?*utm_source=customer_newsletter&utm
> _medium=email&utm_campaign=productA*
> www.example.com/productB/?*utm_source=prospects_newsletter&utm
> _medium=email&utm_campaign=productB*

The additional parameters are name–value pairs. The names (utm_ *name*), are specific to Google Analytics and cannot be changed. Their values—for example *newsletter*—are what are shown in your reports, literally. That is, what you see is what you get. If you make a typo in the value, such as *neswletter*, this will show in your reports. It cannot be corrected later. Similarly, if some marketers specify *utm_medium=e-mail* while others use *utm_medium=email*, your data becomes fragmented, as Google Analytics has no way of knowing if these were intended to be the same.

To begin the setup of explicit campaign tracking, your marketing team first needs to define the data structure—the name–value pairs—in a way that makes sense to them. They have five options to choose from, two of which are compulsory, as shown in Table 6.2.

Note that AdWords referrals can be tracked automatically in Google Analytics. No campaign tracking parameters are required so long as the AdWords account has been linked to the Google Analytics account and auto-tagging is enabled. Organic search (free search engine listings) and sites that link to your content unreservedly (not campaign-specific) are also tracked automatically.

## Using Existing Campaign Parameters

Although you cannot modify the reserved names Google Analytics uses for campaign-specific details (utm_*name*), you can utilize existing campaign parameters and map these to Google Analytics. For example, if you have an existing landing page URL that uses campaign parameters produced by another tool, such as

> *www.example.com/?SM=1&SRC=facebook&campaign=social_responsibilty*

you can automatically map these to Google Analytics utm_*name* pairs using a view filter.[13]

**Table 6.2** *Using Campaign Tracking Parameters (in Hierarchical Order)*

| Parameter Name | Required? | Description and Examples |
|---|---|---|
| utm_medium | Yes | What is the channel being used? For example: *email*, *banner advertising*, *offline print*, *online print* (such as PDF), *social network*, or *affiliate*. This is the top-level grouping of the campaign hierarchy. Define this first. |
| utm_source | Yes | What source is set to send this visitor? This can be a specific website URL, such as *affiliate-1 .com*, *reseller20.com*, *facebook.com*, *twitter .com*, or, if you are using an email list data source, *high_value_customers_uk*. |
| utm_campaign | Optional (though highly recommended) | The name of the specific campaign. This should be channel agnostic so that a single campaign can be compared across all channels (on- and offline). For example: *Spring sale for leather shoes* or *subscription renewal offer*. |
| utm_term | Optional | Used with paid search only, to capture the keywords being targeted. For example: *leather shoes* or *automated widgets*. Not required for AdWords, as this is automated for you. |
| utm_content | Optional | The version of the ad used. This is powerful for testing different design formats. For example: *animated banner* versus *static*; for an email, the *top-txt-link* versus the same link placed as *main-image-link*. |

## Implicit Values

An alternative to specifying the five name–value pairs of Table 6.2 is to use a centralized technique. You can add a single *utm_id* parameter to your landing page URLs and use the Google Analytics administrator interface to import (upload) what that ID corresponds to. For example, www .example.com/productB/?*utm_id=50gB* includes the name–value pair *utm_id=50gB*, which might be defined as follows:

    source: customer_database_uk
    medium: email
    campaign: Upsell Spring

This technique has two advantages: it removes any campaign-sensitive information from your landing page URLs; and it prevents anyone from spamming you with their fake campaign information—the purpose of which is to entice you to click through in your reports to investigate these strange campaigns, therefore generating ad revenue for the spammer.

## Which to Choose

Consider using the implicit technique if a single person (or team) manages *all* digital campaigns for your organization. However, if multiple teams are involved, use the explicit method with a solid process and methodology in place for defining the tracking values. This spreads the workload (freeing up your resources) and allows for separate teams to be creative and to experiment with their needs.

⚠️ *Campaign tracking is for use with external campaigns only—the campaigns you employ to bring traffic to your website. Do not use this technique for monitoring your own internal campaigns, such as your special promotions. Doing so will overwrite your visitor's original referral information (the campaign information that brought them to your site in the first place) and will restart the visitor's session, leading to double counting of visits.*

*If you sell advertising on your site, track clicks on these as events or virtual pageviews. If you have an e-commerce facility, special offers and promotional listings can be tracked with specific transaction-related functions.*

## What Happens without Campaign Tracking?

Even without campaign tracking, Google Analytics still tracks visitors to your website. However, in this scenario the issue for Google Analytics is how to report the visitor's attribution. In other words, what marketing activity or referral source gets the credit for driving the visitor to your site? Campaign tracking ensures the attribution is correct; without it, Google Analytics needs to guess. Table 6.3 lists how Google Analytics assigns attribution in these circumstances.

As you can see from Table 6.3, there is a great deal more insightful information to be gained when campaign tracking is in place. In addition, without campaign tracking the marketing channel (called the *medium*) of *none* becomes a catch-all label for any visitor whose attribution cannot be determined. It is supposed to be related to the number of people that remember your brand name and type your web address directly into their browser. That is a useful number to know. However, without campaign tracking in place, *medium=none* is simply an inflated number for *unknown*.

Similarly, without campaign tracking in place, the marketing channel *referrer* is an inflated figure. An enterprise website may have thousands of different referral domains (thousands of websites and articles linking back to the enterprise). Amalgamating these together with social networks, email, affiliates, and banner click-through visitors makes it a lot harder for your marketing and sales teams to find important information.

**Table 6.3** *Attribution Behavior without Campaign Tracking*

| Traffic Source | Sample Attribution with Campaign Tracking | Attribution without Campaign Tracking |
|---|---|---|
| Email marketing | Labeled as *medium = Email; source = UK_customers_2014; campaign = spring sale* | Labeled as *medium = none; source = direct; campaign = not set* Visitors who use webmail will be labeled as *referral* the same as if a website is linking to your content and sending you traffic. Such referrers are therefore buried among other referrers. |
| Social network site | Labeled as *medium = Social Network; source = Facebook; campaign = corporate responsibility query* | There are two scenarios*: 1. The visitor comes directly from the social website (facebook.com): labeled as *medium = referral; source = facebook.com; campaign = not set* 2. The visitor comes via the social network's mobile app: labeled as *medium = none; source = direct; campaign = not set* |
| Paid search other than AdWords | Labeled as *medium = PPC; source = Bing UK; campaign = spring sale; keyword = leather shoes; content = special offer v1b* | For example, a visitor clicking an ad on Bing.com following a search for "leather shoes": labeled as *medium = organic; source = bing.com; campaign = not set; keyword = leather shoes* |
| Display ad | Labeled as *medium = Banner; source = MagazinesiteA; campaign = spring sale; content = static banner (skyscraper) run of site* | For example, a visitor clicking a banner ad on MagazinesiteA.com: labeled as *medium = referral; source = MagazinesiteA.com; campaign = not set* |
| Affiliate or reseller website | Labeled as *medium = Affiliate; source = affiliate1; campaign = productA* | For example, a visitor clicking a link to your website from affiliate1.com: labeled as *medium = referral; source = affiliate1.com; campaign = not set* |
| Links from within documents (such as a PDF catalog) | Labeled as *medium = PDF; source = catalog 2014; campaign = Widgets section; content = click on image* | Labeled as *medium = none; source = direct; campaign = not set* No information as to which document, or which section within it, is providing your traffic |

* Note that more than half of all social visits occur via a mobile app.[14,15,16]

The bottom line is that campaign tracking is important and its setup needs to be prioritized within your organization.

## ATTRIBUTION

What marketing activities should receive credit for sending you traffic? Which should receive the credit for any resultant conversions, such as becoming a customer or a new lead? These questions are what attribution attempts to answer.

Having campaign tracking properly set up is a key requirement for Google Analytics to report the correct attribution. Even when campaign tracking is in place, how do you decide on the attribution model? Recall the scenario (with campaign tracking in place):

**Day 1**   The new visitor arrives via a Google organic search (clicked on your free listing) and browses a handful of your content pages. *Referrer = Google organic.*

**Day 2**   The same visitor returns via a click on your animated banner advertisement on the MagazineAd.com website (they liked your time-limited special offer). While on your website, they subscribe to your newsletter. *Referrer = MagazineAd.com.*

**Day 3**   The same visitor returns again after receiving your initial welcome email and clicks on a link within it that advertises the original special offer. They check the offer details but are not ready to commit. They leave your website. *Referrer = Welcome email.*

**Day 6**   A few days later you send a follow-up email with a different special offer. The visitor clicks on the link within your email and visits your site. This offer meets their needs, and they go on to become a new customer with you. *Referrer = Follow-up email.*

Which of these four actions (in order: organic, banner, email–welcome, email–follow-up) should be given credit for the conversion that happens on day 6? There are a number of ways to model attribution, discussed next, all of which involve some kind of compromise, because of the complexities of the problem.

### The Default Model—Last Click

Historically, because it is the simplest to implement, the industry assigned credit for a conversion to the last observed click-through. In the example, only email-follow-up will be credited for the visitor's conversion—the organic, banner, and email-welcome drivers are given no credit. Their attribution is overwritten when the visitor returns via a new referrer path.

It is straightforward to reverse this model—to give credit to the first referrer only. However, the point is that only one can be given the credit for the conversion with this model.

Although the last-click model is an oversimplification in a multi-channel marketing world, the purpose of keeping it as an option in Google Analytics is that it maintains simplicity. Knowing what final marketing activity drives the visitor to convert is an important step in understanding your marketing activities—a great deal of optimization can be done with this information. However, there are likely to be other supporting activities that are contributing to your conversions, and these may be significant. Therefore, once you understand the last-click performance of your website marketing efforts, move on to extended attribution models.

### Extended Models

Although last-click models are simple and at least provide a report on the final link in the attribution chain, they are severely limited in the

### The Google Analytics Default

For its default, Google Analytics applies one exception to the last-click model (the model in which the last click is a direct visit): when the visitor types your web address directly into their browser or uses a previously saved bookmark or favorite. For this scenario, the previous attributed referrer keeps the credit for the conversion—it is not overwritten.

To clarify, the visitor is tracked as a direct visitor in Google Analytics. However, the credit for the conversion does not change from its preceding value. In the example, if a fifth direct visit is added, the attribution remains as *email-follow-up*. The Google Analytics default model is the *last non-direct click* attribution model, shown schematically in Figure 6.4.

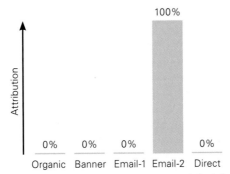

**Figure 6.4** *Last non-direct click attribution (the default for Google Analytics)*

multi-channel world. Where campaigns are launched to target a broad spectrum of channels with the specific intent of having a 2 + 2 = 5 effect, the theory is that the combined impact of using multiple channels is greater than the sum of its parts. Therefore, once you understand the basic last-click levers, move on to extended, more advanced models.

Google Analytics has a number of attribution model templates that you can use. My friend and former colleague at Google, Avinash Kaushik, has a great blog post on this subject, "Multi-Channel Attribution Modeling: The Good, Bad and Ugly Models."[17]

Rather than repeating Avinash's descriptions and comments on them here (they are well worth a read), I illustrate the models graphically in Figure 6.5. The charts are self-explanatory; they show how attribution can be distributed. The key is finding the right model for your organization. If you are ready for attribution modeling, you need to experiment. My advice is to avoid the simplified first- and last-click models and focus on understanding what impact the others have (linear, time-decay, position-based). With these mastered, you can graduate to building your own custom model.

Attribution modeling relies on Google Analytics being able to recognize your returning visitors. If they delete their Google Analytics cookie between visits or use a different device (moving from mobile phone to laptop to tablet, for example), the attribution model will break down. You can overcome this issue by encouraging your visitors to authenticate with you—that is, log in. If they do, your own internal anonymous login ID can be used by Google Analytics to stitch together visits from different devices.[18]

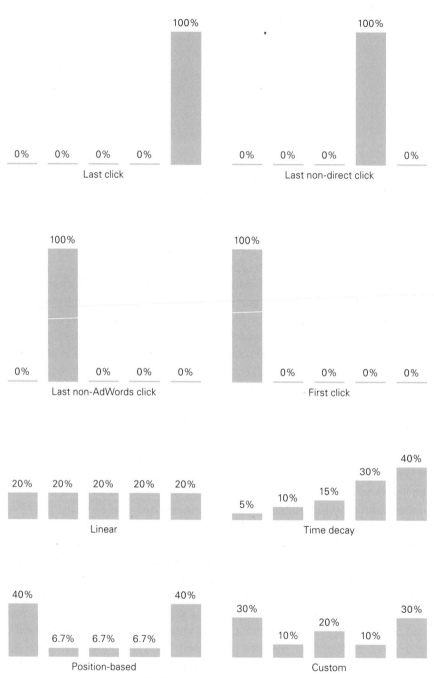

**Figure 6.5** *Google Analytics attribution models*

## A Word of Caution Regarding Attribution Modeling

Attribution modeling is a great recent advance of Google Analytics (launched in 2011). But it is not a panacea for deciding which of your referrers should receive credit for a conversion.

At best, attribution modeling is a powerful guide for your sales, marketing, PR, and content teams to be able to work more cohesively. It is not an exact science. Beyond the oversimplification of first- and last-click models, different models simply tell a different story. It cannot be said that one is right or wrong for you—there are many shades of gray that your analysts will need to appreciate.

For example, the time-decay model may be most suitable when considering affiliates. For assessing paid search, you may judge the position-based model a better fit. If both paid search and affiliates are simultaneous components of a visitor's path, then a custom model should be investigated.

The decisions you make here all require good, sound logical thought experiments. See Chapter 8, "Building Your Insights Team."

This is what sites such as Amazon, Sony, and Walmart do—they provide a motivation for a visitor to be persistently logged in when they visit. The result is that they are consistently tracked across all devices. If you can generate such a motivation for your own customers, it is well worth implementing. (I use these well-known brands for illustration purposes only.)

## TESTING AND EXPERIMENTS

As part of its feature set, Google Analytics has a built-in platform for conducting A/B testing, called Content Experiments. Having a testing platform integrated within your data measurement platform makes sense. After all, both rely on data to be effective. However, another driving force for the integration is that as you experiment with the way you display content—that is, deliver different versions of the same content to different visitors—the impact of that change can be reflected in *all* your visitor reports. So if a test variation produced a better visitor engagement (or sales) than the original version, that impact can be shown alongside the plethora of other metrics available in Google Analytics, not just one conversion metric. Clearly this is a significant advantage compared to a standalone testing tool.

Despite the advantages of integration, I am not a big fan of the current Content Experiments feature. To understand why, let's look at how testing works and what is good—that is, clever—about Content Experiments.

## The Principles of Experimentation

This description is tool agnostic. That is, it is not specific to Google Analytics.

Experimenting with your website content comes in two flavors—either comparing different versions of the same page (A/B testing) or simultaneously changing multiple elements within a page (multivariate testing). The principle of both types of testing is to display different versions of your content to your visitors at random. The specific version displayed is maintained throughout a single visit, so your visitor is unaware of other versions; the test does not interfere with your visitor's browsing experience.

For each experiment you define a goal for its performance to be assessed against. Your goal can be a follow-on click-through to a specific page, the generation of a new lead, a transaction, or a revenue goal. A winner is declared for the test version that drives the most goal conversions, assuming you have enough traffic for the difference to be statistically significant. The hypothesis is that the winner is the version of content your visitors prefer. Once that is determined, the test is complete, and you adopt the winning test page as your permanent content. This is the basis of content optimization—optimizing your content based on solid science.

Marketers are familiar with A/B testing—a binary test to compare the effectiveness of one element, such as a product image, versus another. To test whether one performs better—drives more engagement or more sales for you—an experiment can be set up to show image A to 50% of your visitors at random and image B to the remaining 50%.

If image A is better at visitor engagement than image B, then image A is declared the winner. Similarly, you can test other elements such as headlines, product descriptions, pricing, special offers, page layout, and design. Despite its name, you can perform multiple side-by-side tests—that is, A/B/C/D... tests.

Multivariate testing (MVT) is used to evaluate multiple page elements—images, headlines, descriptions, content, and so on—*simultaneously* in order to understand which combinations provide better engagement. This simultaneity is what distinguishes MVT from A/B testing. For example, the combination of image A, headline B, price C, may be significantly different in terms of driving visitor engagement than image C, headline B, price A.

If you have three variations of each of these elements (A, B, C), then you have a total of 27 combinations to test (3 × 3 × 3). Because of this, MVT experiments take a lot longer to complete than do A/B experiments.

☛ *The Google Analytics Content Experiments platform is currently an A/B testing platform only.*

## What's Cool with Content Experiments?

For controlling content experiments, you can specify the use of the *multi-armed bandit* (MAB) model. The MAB model is a statistical algorithm that allocates more traffic to a winning test combination over time, at the expense of a losing combination. That makes sense, particularly if you are an e-commerce site, where money is being lost if a poorly performing test page is delivered. After all, why would you want your test to remain static when there is a clear winner?

The MAB model is a clever technique used only by Google, unique in the A/B testing industry. However, if you prefer not to use it, you can also select the traditional *fixed* model, where the traffic allocation remains fixed over time regardless of any clear winner—for example, 50% of your visitors view version A, 50% view version B.

### Overaggressive Bandits

In the early days of content experiments, users considered the MAB algorithm overly aggressive. If there was an unexpected peak in conversions, traffic would be reallocated to the winning test version at such a rate that it could not be rebalanced if that condition subsequently changed.

Here's an example to illustrate the issue:

You sell products that are sensitive to the weather. For a page under test, you have both umbrella and T-shirt product information on the same page. The weather turns wet for a few days and you sell a great many more umbrellas than T-shirts. Your umbrellas are declared the winner (they receive significantly more sales for that period) without the algorithm waiting for the weather to change back and equilibrate. National holidays and other one-off events can also mess with your test data in a similar way.

Overaggressive bandits have historically been a problem. This problem was fixed (the algorithm was pacified) early in 2013.

So as a methodology, Google Analytics Content Experiments are perfectly good for A/B testing. (Note that multivariate experiments are not currently supported in Google Analytics.)

### What's Painful with Content Experiments?

In terms of setting up and administering an experiment, Content Experiments are unwieldy, unlike the rest of the Google Analytics product. The reason is that test pages are delivered from *your* server. You host the different test versions yourself, and the Google Analytics experiments engine determines the random sampling—who sees what test version.

With the requirement that test versions be hosted on your own website, it becomes a headache to test pages that are built from multiple *include* components. Consider the simple page template shown in Figure 6.6. The main page is built by including three template files—the page header, navigation menu, and footer (four files in total). Almost all commercial sites are built in this way, as it allows for easy updating and maintenance, such as a change to the side menu that only needs to be made once but then applies across the entire website.

The page structure of Figure 6.6 presents a problem for Content Experiments. In order to conduct a test on different versions of the call-to-action button, the web development team has to build a page delivery system that can process variations of the template files as a *single* URL. In this example, that might mean swapping out the *main-content* file for *main-content-v1b* while keeping the original header, navigation, and footer

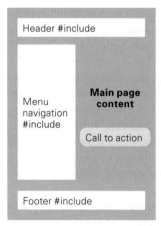

**Figure 6.6** *Sample A/B test page*

templates in place. So, if the original landing page URL is www.example.com /product-abc, your web platform needs to be able to process separate URLs for each test variation—for example, www.example.com/product-abc/ ?content=orig and www.example/product-abc/?content=v1b, where *content= v1b* defines a different variation to display.

This becomes more complicated as you test different sections of the page. For example, take swapping out the header for a different one while keeping the rest of the content untouched. The URL for this could be www .example.com/product-abc/?content=v2c. In this case, your web platform needs to interpret the value of the *content* parameter and determine which version of the *include* files to build the page from.

Building a content delivery system just for A/B testing is a significant undertaking for your IT department that is best avoided if an alternative exists. Fortunately, one does. The alternative approach is to use a third-party testing tool that takes a client-side approach.[19] This technique modifies your test page on the fly, by using JavaScript and CSS *within* the page content as it is loaded. The result is that test variations can be built within an administrator interface rather than on your web servers. Experiments such as Figure 6.6 are then possible in a matter of minutes—without the need to change your website delivery system.

The downside of the client-side method is that there is a slight delay added to your page loading. This happens while the test script figures out the test combination requested and then alters the content on the fly as your page loads. However, in my experience the benefit of a much easier experiment setup far outweighs any page loading delay. The small incremental improvements achieved by deploying numerous quick, easy-to-set-up tests can quickly add up to a significant return for your organization while minimizing any IT overhead.

### Integrating a Third-Party Testing Tool with Google Analytics

If you use a third-party testing tool[19] to manage and conduct your experiments, you can still integrate the data with Google Analytics. The key is to pass the version number or name presented to your visitor as your page is loaded. Typically this is done using a Google Analytics feature called a custom dimension—a one-line addition to your GATC that some testing tools add automatically for you.

Once this is in place, all your Google Analytics reports can then be segmented by the test version that your visitors saw, allowing you to compare how each test version affected *any* metric within Google Analytics.

## EXTRACTING YOUR DATA

You can extract your data from Google Analytics in numerous formats—for example, as a CSV/TSV file, an XLSX (Excel) file, Google Spreadsheets, or a PDF. That is great for a small number of one-off report exports but not suitable when automation or a high volume of report data is required. For this scenario, the solution is to use an application programming interface (API).

As with almost all Google products, Google Analytics has its own set of APIs. If your developers wish to extract data and use it in another application, you can bypass the Google Analytics user interface and work directly with your data. This is the same process as described in the section "Scaling with Automation," in Chapter 5.

There are numerous export examples for the API, including automatic data exports into Excel or PowerPoint, building a customized dashboard, and exporting web traffic data into your CMS or CRM system. There are several Google Analytics APIs to choose from.[20]

Using the Google APIs is a programming exercise—a direction you point your development team in when you need something that is not provided by the Google Analytics user interface or is cumbersome to obtain via the user interface. The following are a selection of what I consider significant third-party applications built using Google Analytics export APIs. You can view the full list at www.google.com/analytics/apps or develop your own.

**E-commerce recommendation engine**   "Customers who bought this item also bought…" is a cross-sell phrase pioneered by Amazon. Google Analytics does not yet have e-commerce recommendation reports to help you directly with this. However, using the Core Reporting API, you can export all of your transactions in your own database and assess correlations using standard database queries.

For example, an insight via the export could be that a visitor who spends less than 30 seconds looking at a product category page will most likely purchase product X. On the other hand, a visitor who spends longer on the category page will most likely purchase product Y. That observation is not available in the current user interface.

Taking this a step further, you could adjust your system's recommendations based on the current visitor's behavior—that is, dynamically change your recommendations based on their time-on-page metric.

**Behavioral personalization**   By extracting your data in real time, you can adjust the content a visitor views according to their behavior. For example, if a visitor has shown a strong interest (engagement) in a particular section of your website but has fleetingly moved to another section, you can personalize the new section to take account of that behavior. Perhaps you wish to entice them back, or maintain a particular navigation menu for them.

**Phone call tracking**   When people pick up the phone while browsing your website, the association between making the call and the fact they were browsing your website is lost—that is, Google Analytics has no record of this. However, you can extract your visitor's Google Analytics ID (the anonymous ID used to track visitors) and associate it with your telephone system, when a web visitor calls. You then send a data hit from your telephone system to Google Analytics using the same visitor ID value.

Because the same ID is used, Google Analytics associates the call data hit as a continuous part of the visitor's web journey—even though it has been generated by a different system (your telephone system). That allows you to analyze what referral source and what behavior leads to making a phone call within your Google Analytics reports. Perhaps you want to minimize or maximize the number of calls received.

## SPEAKING OF KEY METHODS...

| When I hear this... | I reply with... |
| --- | --- |
| Our marketing automation system keeps track of visitor scores—how likely a prospect is to become a customer. How can we use this with Google Analytics? | Use a visitor label for this. For each visitor to your website, pass their score into Google Analytics by setting a custom metric, with its value obtained from your marketing automation system. This technique has been used successfully with the Eloqua system and should work with others.[21] |
| What A/B experiments should we be running? | My general rule is to test only what you understand. For example, test a hypothesis that one product image is preferred versus another, or that one set of value propositions in your page copy is more persuasive versus another.<br><br>In other words, do not test everything just because you can. You will save a great deal of time and energy if you focus on things you have an understanding of. That does not mean your understanding is correct. Rather, if you think you understand what a visitor does on your site, then that is a good reason to test it. |

| When I hear this... | I reply with... |
|---|---|
| We know our visitors access our site via a number of different devices, and this is inflating our visitor count. How can this be fixed? | The way to achieve this (without violating your visitors' trust) is to have your visitors authenticate with you and pass your customer ID back to Google Analytics. That way, the visitor ID is consistent regardless of what device they connected from. The effectiveness with which you motivate your visitors to open a user account and *use* it when they visit your website is the limiting factor here. |
| | If you struggle to encourage your visitors to use their account, combine this method with your email newsletter. That is, append their visitor ID to all links in your newsletter. If such links are clicked, you pass your customer ID back to Google Analytics for visitor tracking. |
| For our e-commerce site, we wish to report the profit margins of our products, not the gross revenue. Can this be done? | Yes, though you will not wish to do this using the client-side JavaScript code that is the default way to track transactions— as this is visible to anyone viewing your page HTML. Instead, you can achieve this by performing a data upload tied to a transaction ID (see Chapter 5), or you can use the measurement protocol to securely send transaction data directly from your server to Google Analytics. |
| | As an alternative to importing the data into Google Analytics, you can export transactions into Excel or a Google spreadsheet. You then configure formulas to calculate your profit. Generally, I prefer this export method, as you can also experiment with different margin and delivery options. After the initial setup, the export can be automated.[22] An example of this is shown in Chapter 9 (Figure 9.9). |

## CHAPTER 6 REFERENCES

1   More information on tracking Android apps:
    https://developers.google.com/analytics/devguides/collection/android/

2   More information on tracking iPhone apps:
    https://developers.google.com/analytics/devguides/collection/ios/

3   You can read a more detailed overview of the Google Analytics platform at
    https://developers.google.com/analytics/devguides/platform/.

4   You can check general data limits at
    https://support.google.com/analytics/answer/1070983.

5   Having fun with the universal measurement protocol:

    http://nicomiceli.com/tracking-your-home-with-google-analytics

    https://learn.adafruit.com/category/learn-raspberry-pi

    www.youtube.com/results?search_query=universal+analytics+example

6       The AOL data leak was the first mainstream press investigation revealing how individuals can be identified from anonymous data: http://en.wikipedia.org/wiki/AOL_search_data_leak.

7       You can specify what percentage of visitors should be tracked by adding a single line to your GATC. Note, this works at the visitor level and is applied statistically randomly. That is, entire visitor sessions are either collected or sampled out: https://developers.google.com/analytics/devguides/collection/analyticsjs /field-reference?hl=en#sampleRate.

8       The technical change required to override the default pageview behavior of Google Analytics to collect virtual pageviews is described at https://developers.google .com/analytics/devguides/collection/analyticsjs/pages#overriding.

9       The code for the tracking of events is detailed at https://developers.google .com/analytics/devguides/collection/analyticsjs/events.

10      The full list of tracking methods is detailed at https://developers.google.com /analytics/devguides/collection/protocol/v1/devguide.

11      The autoLink plugin developed by Google is a clever idea that essentially removes the pain from having to modify all your cross-domain links. By adding only two lines of code to your GATC, all your cross-domain tracking is automatically taken care of for you: https://developers.google.com/analytics/devguides /collection/analyticsjs/cross-domain.

12      Google acquired Urchin Software Inc. in April 2005. The founder of Urchin, Paul Muret, is still the main driving force behind Google Analytics development. He is currently VP of engineering at Google.

13      More on Google Analytics profile view filters at https://support.google.com/analytics/answer/1033162

14      In May 2013, according to a compilation of statistics by Statistic Brain, 60% of tweets came from third-party applications: www.statisticbrain.com/twitter-statistics.

15      From Facebook's quarterly earnings slides (Q2 2013), 71% of Facebook users access via a mobile device. Of course, not all of these will use the Facebook app, but my opinion is that the majority will: http://www.cnet.com/news /facebook-earnings-by-the-numbers-819m-mobile-users/.

16      From Twitter marketing emails (Q1 2014), 76% of Twitter users access via a mobile device. Of course, not all of these will use the Twitter app, but my opinion is that the majority will.

17      Avinash's blog post on attribution modeling: www.kaushik.net/avinash /multi-channel-attribution-modeling-good-bad-ugly-models/. See also my comments on his post at http://brianclifton.com/multi-channel-attribution.

18      Using your own visitor ID to track visitors in Google Analytics: https://developers .google.com/analytics/devguides/collection/analyticsjs/user-id

19      Optimizely and Visual Website Optimizer are two well-respected testing platforms that use a client-side (on-the-fly) approach to testing pages.

20      Google Analytics API documentation can be found at https://developers.google.com/analytics/devguides/reporting/.

21    Eloqua is a marketing automation tool (**www.eloqua.com**). Other examples include Silverpop (**www.silverpop.com**) and Pardot (**www.pardot.com**).

22    An excellent walk-through tutorial on automated data exporting using the Core Reporting API and Google Spreadsheets is provided by Nick Mihailovski of the Google Analytics developer team: **http://analytics.blogspot.co.uk/2012/08 /automate-google-analytics-reporting.html**.

# 7

# Data Responsibilities

**When you collect data on** people, you automatically inherit responsibilities for that data. In all developed countries (and in most of the world in general), there are data protection laws that govern this, and you should at least be aware of the basic principles. For example, in Europe, the fundamentals are that you put the end user first and that you ask for permission before collecting data. From that guiding baseline you can build and refine for your specific requirements—such as defining what constitutes permission (explicit verses implicit).

This chapter discusses the privacy debate—in general terms and specifically in relation to the European Union (EU). It includes an approach for evaluating your privacy level with best-practice tips on protecting your reputation in this area and building visitor trust. Beyond privacy considerations, it discusses how to structure and protect your data from accidental (or deliberate) pollution and deletion and plan for future changes in the fluid data protection landscape.

## ALL ABOUT PRIVACY

Although I always try to base my decisions on good data, I am also a strong privacy advocate. Those two ideals are not mutually exclusive. Data enthusiasts are always on a quest to find more supporting data or better-quality data, but end-user privacy is a fundamental human right to be respected.[1,2,3]

A detailed view of differing privacy attitudes by geography can be found at the *Economist*,[4] but in general privacy concerns vary by region as follows:

- In the US the "average person" is concerned with government intrusion and a bureaucracy overhead when they think about online privacy worries.
- In Europe (more specifically the EU), the concerns tend to focus on advertisers and companies harvesting information to sell to third parties or to bombard you with spam.
- In Asia, in general the concern when discussing privacy is about a "surveillance state." This is probably connected to the fact that only 6 of 23 countries in this region are democracies.[5]

### The Privacy Debate
Online privacy is a surprisingly complex subject. Apart from the cultural differences of what defines privacy in different parts of the world, there

## Tracking Versus Spying—The Snowden Impact

The Edward Snowden "affair" took the existing privacy debate to a much broader audience. To the general public, the tracking of visitors for commercial reasons appears no different from government security agencies surreptitiously trawling the Internet en masse. The resultant perception is that all tracking is scary and invasive and may one day be used against you. Although I advocate that people should be more aware of their online privacy footprint, the concern in the digital analytics industry post Snowden is that people will start to block commercial tracking techniques more affirmatively—for example, using ad-blocker software, opting out when requested, and blocking or deleting cookies.

Regardless of whether this happens, the reality is that if you use the Internet, some degree of tracking is inevitable. After all, your IP address has to be transmitted to the destination you connect to in order for it to work. Hence there are degrees of privacy (shades of gray).

If analysts, marketers, website owners, and all the other interested data parties take care and respect end-user privacy, there are good reasons for visitors to continue to share information—it benefits both the end user (with better-performing websites and sales offers) and website owners (with an increased return on investment because of their ability to make better, more targeted decisions). This of course is circular: as ROI improves, consumers get increasingly better deals. However, if a mass evasion of tracking by end users ensues, the digital world will, by necessity, take a very large step back—reverting to the bad old days of interruption marketing.

are also different levels of privacy invasion from a visitor's point of view, ranging from "Tolerable if it provides me a benefit in return" (such as providing access to high-value content on your website—support areas, white papers, discount pricing and so forth) to "Alarming. I wasn't expecting or even aware of that" and "That should not be allowed. It is a loss of my trust."

To compound matters, parts of your website may operate at different privacy levels—making it hard to establish an overall statement on your approach. Common examples include the embedding of content from elsewhere, such as social share buttons (Tweet, Like, Google+, and so forth); embedded video from YouTube, Vimeo, and other video-hosting websites; embedded third-party images, such as certifications; and third-party tools such as the DoubleClick ad network, visitor survey tools, live chat, and A/B testing tools.

Figure 7.1 illustrates the different levels of privacy with an analogy. Suppose you wanted to gather data on the impact of traffic on your community. The question you want to answer is "How busy is this road?"

From a tracking perspective, there are three privacy levels:

**Green: Aggregate, non-personal data**    When nothing is collected that identifies individuals or tracks individual behavior, because all data is aggregated, you have a green flag to collect all the data you want. You can do a great deal of analysis without personal information. If you want to know how busy a road is, you have no reason to collect anything at the individual, or personal, level.

**Yellow: No personal data, but individuals tracked**    Proceed with caution when you start tracking individuals, even though they're still anonymous. The data by definition becomes more invasive. This kind of tracking allows you to profile individuals and target them for advertising, even though you don't know who they are. Because of this, it can be argued this data is personal. There is also the fear for many users that given enough anonymous information, an individual can be identified by triangulation.

**Figure 7.1** *Three different levels of online privacy: The organization gathering the data is analogous to a website owner or marketer (you). The road represents the web infrastructure. A car represents a visitor's browser. The people in the cars are the visitors. Destinations (shops, schools, houses) are websites.*

By building individual profiles, you make the data more valuable. But to many people that means either you spam them or you sell the information on for others to spam them.

● **Red: Personally identifiable information (PII)**   When you obtain personal details such as a person's name and address, you need the explicit permission of the user. Otherwise, stop. Imagine yourself in the driver's seat of one of the cars in Figure 7.1. Would you feel comfortable being tracked by surveillance cameras or tracking devices without giving your explicit permission? And if you gave your permission to be tracked only for this specific study, you would not expect to be tracked for all time, or to have the permission applied retroactively to data collected before you gave permission.

Moving from green to red, the tracking activities become more invasive (more personal), and the end-user privacy concerns grow. Legal obligations with respect to privacy increase, and more work is required to keep on top of best practices so that your visitors maintain trust in your brand.

**EU Privacy Law**
In May 2011 an EU directive called the ePrivacy Directive came into force. In the UK this was implemented in the form of the Privacy and Electronic Communications Regulations (PECR). Distilled to its fundamentals, the law's aim is to protect the privacy of individuals online from people and

---

### Summary of Privacy Color-Coding
Using green, yellow, or red to indicate the level of data responsibility for your organization is applicable to all platforms, such as mobile apps, not just to the web.

● Green designates methods with the lowest risk to your organization, those most trusted by your visitors. This level entails the least data responsibility and is the easiest to manage.

● Yellow allows for visitor profiling, which can be interpreted as personal data because profiles can quickly get very specific. The risk to your organization and the management overhead are significant.

● Red is reserved for methods that capture PII and therefore carry the highest risk to your organization. These are the methods that are least trusted by your visitors. They require the most effort with regard to data responsibility and management.

organizations that collect personal information about them or use behavioral targeting techniques to profile a visitor across the web.

PECR is often referred to as the "EU cookie law" online and in the press because it states, unfortunately in a quite broad and ambiguous way, that cookies cannot be set without a visitor's consent. However, the law is technology agnostic. That is, it is based on privacy levels, not on whether an HTTP cookie, or other technology not yet invented, is used. The law applies in all 27 EU member countries.

As you can imagine, the implementation of this law caused some consternation in the digital industry, where cookies have become as fundamental as HTML and JavaScript. Google Analytics and many other embedded functions rely on cookies to work. In principle, PECR is a good and much-needed law, as behavioral targeting and the abuse of private information were becoming pervasive. Collecting benign, anonymous, aggregate data, such as that provided by Google Analytics, is not the target of this law.

The difficulty the EU legislators faced was wording the law and guidelines in a technology-agnostic way that deters privacy abuse while protecting the legitimate need of website owners to know what is going on with their websites—for example, using Google Analytics.

☞ *Although my comments are from a UK perspective (my native land), they are applicable to all EU member countries. Even outside the EU, governments are looking closely at what happens in the EU to establish similar privacy laws. Therefore, understanding this is important, as it is the direction that web privacy is inevitably going— more privacy-centric, with more user consent.*

### What This Means for Web Analytics Users

Ultimately you will need to follow the advice of your own legal counsel in the light of rules published by the data protection authorities in the countries where you operate. I am offering my lay interpretation of the law here as a guide to best practices.[6]

⬤**Green level**  If your website only uses anonymous, benign, first-party tracking techniques and the resulting data is stored and reported in aggregate (that is, not at the individual level), you do not need to seek explicit consent from your visitors in order to track them. This law is not about hindering benign first-party tracking techniques. The use of Google Analytics *generally* fits into this category.

I must emphasize my use of *anonymous* and benign *first-party* tracking techniques. *Anonymous* means just that. It does not include an anonymized unique ID that can be tied back to an individual via your CMS. *First-party tracking* means that the website the visitor is actually viewing is the same website that is collecting the data—not a third-party website or advertiser. In other words, the collecting of the data is owned and is completely controlled by your organization.

In addition, the entire tracking process is transparent to your visitors and readily available, not buried deep in a privacy policy that is difficult to find or comprehend.

⬤**Yellow and** ⬤**red levels**   If your website tracking is not completely anonymous, or your data collection is owned or set by a third party, you need explicit consent from each visitor in order to be compliant with the law in the EU. That is, you must ask each visitor if they accept your tracking and privacy approach. If they agree, you can continue to track. If they opt out, you must remove all tracking of those visitors before they continue to browse your website.

The same approach of transparency and accessibility is required for your privacy policy.

Although these guidelines appear straightforward, the difficultly for website owners is in assessing the level that is applicable to them. For example, on the surface it would appear that if you are only using Google Analytics to track your visitors, you have little to worry about. However, that is not always the case.

### Common Pitfalls (Even If You Are Using Google Analytics)
Listed in no particular order, here are five common pitfalls to avoid when assessing your privacy responsibilities:

- It is possible to capture personal data inadvertently with Google Analytics. For example, this can happen when a visitor receives a confirmation email for an email newsletter sign-up, site registration, or the like, and the confirmation link the visitor must click includes a clear text version of their email address in the URL. Google Analytics tracks URLs by default. When your subscriber clicks the link to confirm and arrives on your website's thank you page, their email address is captured in your reports. Ensure you have checked your data for any personal information. To do this, check your content reports (pages and events) for captured usernames or email addresses.

Collecting personal data is also against the Google Analytics ToS. If you discover such data, you will need to close and delete the Google Analytics data collected for that web property. See Chapter 4 for more details.

- Often, other tools and scripts are in place on your web pages that track visitors—and these may not be anonymous or first-party. Assess these separately from Google Analytics—see the section "Assessing Your Website Privacy Level."
- Site owners must have a best-practice privacy policy in place and make it easily accessible. This is also a part of the Google Analytics ToS.
- If any personal data is captured, explicit consent *must* be requested from your visitors. Captured personal data can be from your visitors completing a purchase or subscribing to a newsletter, for example. For these, visitors are completely aware they are handing over their personal data and therefore knowingly agree to do so by making their purchase or subscribing. No additional request to track is required. (This is not, strictly speaking, *explicit* consent. However, the action of completing a purchase is so obvious to the visitor that it goes way beyond implied consent).

   If the collection of personal data is not so obvious as I have described, consent must be asked for separately.
- If personal data is captured by consent, it must not be used to back-fill data. That is, you cannot associate the personal data with the visitor's actions *before* their point of consent.

### Assessing Your Website Privacy Level

To assess which privacy level your website fits, work with your web development team to conduct a privacy audit. This is a technical audit requiring a strong understanding of what is happening behind your pages. Use the following steps and document your findings:

☛ *The generic term* tracking widget *refers to any script, tool, plugin, or other content that can track the activity of your visitors.*

### Identifying What You Have

Identify what tracking widgets are in place on your pages. List these by vendor name, with a brief description of their purpose. You may be surprised how many you find. On my own website (brianclifton.com), I at first assumed that I only track with one widget—Google Analytics. But I found these six widgets tracking visitors and their interactions:

- Google Analytics, tracking all visits by default.
- The AddThis social plugin widget that allows visitors to share my content across multiple networks, tracking all visits by default.
- A click on many of the AddThis social share buttons, such as Tweet, Like, or Google+, also sends visitor data back to those networks, tracking a visitor if a share action is clicked.
- A page testing widget (Optimizely): I run experiments on the layout of my site to test the effectiveness of different call-to-action designs, tracking all visits by default.
- The SiteApps widget, an embedded plugin that highlights content of interest using a sticky note–type display, tracking all visits by default.
- A feedback survey widget (Kampyle) that allows visitors to tell me what they think of my content or to flag a problem (qualitative analytics) tracks visitors if they submit feedback.

I built my own website, so I should know there are multiple tracking widgets. However, as with any active website, my content is evolving and additional functionality is continuingly being added (widget creep). In general, I use widgets to provide a better visitor experience—for example to make it easier for them to find and share content. That is, tracking is not my purpose for using the widgets. I forgot that they also have tracking functionality, not specifically for my benefit as the website owner.

For any third-party widget placed on your website, the widget vendor is almost certainly tracking its usage—that is, sending data back from your website to the vendor. That can happen even if the widget is provided for free. In fact, I find the lower the price of using a widget, the more likely this type of third-party tracking is taking place below your radar. Data can be more valuable to the widget vendor than charging you for using their widget.

### Culling Redundant Tracking

During an audit, I often find organizations inadvertently collect way more information than they actually need. This is usually due to legacy and redundant widgets on pages that are no longer used but are still setting and collecting data. Unless you are using these, remove them to save the headache of managing the privacy implications.

Ask the following about your widget usage:

- Who does the collected data go to—our own organization, or a third party?
- Do we or the third party need the data collected by it?
- If we need the data, how does it help us optimize our website content or marketing efforts?
- If we need the data, can it be collected in a different way—within Google Analytics, for example?

If there are no convincing answers to these questions, the widget is a prime candidate to be culled. You need to be quite firm here. There need to be compelling reasons for using a widget that is collecting data and thereby adding to your organization's privacy overhead.

On my website I can justify the use of the six widgets. They cover my needs of requiring both quantitative and qualitative data on my visitors so I can better identify and serve the needs of my target audience (Google Analytics, Kampyle); provide convenience features for my visitors—such as helping them locate and share content (AddThis, SiteApps, share buttons); and enable me to improve the website by scientific experiments (Optimizely).

If the widget itself is needed but the data collection feature of the widget is not required, it may be possible for this to be switched off.

### Checking for Personal Information

If Google Analytics is in use, confirm no personal information is collected. If it is, you are in breach of the Google Analytics ToS and you will need to remove this data. See Chapter 4 for how to do this.

For each of your other widgets, a similar check is required to ensure compliance with its usage and also to ensure you fully understand the privacy implications. An important motivation for investing in web analytics in the first place is the desire of website owners and marketers to *individualize* data and get *personal*. Individualizing data provides the prospect of tailoring content and marketing campaigns to specific visitors' needs, leading to a better engagement and cross-sell and upsell opportunities (business nirvana). There is nothing wrong with that desire per se, so long as you gain the explicit consent of your visitors first, and stop tracking them if they say no.

The golden rule is to ensure that your visitors are fully aware of what personal information you are collecting and that they explicitly agree to its collection.

## Color-Coding Your Privacy Levels

After you have culled unnecessary widgets, assess the privacy level of those that remain by using color codes. If the widget is classed as green, then no explicit consent is required from your visitors. If the widget is classed as yellow or red, you will need to provide a consent mechanism.

☞ *The most likely outcome of this exercise is that your pages contain a mixture of privacy levels due to the mix of different widgets present on your pages. Even if you have a large proportion of pages that are classed as green only, a scenario in which a visitor views only these pages and none that are classed as yellow or red is unlikely. So you need the consent of all your visitors before you can track them. In essence, this is what the EU privacy law states.*

The Information Commissioner's Office (ICO) guidance document has some excellent examples of nonintrusive consent mechanisms.[6]

Gaining explicit consent encumbers the visitor journey. It raises a red flag to visitors by highlighting privacy issues, and that is likely to put off some of them. The reason is not necessarily that they fear you are doing

### The Hidden Tracking Code on Your Site

The plethora of useful third-party widgets and plugins for websites means that pretty much all websites have some form of tracking that takes place below the radar—data collected and sent back to the third-party widget owner. Often, website owners themselves are unaware of this. If you have any of the following deployed on your site, you are collecting more than just green information and need to assess the privacy impact:

- DoubleClick
- Google Maps
- AdSense
- Disqus
- YouTube
- ShareThis
- LivePerson Chat
- Social plugin buttons (Tweet me, Follow me, Facebook Like, Google+, LinkedIn, and so on)
- AddThis
- UserVoice

All of the above set third-party cookies that track individuals (though anonymously).

## The Real Privacy Debate—the Triangulation of Anonymous Information

If websites collect only anonymous data, is end-user privacy safe? In other words, are individuals guaranteed anonymity if that is what they choose? Unfortunately, no.

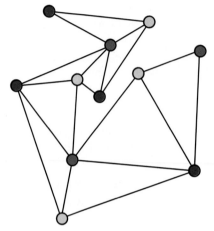

Widgets that deploy third-party cookies, although they track anonymously, can track visitors *around the web*. This can happen even if you do not interact directly with the widgets themselves. Some widgets track your path to different, unrelated websites you visit, and they track what you do there.

This is possible because of the ubiquitous nature of these widgets—they are placed on millions of websites around the globe and on numerous megasites (the super-high-volume websites with billions of visits per month). Each site that uses these widgets is sharing its visitor data with the widget vendor. Most people, including the website owners themselves, are unaware of this hidden tracking.

The privacy concern is that widget vendors are amassing huge data volumes at the individual level. Even if this all remains anonymous, given enough information an individual can be identified by triangulation of the data points.

A famous example of this is the 2006 AOL search query release. This intentional release of "anonymous" data was made public and intended for research purposes. However, the *New York Times* was able to locate an individual from the records by cross-referencing search terms with phone book listings.[7]

In my view, this is the real privacy debate. However, the complex interconnections of privacy (green, yellow, red) even within the same page are what obfuscate the discussion. The same triangulation concerns also apply to companies that provide web browsers, computer and mobile operating systems, and Internet access.

Related links:

BBC news article: www.bbc.co.uk/news/technology-21499190

European Commission's Directorate General for Justice:

http://ec.europa.eu/justice/data-protection/minisite/

something bad but that privacy is a complex subject with many ramifications. Until you mention the issue, your visitor does not realize they have to contemplate these complexities when they visit your site. That extra and unexpected workload of thought creates doubt in your visitor's mind. Doubt leads to caution—opting out of your tracking and hence depriving you of valuable data. This is why culling unnecessary widgets is important.

## Best-Practice Tips

What I have learned in over 17 years of building, promoting, optimizing, measuring, and analyzing websites is that there is no one thing that determines online success. It is a culmination of many things, the whole of which can be much greater than the sum of its parts. Privacy, and your approach to it, is one of those small and often overlooked parts that few people consider to be important until they stop to think about it.

The value of your privacy approach to your visitors is hard to measure directly. However, privacy forms an important part of the trust your visitors, your customers, and your potential customers have in your brand. As any sales or marketing person can tell you, building trust is part of the selling process.

Here are best-practice tips for collecting visitor data while maintaining customer trust.

### Being Transparent

Being transparent with your visitors about the privacy of their data will stand you in good stead. Explain in clear, concise language what data you collect, what you do with it, and how a person can opt out of tracking or have their data removed. If necessary, consider explaining what your site doesn't do. This can be particularly helpful if your site is targeted at people who may have heightened concerns about privacy—for example, if you are in the health care industry. Your privacy policy should be written for your visitor's benefit, not for the protection of the legal team.

### Avoiding Confusing Statements

Don't combine your privacy commitments for non-personal data with those for personal information. Treat the two categories separately. Most of your site visitors will not be required to provide you with their personal details—they are simply browsing your website for information. There is no point in alarming these visitors with statements about personal information when such statements are not relevant to them.

Your privacy statement should also be easy to find. At the point you request PII, state prominently what will happen to that information.

### Getting Permission to Track

While you do not need permission to track anonymous users in order to comply with the Google Analytics ToS, you *do* need to get your visitors' permission before tracking them if any widget on your site is assessed at the yellow or red privacy level and you conduct business in the EU.

Furthermore, for business you conduct in Germany, regardless of where your website is hosted, even a privacy level of green requires permission to track unless you anonymize IP addresses first.

### Anonymizing IP Addresses

Google Analytics does not report any visitor IP address information—it is not available in any report. However, by default IP addresses are captured and stored by Google Analytics. The only use Google Analytics makes of a visitor's IP address is to provide geo-location reports of where visitors connect from when accessing your website. This is accurate to within approximately 25 miles (40 km)—an area of almost 2,000 square miles.

Some countries—most notably, Germany—consider IP addresses to be personal information, making it illegal to store these by any method without the explicit permission of your visitors.

To provide greater control over this issue for administrators, Google Analytics has a setting that instructs it to remove the last three digits of a visitor's IP address (the last octet). This occurs at the point of Google's receipt of the data and within the server's memory. For example, an IP address of 212.113.144.144 becomes the anonymized version 212.113.144.0. The full IP address is never written to disk. Setting this option requires a one-line change to your GATC.[8]

I recommend you enable the Anonymize IP option by default—for all your pages. By doing so, not only do you send a positive signal to your visitors about your privacy vigilance, you also protect yourself from privacy law changes in other countries.

### Accuracy Considerations

The use of the Anonymize IP function will affect the accuracy of reports containing geo-location information, but the accuracy loss is minimal.

For example, MaxMind is a leading geo-IP intelligence company. They originally provided the geo-location feature for Google Analytics, though it was replaced by Google shortly after their acquisition of Urchin (the forerunner of Google Analytics), in order to align with the geo-location reporting used for AdWords. At the country level with the full IP address, MaxMind reports an accuracy of 99.8%. They estimate the impact of anonymizing the IP address as a reduction to 99.6% accuracy.[9]

The accuracy of identifying cities in different countries is shown at www.maxmind.com/en/geoip2-city-accuracy. With the full IP address, approximately 30% of city information is either inaccurate or not available. MaxMind reports that with Anonymize IP enabled, city level accuracy will drop by approximately 3%. At region or state level, the accuracy drop is estimated at 0.5%.

## GEOGRAPHIC DATA STRUCTURING

There are a number of ways to structure your data geographically in order to build reports that include only visits relevant to a specific country or region.

A common scenario is an organization that has a single website with location-specific content, such as

www.example.com/US

www.example.com/UK

www.example.com/DE

www.example.com/CN

### What About Historically Collected IP Addresses?

If you have historically collected and stored the full IP addresses of your German visitors in Google Analytics (the default behavior) without explicit permission from your visitors, the German data protection authorities require you to delete and close the reports for that web property. In order to continue using Google Analytics, you will need to open a new, compliant web property data set within your account—either with all users granting you permission to track them in this way or with all IP addresses anonymized.

Although this in itself is a significant setback to your organization, your loss may not be confined to German visitors. Potentially, you could be forced to delete *all* data from all your visitors. Unless you have structured your Google Analytics account geographically into separate profile views, visitors from different countries will be blended together. These cannot be separated at a later stage. Therefore, the demand from the German data authorities poses a risk to all your data.

The subdirectories define where the country-specific information is located. This URL structure is typical for many organizations because of its ease of setup and management from a CMS perspective. But the implications for data responsibility are often overlooked.

Your organization may have semiautonomous area offices, each wanting a report view just for their country or region (Figure 7.2). The US country manager is given access to the US report view. The UK country manager is given access to the UK report view, and so forth. The intention is to allow the full extent of Google Analytics' 100-plus reports to be available to each country office, populated with data only relevant to them.

On the face of it, creating specific geographic report views is straightforward. You might be tempted to set up filters by subdirectory name,[10] grouping all visits to the US subdirectory into the US report view, grouping all visits to the UK subdirectory into the UK report view, and so forth. However, there are two important issues with this approach. One concerns accuracy. The other relates to what to do if you need to isolate visitors by country for legal reasons—for example, should the data protection laws of that land change.

## The Accuracy Implications

By filtering visitors based on a country-specific subdirectory, there is a possibility of visitors from one country viewing content in another country's section of your website. Travelers or resident immigrants might want to view your content in their native language. This could be a US traveler connecting from their hotel room in Germany.

Because of this, your filtered reports for the US market will also contain visits from Germany. This casts doubt on your data because it is

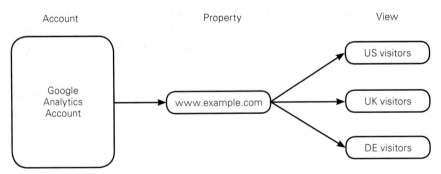

**Figure 7.2** *Google Analytics account hierarchy showing three geographic report views*

impossible to say for certain why this is (it could equally be a German citizen wishing to view an English page out of preference). For global brands, I have found that around 2% of visitors access a country subdirectory that is different from the country they connect from. That is neither good nor bad; it's just something to be aware of.

In addition, it is a common practice for a web server to automatically redirect a visitor to content that matches the country they connect from. A visitor connecting from Germany to the home page of www.example.com is automatically redirected to www.example.com/DE. But our US traveler in Germany will immediately switch to the US page.

In this case, your filter will count the visitor twice—one single page visitor to /DE and one visitor to /US. Referral information is also lost in your /US reports because Google Analytics determines what campaign drove the visitor to your website from the visitor's landing page (/DE), not subsequent pages (/US). Therefore, when you view the US reports, the campaign and referral information is lost.

Both these inaccuracy issues are relatively small, but they have significant legal implications for protecting your data.

## The Legal Implications

In 2011, the data protection authorities in Germany started to take an interest in Google Analytics and its privacy implications. Their decision was that German website owners had to explicitly ask visitors to opt in to being tracked—whether by Google Analytics or by any other tracking tool. Previous data collected without this opt-in was required by law to be deleted. This affects all website owners based in Germany, with implications for others conducting business in that country.

Place yourself in one of the following two positions:

**Scenario 1** You are a Google Analytics administrator and have *no* geographic filters in place. All your visitor data is aggregated, and there is no mechanism to unpack it and remove only visitors from Germany. The requirement to delete historical data from German visitors means you must remove *all* visitor data.

**Scenario 2** You are a Google Analytics administrator and have geographic filters in place that are defined by subdirectory usage. At first you may feel safe in the knowledge that only historical /DE data needs to be deleted, painful as that might be. Unfortunately, you too are required to delete *all* data. This is because of the accuracy issue. German visitors (in fact, any visitor) can change their subdirectory preference on your website and view different country content. Subdirectory filters cannot account for this, and therefore your visitors are blending—albeit at small levels. Some of your German visitors may be in your US reports. Analogous to mixing two liquids, once blending happens, and no matter how small a proportion of your traffic this represents, there is no mechanism to remove only the visitors from Germany.

## The Solution

Solving both the accuracy and legal issues is straightforward—instead of filtering by subdirectory, you filter geographically based on which country your visitors *connect* from. Your reports then show visitors by their location, not by content viewed. This is a very different definition, though the numbers may not differ by much.

By filtering in this way, you also protect your organization from future changes in national or regional laws. Should a country change its laws with respect to data privacy or anything else connected with the operation of your website, you can react to that change within a self-contained (walled) geo-location report set for all visitors who connected from that country. For the example of what happened in Germany, you would still have lost your German data, but the loss would be contained only to that report set. The rest of your data would remain safe.

◆ *Online privacy is a dynamic area in law that is still a long way from being solidified. However, the direction is clear from governments that are looking into this—the law is likely to get stricter on what online information can be collected without your visitor's explicit consent. Employing geographic filters based on your visitor's country of connection is a best-practice tip to protect and minimize any disruption to your organization.*

## ACCESS CONTROL

I am a big advocate of democratizing data—sharing reports with all those within your organization (and a select few outside) who have an interest. However, it is important to consider the implications of this. Access control determines who can view your reports and at what level. Apart from viewing reports, users with access can make changes to your account structure, make changes to the data structure, add other users, change permissions for other users, delete a data set (profile view), even delete the entire account!

Take access control seriously. Many people who shouldn't be are granted arbitrary access to sensitive company information—e-commerce revenue, marketing strategy details, test results, demographic data, cost data, and other invaluable information. Even humble traffic volumes can be invaluable to your competitors. Inappropriate access to data can even lead to charges of insider trading.

Why is valuable information not managed rigorously? It appears to me that because Google Analytics makes data available free of charge, data governance is not taken seriously. But the cost of the data is independent of its value. Whether the data is collected for free or not, you should have guidelines in place to determine who should have access to it and at what level. Review user access regularly to purge ex-employees and ex-agencies.

Following a user purge, consider what level of understanding each of your remaining users has. For example, a senior manager may open a report and take a number at face value, without an understanding of any setup caveats or applying the correct segmentation, filters, or groupings. Without a solid understanding of the reasoning behind the numbers, the wrong conclusion can be reached.

Also consider the level of responsibility each of your users has. I have come across users who have set up a data filter incorrectly and ended up deleting data by mistake. The issue for you is that once data is deleted it cannot be recovered. Such mistakes are common, but they can be mitigated by good account governance (see Chapter 4). Users who are not adequately trained and experienced should have view-only access to the reports until you are confident they know what they are doing and until they have an actual job-related need to have additional permissions.

Managing user access and configuring the appropriate permissions are done within your Google Analytics Administration interface.[11]

☛ *The Change History feature within the Administration interface allows you to view what changes have been made to your account and by whom. The log covers the last 180 days.*[12]

## PROTECTING YOUR DATA

A user with the correct level of access permissions can inadvertently (or maliciously) play havoc with your data. This can be the pollution, or deletion, of the organization's data—even the deletion of your entire Google

Analytics account. Controlling who has access to your account and at what level is a large part of protecting yourself from mistakes. Here are some other strategies for maintaining data integrity:

**Apply hygiene filters** Filters allow you to modify or delete data.[10] They are a powerful feature and should be applied only by experienced users. Regardless of what specialist filters you may apply, I recommend that the following hygiene filters be set as your default:

### Include only your own domains

Apply a filter so that data will only be included if it originates from your domains. This prevents people hijacking your GATC and sending you useless data (I have seen this happen by mistake and also maliciously).

### Remove monitoring bots

There are numerous automated robots on the web that can be employed to check your website, such as a robot to verify that your website is up and running and accepting orders, alerting your IT team if there is a problem. Such tools generally trigger the GATC and can inflate your visitor and pageview counts significantly. Filter these out from your reports using an exclude filter.

### Remove staff visits

Generally, your own staff visits to your website are not important to you, but they can account for a significant portion of your total traffic. Remove these from your reports. If tracking your own staff visitors is important, filter these into a separate profile view so that they can be analyzed separately.

### Remove agency visits

As with staff visits, remove agency visits from your main reporting view. Such visits may be relatively low in number. However, they can be disruptive as they are likely to trigger high-value engagements (agencies like to verify calls to action are working correctly). Typically, you will want to keep such visitors in your test profile view for troubleshooting purposes, but not in your main report view.

**Create a backup view** Keep a backup of your main reporting data set (profile view). To do this, create a copy of the data with only your hygiene filters applied, no others. You can then refer to this if an error is made in your main report view.

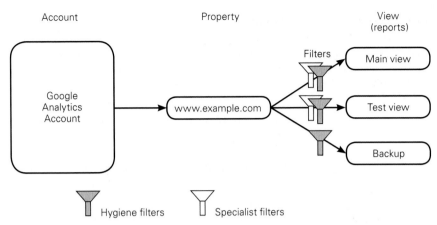

**Figure 7.3** *A best-practice account structure for a single-domain website*

**Create a testing view**   Use a copy of your main reporting data set for testing and verifying new filters and new configuration options. Once you have confirmed these are working correctly in your test view, apply them to your main report view.

With the above best-practice recommendations in place, a simple account structure may look similar to that shown in Figure 7.3. If you have a single website focused on a single market, you will have three report views (Main, Test, Backup). However, things can readily get more complex. For example, combining the structure of Figure 7.3 with the geographic requirements shown in Figure 7.2 produces nine report views—three for each country.

If you have multiple websites, mobile apps, and event and store data all coming into your account, data structuring becomes an important project in itself. In fact, because of its complexity and because of the limit of 100 report views in Google Analytics, you would probably take a different route to your geographic requirements—for example, grouping by region or highest-performing markets.

## SPEAKING OF DATA RESPONSIBILITIES...

| When I hear this... | I reply with... |
| --- | --- |
| My company is based outside the EU. Are the EU privacy laws applicable to me? | Yes. If you conduct business within the EU and you target EU visitors as part of your visitor acquisition strategy, you are expected to follow the laws for that region. |

| When I hear this... | I reply with... |
| --- | --- |
| Do we need to color-code our privacy levels per page? If so, how do we determine our overall privacy level? | If you can restrict what pages your visitors view—for example, via a login area—grouping your privacy into two sections makes sense. Automatically crawl your pages looking for all widgets that collect data.[13] Using this list, cull any widgets you do not need. Then assign a privacy level (color) for each of the remaining widgets. Your overall privacy color code is the highest common denominator for that section. That is, if some pages contain red widgets, effectively your entire section privacy level is red. |
| We have historically split reports to our country managers by filtering visits based on subdirectory. If we change this, as you suggest, to the visitor's connecting country, should we continue to store the data in the same profile views, or start again? | It is cleaner and easier to manage if you take the plunge and start afresh. Timing this with a new web design launch or other major event is usually a good idea.<br><br>However, if historical data is *critical* to your organization, consider using multiple trackers (multiple GATCs) on your pages: simultaneously send data to two profile views—a new one to protect your organization and the original profile view for continuity.<br><br>Having multiple GATCs on your pages requires additional overhead from your web development team. The good news is that in time, usually about a year, you should be able to switch your users over to view only the new protected report sets. Most people do not look back at more than one year of data. |

## CHAPTER 7 REFERENCES

1   Opening Statement by Ms. Navi Pillay United Nations High Commissioner for Human Rights at the Human Rights Council 24th Session: www.ohchr.org/EN/NewsEvents/Pages/DisplayNews.aspx?NewsID=13687

2   From Liberty—an independent human rights organization that works to defend and extend rights and freedoms in England and Wales: www.liberty-human-rights.org.uk/human-rights/privacy

3   A right to privacy is explicitly stated under Article 12 of the Universal Declaration of Human Rights, although it has no basis in law or enforcement: http://en.wikipedia.org/wiki/Universal_Declaration_of_Human_Rights.

4   The Economist Daily Chart: www.economist.com/blogs/graphicdetail/2013/11/daily-chart-2

5   Taken from "The State of Democracy in Asia," a lecture given by Brian Joseph, senior director of the National Endowment for Democracy, at Colorado College: www.ned.org/about/staff/brian-joseph/the-state-of-democracy-in-asia

6   My views on data responsibility are based on discussions with the UK's privacy protection agency (the ICO); panel discussions at events such as the eMetrics Summit; and studying the ICO guidance document for this law (specifically the section "Implied consent as a basis for compliance . . .").

The ICO guidance document (PDF) is one of the best thought through and most detailed documents on the subject of the EU cookie law. It is available at http://ico.org.uk/for_organisations/privacy_and_electronic _communications/the_guide/cookies. While my recommendations are based on logical arguments and interpretation, they do not constitute legal advice.

7    The AOL data leak was the first mainstream press investigation revealing how individuals can be identified from anonymous data: http://en.wikipedia.org/wiki/AOL_search_data_leak.

8    A technical explanation of how Google Analytics anonymizes IP addresses can be found at https://support.google.com/analytics/answer/2763052.

9    MaxMind geo-IP intelligence at country level: www.maxmind.com/en /country and city level: www.maxmind.com/en/geoip2-city-accuracy. Information relating to the impact of using Anonymize IP was communicated via direct correspondence.

10   Filtering data in Google Analytics is detailed at https://support.google.com/analytics/answer/1033162.

11   Managing users and their permissions: https://support.google.com/analytics/answer/2884495?ref_topic=1009690

12   More information on viewing the history of account changes can be found at https://support.google.com/analytics/answer/2949085.

13   There are a number of tools that can crawl your website and report back on what tracking widgets are on your pages. Some can also work with mobile apps. These were discussed in Chapter 4 in the section "Tracking Code Deployment."

# Building Your Insights Team

**The digital analytics team has** many roles, though ultimately its purpose is to provide insights—not data reports—to the business. I use the terms *digital analytics team* and *insights team* interchangeably throughout this chapter. I recommend the latter when naming a team within an organization.

A common mistake is to confuse digital analytics with the more traditional business intelligence that already exists (also known as customer analytics). Although the skill set required for each is very similar (the main reason for the confusion), the important difference is the certainty that can be assigned to the data for each—that is, its accuracy.

Working with fuzzy data is a constant challenge of the digital analytics team, one that is quite different from the certainties of the customer analytics department. Customer analytics works with definite data—customers are identifiable people with a confirmed set of demographic information, such as location, gender, age, ethnicity, language, home ownership, employment status, and so forth.

On the other hand, the vast majority of digital analytics data is anonymous—with typically only 3% of website visitors identifying themselves.[1] The result is that any demographic information can only be approximated or inferred. For example, location detail is at best within a 25-mile or 40-km radius. That may sound quite accurate, but it covers an area of about 2,000 square miles. Putting that into context, Greater London encompasses 611 square miles with a population of 7 million.[2] Age and gender information is inferred by what other websites your visitors have previously visited (assuming these websites display banner ads from the Google advertising network).

In addition to the difficulty of working with anonymous data, digital analytics is constantly at the mercy of *any* change to your marketing campaigns, your website pages, mobile apps, or other tracked devices. A new

### Data Contamination

Once data is contaminated with errors in Google Analytics, it cannot be cleaned. Of course, the errors can be corrected moving forward, but the previous affected data cannot be cleaned. This is because the vast majority of data (typically around 97% for websites) is from anonymous and therefore aggregated visitors. Unlike working with data of known customers, there is no way to pick apart the data and discard the bad parts, any more than you can separate blue-colored water from red-colored water after you've mixed them.

web page may not have the GATC added or may be deployed with a default setting when a customized version is required (the most common mistake). As websites are in a constant flux, data quality is a significant challenge for the insights team, as discussed in Chapter 4.

## WHERE SHOULD THE DIGITAL ANALYTICS TEAM SIT?

Where is the digital analytics team best placed in an organization? Who should they align with? These questions are not straightforward to answer, because digital data—the plethora of data points that can be collected online—can affect all parts of the business. These include the obvious departments of sales and marketing and the not-so-obvious parts of the business such as product design, manufacturing, support, and customer service. All of these are your potential stakeholders, though some will align better than others.

☛ *Calling your Google Analytics specialist team the* digital analytics team *is a reminder that Universal Analytics allows you to collect data not just for web pages viewed on a computer but for any device or interface capable of sending a URL over the Internet, such as barcode scanners, turnstiles, doors, and so forth.*

If you have an existing business intelligence (BI) unit, it makes sense for the digital analytics team to be a part of this structure, because the skill set required for digital analytics is similar to that for the BI team. However, the quality of the collected data is owned, managed, and monitored by the digital analytics team themselves (described in Chapter 4). The BI unit will have its own procedures for checking data quality. But the digital analytics team, not the parent BI unit, must own the data collection process, as it is critical for their analysis.

Most organizations do not have a BI unit and are not ready to create one just yet (though this book is about influencing that decision). If this describes your organization, then there are a number of options available to align the digital analytics team. You can

- Outsource to an agency (the most common scenario).
- Make it a part of the marketing or communications department.
- Make it a part of the sales department.
- Make it a part of the strategy and operations department.
- Make it a part of the IT or web development department.

**Outsourcing digital analytics** Because of the difficulty in finding digital analytics experience internally and because knowing where to locate the digital analytics team can be tricky in the early stages, many organizations prefer to outsource the work. Making use of the skills and experience of a third-party consultancy or agency will stand you in good stead. I recommend this approach for *all* organizations (for transparency, I should add that I run a consultancy that does just this). But the extent of outsourcing requires careful consideration.

Getting the right mix of in-house and outsourced expertise can have a dramatic effect on the success of the digital analytics team. Too little outsourcing and you risk missing opportunities (the benefit of collective experience) and making poor decisions due to lack of knowledge. Too much outsourcing and you end up creating a silo, building insights that the rest of the business is not fully engaged in. A fully outsourced digital analytics team is too far away from the business to be able to understand its day-to-day needs, drivers, strategy, opportunities, and pain points. Creating a silo is a problem whether you outsource some of your digital analytics requirements or not.

Using a GACP is the best fit for outsourcing requirements. The GACP network is a global network of over 200 certified partners (www.google.com/analytics/partners). They range in size and services offered, from management consultancies to marketing agencies and web development firms. All are certified as product experts and can help you with the different aspects of digital analytics (data strategy, implementation, training, insights, and analysis).

Unless your digital analytics team is capable of covering *all* of the analytical roles in depth that I describe in this chapter, partner with an experienced GACP. However, your organization still needs to pay close attention to the management of the GACP relationship. That is, alignment is still required with the rest of the business.

**Aligning with marketing or communications** In most organizations, digital analytics is aligned with the marketing or communications department. This is a natural first choice, as the website is usually a function of the organization's marketing activity. The alignment can work well if the marketing team is digitally savvy and they are working toward an integrated approach, where persuading a potential customer to visit your website is the focus of *all* marketing campaigns—not simply an afterthought.

However, if your website is not the focus of the marketing or communications team, then this fit can be difficult. Progress—the propensity to make a change based on data insights—tends to stagnate. The result is that the digital analytics team becomes a set of report monkeys, not the insight analysts they train and aspire to be.

**Aligning with sales** If e-commerce is a significant part of your business, aligning digital analytics with the sales team can be a rewarding fit. Sales teams live and breathe by their numbers, so you will have an engaged audience that is open to experimentation and change. The digital analytics team can also have the biggest impact here. Changes made to the website design, navigation, site search results, traffic acquisition strategy, special offers, and purchase funnel can produce immediate and significant results—results measured in monetary terms. Everyone understands $$$ metrics.

**Aligning with strategy and operations** Business intelligence is part of strategy and operations. If your organization does not have a BI team, and if digital analytics is a significant part of the overall business model, then putting the digital analytics team in the strategy and operations area makes sense. If it is not a significant part of the business model, then avoid aligning the digital analytics team here. This is because the rapid tactical decisions the team will want to make may cause friction in an area that is planning for a longer-term approach.

**Aligning with IT** Historically, digital analytics aligned with an organization's IT team. This was because the tools were technically difficult to set up and reports were stiff—visually unappealing and requiring a detail-oriented mind and considerable time to extract insights from them.

The launch of Google Analytics in 2005 was transformative in that respect. Its aim was moving digital analytics away from being an IT "project" to be more closely aligned with marketing and communications. IT, and more specifically the web development team, is still an important stakeholder in the digital analytics world. However, unless the IT team is already tightly integrated with marketing, the digital analytics team's requirement for experimentation, usability improvement (reducing friction), and reacting to the dynamism of marketing means this is not a good place for digital analytics.

## TEAM STRUCTURE—DON'T BUILD A SILO

Building silos is an unfortunate downside of large organizations. It is after all easier to build a self-contained team with its own budget, staffing, walled responsibilities, and clear chain of command than to maintain an integrated cross-functional organization. However, in the digital economy, success is determined by how well integrated your approach is. That is what drives a visitor to your website in the first place. Their expectations, their user experience, their propensity to become a customer (or advocate your brand), the value of that relationship, and ultimately the value of your website to the organization are primarily determined by how well you integrate all the digital touch points your visitors will use.

I have seen large, famous brands fail miserably online and small, unknown brands rise spectacularly, based on how well they have integrated their digital approach throughout their organization. Consider the simple Venn diagram of Figure 8.1—a report pulled directly from Google

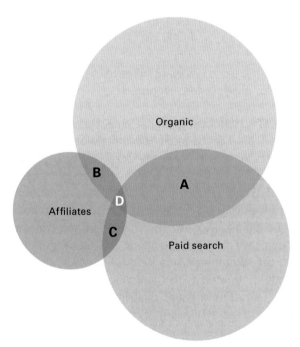

**Figure 8.1** *Multi-channel report showing the volume of sales by marketing channel*

Analytics for a travel website. Each circle represents the volume of sales from a specific channel—organic search, paid search advertising, and affiliates.

The bigger the circle in Figure 8.1, the more sales generated from that channel. Overlapping circles represent sales from visitors who came to the website via multiple channels. For example, a visitor first clicks on your organic listing on Google.com, visits your website, and leaves without purchasing. They come back another day via a click on your text ad on Google.com (AdWords), visit your website, and purchase. For this scenario, two of your marketing efforts influenced the visitor to become a customer. This is represented by area A of Figure 8.1. The order is not represented in the Venn diagram—visitors who click on your ad first and then follow up after an organic search and become a customer are grouped with those who do the reverse. However, other reports can differentiate these scenarios.[3]

Area B represents those visitors who were influenced by one of your affiliates and organic search engine results. Area C is the overlap of affiliates and your AdWords advertising. Area D is when all three of the digital channels overlap. This represents visitors who came to your site at least three times, having been influenced by each digital channel, and then became a customer.

The overlaps shown in the Venn diagram can get very interesting and quite complex—showing the extent of a mixed marketing approach. To keep things simple, I only consider three marketing channels in Figure 8.1, though many more may be involved for your business—including offline marketing if that is tracked in Google Analytics.[4] However, my point is to illustrate that visitors rarely discover your brand or product in a silo—there will be multiple digital touch points your potential visitors are exposed to. If your organization's marketing efforts are working in a silo (separate from your measurement department), your team may only be aware of a small part of the overall picture.

For example, I often find that for website tracking, the influence of email marketing efforts is completely forgotten about. This is because those efforts arise from a different part of the organization—usually customer retention. Email marketing may well be tracked, but it is separated and siloed away from the digital analytics team. The result, when someone asks the sensible question, "How do sales and leads from our email marketing efforts compare with our website traffic acquisition efforts?" is that they don't—it is comparing apples with oranges.

When working in silos, you face the same comparison issues when considering offline marketing, web design and architecture improvements, the mobile experience, and sales and support. Organization limitations can be hard to overcome, but you can mitigate against them.

## Management and Stakeholders

As I have mentioned, the success of a website is determined by how integrated the digital strategy is with the rest of the business. The approach for integration is straightforward in principle:

- First, start building your core team.
- Running in parallel, integrate your team with your organization's stakeholders.

### Building the Core Team

Plan to build a core team that focuses on data collection, its quality control, and the provision of fundamental insights for the business—insights that tell a story with data. These are a mix of the must-have KPIs for the business and visualizations to aid the understanding of what visitors and customers do on your website, such as the flow of visitor traffic between different parts of your website.

Insights require a formal presentation from your chief storyteller (your data scientist), though once they are understood and agreed upon, they can be automated into a dashboard format. An insights presentation may include a story describing how the following values have varied during the past quarter and how they compare to the same period last year:

- The total revenue generated
- The checkout conversion rate (engagement rate for non-transactional sites)
- Conversion funnel visualization—how visitors migrate from anonymous visitor to customer or brand advocate
- The volume of social likes and social sharing
- The current marketing spend
- PR activity

Segmenting your insights geographically, by language, by product section, by website domain, by connected device (phone, tablet, desktop), is a natural progression for your insights reports. The above list can therefore grow very rapidly.

So far, everything can be achieved in a digital analytics silo—there's nothing wrong with that, and the digital analytics team's work is communicated throughout the organization. However, unless there is an obvious, no argument, no excuses red flag shown in your reports, nothing significant will change with your website's content, its architecture, or its marketing approach. Without making changes and showing its impact on the business, your future insights audience will dwindle—you are repeating the same old story. The solution to this very real problem is to find your business stakeholders and then integrate with them.

### Integrating with Stakeholders (Multiplying Investment)

Establishing the core digital analytics team is an important step in an organization's measurement strategy. Unfortunately, most organizations stop at this point—the go-to data team is in place, job done, right? As I emphasize throughout this book, the digital analytics team is *not* the go-to data team—it is the agent-of-change team that uses data to tell its story. That is not a play on words; it defines the core purpose of the team itself.

As I discuss at the beginning of Chapter 2, change is difficult for any organization. To overcome the natural human resistance to change, the digital analytics team needs its supporters at all levels—you will not be able to drive change on your own. Gaining support is not just about obtaining consensus that the objective to change is a good and interesting pursuit. Rather, it is the integration of senior managers who can directly affect or be affected by the team's success. These are your stakeholders—they are your investors, sponsors, even direct participants.

Who are your stakeholders?

Your stakeholders are the same organization departments you wish to align with, as shown in Table 8.1. In the first instance, all of these contenders should be canvassed to ascertain their interest level. Most if not all will go on to be active stakeholders. These people help you define what is important to measure from the business point of view and to prioritize it. When meeting with your stakeholders, ask the following:

- What data is actionable and why? That is, what action will be taken if the number changes significantly?
- What data is good-to-know but not necessarily actionable information?
- How are your stakeholders used to receiving information? (They are very unlikely to want access to Google Analytics themselves.)

**Table 8.1** *Potential Stakeholders for the Digital Analytics Team*

| Stakeholder | Description |
|---|---|
| Head of marketing | Potential owner or parent of the digital analytics team, as websites are most often a function of marketing. Even if not, the marketing department is usually the strongest stakeholder for digital analytics because of their need for accurate, easy-to-access, and low-acquisition-cost data. |
| Head of web development | As the team responsible for delivering and maintaining the website, the web development team is obviously interested in understanding its performance. This relationship is two-way—the digital analytics team requires the help and support of the web development team to ensure that good quality data is being collected. |
| Head of PR and communications | A large part of public relations and communication takes place on social networks. Google Analytics can help you understand this activity in two ways:<br>• It allows you to see visitor reports from people who come to your site via a social network.<br>• It allows you to see how your content is being shared or interacted with across a social network (outside your own site*).<br>As with the marketing team, the PR and communications team can get a great deal of value from Google Analytics. |
| Head of sales | If sales are made directly online, then this is an obvious stakeholder to include. Even if sales are completed offline, your website is likely to be generating qualified leads. Understanding the onsite–offsite relationship as well as all the other corresponding metadata (what people search for, terminology used, other products viewed, and so on) can provide powerful insights to the sales team. |
| Head of customer service | If you can identify a visitor as an existing customer (for example: if they log in; use a coupon code; arrive via an email link), it is relatively straightforward to generate an entire report set just on existing customers—what they search for, terminology used, products viewed, and so on. This is powerful information for anyone interested in the after-sales process. |
| Head of business intelligence (may also be called consumer insights) | This is a natural stakeholder if such a department exists within your organization. The potential to integrate web data with other offline data makes this an extremely valuable relationship to cultivate. |
| Head of strategy and operations | Another natural stakeholder. The purpose of the digital analytics team is to enable the business to understand the digital world it operates in. However, Universal Analytics has the potential to collect and report on any data. That is valuable information for any business strategist or operational leader. |

* Viewing social activity that takes place away from your website is something Google Analytics is able to show for those social networks that are a part of the social data hub.[5]

While discussing the above list, subtly ascertain your stakeholders' levels (and their teams' levels) of metrics understanding.

In many cases, because of the organizational positioning of a website, the digital analytics team reports to the head of marketing. That is a good position to be in. However, as shown in Table 8.1, the scope of digital analytics is much broader than marketing alone; there are other people within the business who also want access to this valuable data.

This is good news for you because with such interest can flow investment. If a stakeholder requires insights beyond the current (or planned) capabilities of the digital analytics team, there is a clear case for further investment—driven by your stakeholders. Having other senior people in the organization banging your drum for further digital analytics investment—be it budget, head count (see the section "Scaling with Power Users"), or other help—will allow you to grow your team quickly and with minimum overhead. The justification is made on your behalf—a nice position to be in as a senior manager!

☛ *Building a network of power users—not a silo of digital analytics experts—is probably the most important lesson I learned while working at Google.*

With your stakeholders in place, map out your team's capabilities using a radar chart, as shown in Figure 8.2. The capabilities axis scales from 0

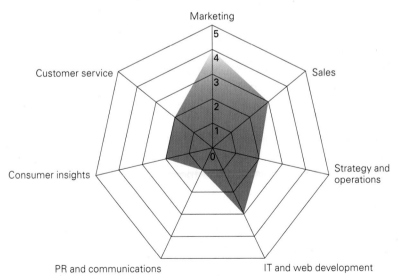

**Figure 8.2** *Mapping stakeholder needs to team capabilities*

to 5, with 0 representing no availability for this stakeholder and 5 representing full availability to meet all requested needs. *Capability* refers to whether a resource is at hand: is there a qualified person in the digital analytics team (or via working with a third-party agency) that can fulfill the stakeholder's need; and if so, are they available (do they have time, or is there budget)?

With your capabilities mapped this way, it is then easy to identify how your team needs to grow.

## Scaling with Power Users

Power users are people who have other day-to-day roles in the business not directly related to digital analytics. For example, a digital marketer—a person who is numerate—may require access to the data, yet is not an analyst nor someone who requires deep-dive analysis to do their job. Their requirements are to understand and monitor a certain subset of the data. By training a group of power users, you both empower other teams within the organization and scale the core digital analytics team efficiently.

As discussed in Chapter 3 (see Figure 3.7), building a Google Analytics power user network within your organization achieves a number of objectives:

- It raises the level of metrics understanding throughout the business and absorbs the more basic reporting questions on your team's behalf.
- It allows for users to be self-sufficient in accessing data as and when they need it.
- Power users are the bridge between the data-intensive analytics team that is focused on the central digital strategy and the local office (or specific product team), which has different day-to-day data needs.
- Power users are a great recruiting base for new members of the digital analytics team. Good digital analysts are notoriously difficult to recruit—there are very few of them.

### Recruiting Power Users

Rather than going around your organization and selecting suitable power user candidates, set up a training program for any interested party, such as a 12-month program of staff development. Typically, in order for a power user to be useful when they go back to their respective team, an initial two-day end-user training course is sufficient. Regular calls supplement the training, perhaps every two weeks. Then in six months' time, follow up with a one-day refresher course—solidifying the material covered previously and extending as necessary. Repeat twelve months later.

Building and supporting a power user network is clearly a significant commitment—both for your team and from those that sign up for the training. It is therefore important that part of each power user's staff performance review include the progress they have made with digital analytics. Creating an aptitude test and awarding a certificate of competence if passed is a great way to signify this and reward power users.

Because of the investment required from your powers users, they won't just be turning up for a time-out from their regular job. Becoming a power user requires the buy-in from their manager—both for the initial time commitment and travel expense, and for keeping up with the continuous product changes. Hence, communicate the benefits of the power user network well, and your candidates will self-select. Applicants will come from teams who have a real need to be data and Google Analytics savvy and are able to commit the time and effort to do this.

The training of the power user network comes from the digital analytics team—it's a great way for them to fine-tune their presentation, communication, and storytelling skills. After all, you can only consider yourself an expert if you are able to explain complex matters to non-experts. The number of power users the team can support therefore depends on the size of the digital analytics team. Allow for 5–10 power users per member of the digital analytics team. If you have more than that, you will need to consider a dedicated power user trainer–manager. However, you may find power users who wish to train new power users (train the trainer)—a great way for them to grow their knowledge and professional development.

## Team Development

There is a strong overlap in the skills base for all roles within the digital analytics team. All are numerate, usually with a degree in science, engineering, or economics. That said, candidates with degrees in philosophy and linguistics can also prove successful. It comes down to structured, evidence-based thinking (analysts are sticklers for accurate facts, and they hate data noise!) and a curiosity and passion to investigate the why of things.

You will have noticed that I have not mentioned statisticians as potential analyst candidates. Scientists, engineers, and economists all have strong statistical knowledge. The question is, does a digital analytics team need a full-time statistician? I don't think so. My reasoning is that modern tracking tools like Google Analytics take care of the heavy statistical lifting for you. For example, Google Analytics can alert you when numbers do not match the expected range; automatically calculate page value and visitor values; and inform you about the statistical significance when experimenting with A/B testing on your site or app.

There may indeed be times when a more rigorous statistical analysis is required than what is provided out of the box in Google Analytics. However, because Google is processing your data into reports for you, the need to process the raw data yourself is typically rare. Even without a dedicated statistician, your team will have a strong statistical understanding from their educational background. It is a key requirement for the team.

Developing the digital analytics team includes the following areas:

**Building presentation skills**   The ability to tell a story using data is the most important skill that requires development. Analytics people are analytical (that's why you hire them). By nature they are not charismatic communicators, but they are creative and pedagogical. They want to explain what they do; it's just hard for them to do that to others who are not working so deep as they are. This is so important to the success of the digital analytics team that it is worth seeking professional help with teaching presentation skills.

**Sharing skill sets**   Members should cross-train so that, for example, a tactical marketing analyst knows enough about the implementation fundamentals to identify data signals that indicate a possible implementation issue.

**Maintaining product expertise**   Google Analytics is a rapidly evolving product. Significant new features appear monthly. Being able to understand these and use them to the organization's advantage requires time. Allow 10% time (half a day per week) for your team to stay on top of, digest, discuss, and experiment with the latest bells and whistles.

As you can see, team development is all about learning. It is what analysts care most about—not being bored. This is why analysts generally prefer to work in an agency environment, where they can multitask on diverse projects in different industry sectors. It is why hiring analysts in non-agency organizations is so difficult (see the section "Recruiting Talented Analysts" later in this chapter).

## Working with a Third Party

Unless your team can cover all the digital analytics roles required in order to provide insights (I describe the necessary roles in the next section), you will need help to plug the gaps—otherwise, you are missing out on opportunities. GACPs can do just that.[6]

However, it is important not to outsource your *entire* digital analytics team. Otherwise, you end up creating an external silo. Therefore, ensure you have two important things in place:

**A dedicated internal resource**   You need a person who can act on the recommendations of the GACP. This person is involved in the day-to-day work with the third party. They are familiar with the digital analytics objectives, work processes, and results. Digital analytics is a major part of their job description; they work with it almost daily, and they have a broad view of the business requirements.

**An active senior sponsor**   You need a person who can make strategic decisions based on the advice given. For example, if the advice given by your GACP is that your site search functionality (that is, how people find information once on your website) is a significant pain point and needs to be replaced, this person can make that decision and make it happen (can approve the change, or at least has the ear of the person that can). This person is actively involved in the digital analytics project, receiving regular status reports (monthly) and chairing strategic workshop meetings with the partner—usually once per quarter.

This person is likely to be you!

## BUILDING THE TEAM

I have often been asked, What is your analytics dream team? If I worked in a global organization with no budget limitations and was asked to build the perfect digital analytics team, how would I go about it? It's an interesting mental exercise that I have mulled over for years. What I've arrived at is a framework and approach that can scale in both directions: If you have the organizational size and commitment, what team should be built now and how would it scale further? On the other hand, if you don't have the size or commitment yet, the same framework can be used with fewer personnel.

In this section I describe how to do this based on the five roles that digital analysts perform:

- Tactical marketer
- Strategic marketer
- Technical specialist
- Engagement and conversion optimization specialist
- Data scientist

It's obviously a nice position to be in if you are able to justify (and get the budget for) a dedicated person in each role. That can happen for a purely digital business, or where e-commerce revenue is a very significant part of the business model. However, a common scenario for most organizations is to start with a single person performing all of the different analyst roles to a greater or lesser extent.

### The Dream Team

If you have the mandate to build a team to cover all of the analytical roles from the beginning, start by recruiting the most senior person first—the data scientist. Based on studying the data and the business requirements, the data scientist will identify the need and opportunities. You then work with that person to map out a recruitment plan. A well-balanced team (the dream team) is shown in Figure 8.3. Growth of this team is then organic, based on need.

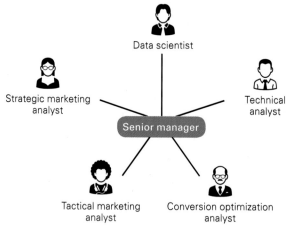

**Figure 8.3** *A balanced digital analytics team (the dream team)*

## Scaling the Dream Team

If your organization has a complex brand architecture[7] with multiple product, divisional, or country-specific websites, more technical analyst investment is required to ensure consistent data quality and coverage. Universities, government departments, and corporate parent brands (such as Coca-Cola, P&G, Virgin Group, Hershey, General Motors, General Electric) come under this description. For these types of organizations, further technical analysts may be part of the core digital analytics team or part of your power user network. The latter can work well if the website content is not centrally managed.

For transactional websites, hiring additional engagement analysts (conversion optimizers) can have a large impact on the business. Such people identify and remedy pain points (friction and visitor confusion) in order to increase your sales, new customer sign-ups, and average order size. These people make you more money!

If your organization is investing heavily in marketing, adding tactical and strategic marketing analysts will help guide that investment to ensure it is placed to best advantage. A common scenario is organizations investing in social media channels. Your tactical and strategic marketing analysts provide the data and analysis to ensure the social strategy is built on solid data foundations, and not a whim, as so many social "strategies" are.

## Starting Small

What if you do not have a mandate for building the dream team yet? This is the reality for most organizations, where resources are limited until the digital analytics team can demonstrate its potential. Here you need a scalable plan that allows you to focus on quick wins—the most important areas that have the biggest impact.

For this scenario, working with a GACP is key. As a senior partner in the data relationship, an experienced GACP identifies and then plugs the gaps between your current analytical abilities and business data needs, guiding you first through the setup process to ensure that good quality data is collected, then providing insights for your organization. However, it is important not to outsource the *entire* digital analytics process. A third party is too remote from the business to be able to drive change on its own—the reason for the data analytics in the first place. Hence, at a minimum you will require a junior analyst and a part-time technical specialist, as shown in Figure 8.4.

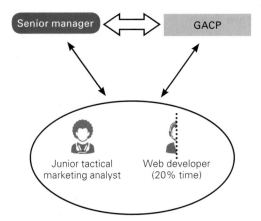

**Figure 8.4** *Minimum requirements for building an analytics team*

Figure 8.4 illustrates the most common team structure I encounter—a junior tactical marketing analyst, often a trainee from the digital marketing team, working with a web developer for technical support. The web developer is there to implement tracking code and advise on complexities and unforeseen consequences of the tracking recommendations. This is not a full-time position at this stage.

The GACP drives the process of building best-practice techniques and advising the digital analytics team with recommendations for collecting accurate data and its analysis. A good GACP brings to the table all the analyst roles.

The junior tactical marketing analyst is there to

- Help determine the scope of work within the available budget.
- Communicate the business needs to the GACP for tracking requirements and vice versa—to communicate back the tracking requirements to the business.
- Ensure action items from the GACP and business have project owners, and coordinate those items.
- Manage expectations and timescales.

Shadowing the GACP, the junior analyst grows their knowledge accordingly and will take ownership of some of the action items. Often this person goes on to develop into the role of tactical marketing analyst or strategic marketing analyst depending on their skills strength.

An alternative initial team structure starts with a web developer who has a strong interest in analytics and is assigned the technical specialist role. The time commitment of the roles in Figure 8.4 is therefore swapped.

## Why the Minimum Is So Important

The percentage of time allocated for a particular role should be measured in days, with 20% being equivalent to one day a week. I use 20% as the minimum to engage with the digital analytics team. An important part of the team-building process is to start with a least one *dedicated* person. I deliberately emphasize the word *dedicated*. It is not worth embarking on building digital analytics knowledge within your organization unless you can commit at least one dedicated resource to the task. Allocating this as part of a person's other day-to-day role does not work. Digital analytics involves too many detailed techniques and methods and requires complete focus.

Without a dedicated person involved, analytics just becomes reporting, with no insights at all.

That is, the technical specialist is full-time, with the junior tactical marketing analyst working 20%. This person often goes on to develop into the role of conversion optimization analyst.

## Scaling the Small Team Up

Following on from Figure 8.4, what is the best way to scale the digital analytics team as you journey from the minimum requirement to the dream team? Figure 8.5 illustrates a common four-step scenario. Key points in Figure 8.5:

- Until you complete the dream team setup, a GACP is an important partner so that you have all the expertise required. By their working with an experienced GACP, the whole team's knowledge base grows.
- From Team A, the junior tactical marking analyst has a career path to become an experienced tactical analyst (Figure 8.6) and then a strategic marketing analyst (Figure 8.7).
- The web developer position of teams A–C has a career path to become the technical analyst or conversion optimization analyst (Figure 8.7).
- Unlike the strategy for hiring the dream team, if you take this evolutionary growth path, the data scientist is hired last. The experienced GACP will perform this role until your organization is self-sufficient.

It may take several years to achieve this and you may find that one of the intermediate phases suits your organization's needs well; Team B

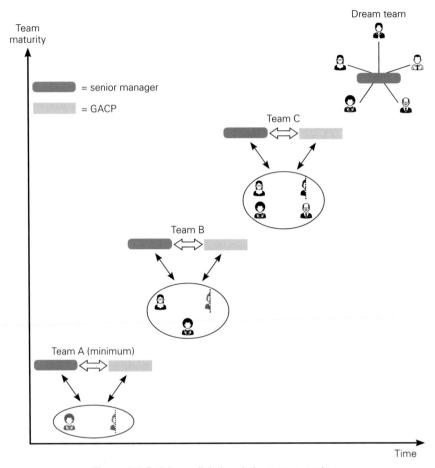

**Figure 8.5** *Building a digital analytics team over time*

(Figure 8.6) is a common stopping point, for example, with the majority of insights driven by the third-party GACP.

## ANALYST ROLES

Each of the following roles may or may not be a full-time position for your organization. Perhaps you can get 20% time (one day per week) from a member of the web development team to support your more technical requirements, such as keeping on top of data quality. My point is that you need a person to at least take ownership of each of these roles if making digital analytics a significant part of your business is to be a success. The

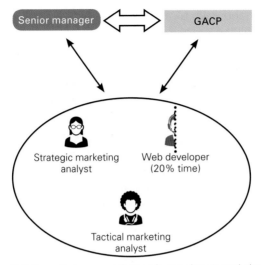

**Figure 8.6** *Team B: the second stage in growing an analytics team*

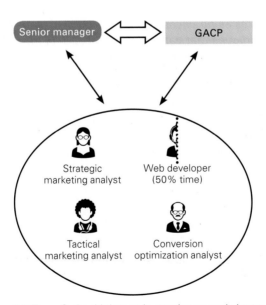

**Figure 8.7** *Team C: the third stage in growing an analytics team*

key is to understand each of the roles and then build a training or recruitment plan to fulfill them.

## Tactical Marketing Analyst

The tactical marketing analyst is responsible for ensuring all day-to-day marketing activities are tracked accurately and consistently to ensure, for example, that the performance of email marketing can be compared with the performance of display advertising (banners), search engine optimization (SEO), AdWords pay-per-click ads, and so forth. The analyst has to build a data structure to allow both the roll-up of campaign information—so different campaigns can be compared side by side—and the roll-up of channel information—so that different channels can be compared side by side (email versus display versus organic versus social and so on).

The analyst has to put in place a process to define all marketing channels for Google Analytics reports. As well as online channels, this can also include offline advertising such as TV, radio, print, display, and links embedded in PDFs. Essentially, whatever medium or method you are using to drive traffic to your website, it can be tracked. For large organizations, training other teams to be self-sufficient in this technique is an important part of the role.

☛ *Tracking offline activities in Google Analytics is less accurate than online activities as no physical "click" is present. Nonetheless, there are tracking techniques that can provide usable data for offline activities so you can compare these side by side in your Google Analytics reports.*[4]

A tactical marketing analyst spends a great deal of time comparing what has happened in the past to what is happening right now. Testing and experimentation are important parts of their role, and they work closely with the strategic marketing analyst.

For developing insights, the focus for the tactical marketing analyst is on understand the marketing mix—that is, how different marketing activities intersect and overlap, as shown in Figure 8.1. Digital marketing rarely (if ever) works in isolation. Hence, attribution modeling—understanding what value should be attributed to different referral sources—is a key strength of the tactical marketing analyst skill set. The analyst answers questions such as whether a visit coming via a click-through on Google organic search is more valuable than one coming from a social network. On the surface this appears a simple question. But it does not have a straightforward answer, as many visitors will use both (and other referral sources) on their journey to becoming a customer. This is a specialist area of the tactical marketing analyst. The attribution modeling feature of Google Analytics is discussed in Chapter 6.

## Strategic Marketing Analyst

The strategic marketing analyst is a natural complement to the tactical marketing analyst, in terms of both skill set and objectives. The main differences are in the scope and time frame. The strategic marketing analyst has a broader scope and takes a longer-term view—for example, year-on-year analysis. Often other data is brought to the table to supplement the story, such as market research, consumer surveys, competitor analysis, and so forth.

Working with the tactical marketing analyst, the strategic marketing analyst spends most of their time looking at the best marketing mix going forward, based on what happened before, and supplementing with additional research data. This can involve altering onsite factors such as design, navigation, and content, as well as inbound marketing factors, such as which channels to use, where and when to use them, and how much to invest.

Experiment design (A/B and multivariate testing), attribution modeling, and forecasting are key elements of this role.

## Technical Analyst

As the name suggests, the technical analyst focuses on the more technical aspects of tracking. This person supports all members of the team and is responsible for data collection, automation, integration, and quality control—whether the data is coming from the website, mobile app, or other sources.

If you run a single website domain without transactions, the technical analyst can be a part-time role. Perhaps a member of the IT team who has a strong interest in data analysis would like to work one day per week supporting your team. That can work well. However, if you have multiple websites (multiple domains and subdomains), or rely on multiple third parties to fulfill important processes for you (shopping carts, travel booking systems, affiliates, and so on), this role becomes increasingly important. As complexity grows, your data quality becomes more vulnerable.

If you have a strong need to integrate other data sets with your Google Analytics data, aligning that data correctly as well as automating the process to be efficient requires a technical analyst—that is, a person with coding and database query skills. If your organization has a large number of stakeholders—country managers, product managers, brand managers—then the building and maintaining of custom dashboards is also a key part of this person's role.

## Conversion Optimization Analyst

There are two halves of a successful website strategy—visitor acquisition and visitor engagement (also referred to as conversion). Both are equally important, though I often find organizations forget about the latter. That is, once traffic has been acquired, whether or not visitors engage with your content once they are on your website is perceived as being set in stone. Of course, that is not the case, and it is very easy to make changes and updates in the digital world.

*Engagement* (also called conversion) is about persuading visitors to do something more valuable than just browse a few pages on your website. You try to build relationships with your anonymous visitors in the hope they like and trust your brand enough to provide their contact details. Until this point, any visitor is completely anonymous to you. The ultimate engagement (a goal conversion) is that they become a customer.

Engagement is an alternative name for your *sales funnel*—all the little things you want your visitors to do so that they progress closer to becoming a customer. Visitor acquisition brings people to the top of the sales funnel. Improving how efficiently they traverse through it is conversion optimization.

This role requires an expert in website persuasion—a combination of website usability (web design, website architecture) and sales psychology. The conversion optimization analyst uses data as the key to identify what to improve (what will provide the biggest bang for the buck) and what the result of that change is. They are expert experimenters in both A/B and multivariate testing.

## Data Scientist

Providing the organization with insights is about providing the reasons for change. The analytics team is therefore the agent for change in your organization. As such, to be credible the reasons for change need to be based on solid scientific thinking. Hence the need for a data scientist.

The role requires a strong scientific or statistical background—used to analyze data and build hypotheses from it (or use the data to confirm an

## What About the Senior Manager?

As you will have noticed for teams A, B, and C in Figure 8.5, the senior manager does not have an analytical role—they are too busy building, coordinating, and integrating the team (between roles and between organizational stakeholders) to have the time. However, as the team's maturity grows, the analytic skills of the senior manager come to the fore. For the dream team, the senior manager is the central role, ensuring a tight integration between data, analysis, and the business as a whole.

The storytelling skills of the senior manager—working closely with the data scientist—provide a helicopter view of events that takes into account the broader business objectives. Having a successful senior manager means the digital analytics team is consulted, from an early stage, on future business strategies—both digital and non-digital.

existing hypothesis). This person will have performed extensive work in all of the other team roles. Hence this is a senior position.

Your data scientist is your chief storyteller. They have the necessary expertise and experience to weave together hypotheses to form a coherent reconstruction of what is currently happening on your website and a road map of what is required to improve it. They use the skills base of all members of the team. Effectively, the data scientist is your number two.

## RECRUITING TALENTED ANALYSTS

Recruiting an analyst is hard—at any level, in any part of the world, for any organization. Part of the recruitment difficulty is because of a global skills shortage: in this industry the main universities do not yet provide degrees dedicated to e-metrics or digital analytics. Another key difficulty is the way organizations approach hiring e-metrics specialists: job descriptions are over-specified—a mishmash combination of roles and skills. The result is you end up looking for unicorns. And as with all hires that are difficult to accomplish, once you get them on board, you will want to keep them.

### The Candidate Profile

Apart from being a candidate myself in the past, I have hired over 20 analysts during my career—for my own teams and for others. The candidates

I target are problem solvers (structured and heuristic), are analytical thinkers (they take nothing at face value), and are evidence-based thinkers (meticulous fact checkers).

Such people like to learn—continuously developing their skills. What analysts care most about is not being bored. Good analysts generally prefer to work in agency environments where they are able to multitask on diverse projects and in different industries. If you are not an agency and you wish to recruit the best talent, you will need to doubly emphasize learning as part of the job description. Surprisingly (that is, if you are not an analyst), research shows the attitude toward learning does not diminish with seniority of the analyst's position.[8]

Greta Roberts, CEO of Talent Analytics Corp., nicely sums up the characteristics of data analysts as follows[9]:

- They have a cognitive "attitude" and will search for deeper knowledge about everything.
- They are driven to be creative and will want to create not only solutions, but also elegant solutions.
- They have a strong desire to "do things the right way," and will encourage others to do the same.
- They have an extremely high sense of quality, standards, and detail orientation, often evaluating others by these same traits.
- They tend to be somewhat restrained and reticent in showing emotions, and may be less verbal at team or organizational meetings unless asked for input or the topic is one of high importance from their perspective.
- They may take calculated, educated risks, but only after a thoughtful analysis of facts, data, and potential outcomes.
- They persuade others on the team by careful attention to detail, and through facts, data, and logic, not emotion.

These descriptions can be applied to any of the five analyst roles listed above. As you can see, "charismatic communicators" is not on the above list. Obviously, good communication skills are important in any team role—candidates need to be able to explain what they do and its relevance to the business. However, in the analytics realm people are working with data day after day, and that means it does not attract extraverts. Rather, in this area I look for good pedagogical skills, the ability to explain complex issues to non-experts and extrapolate the relevance to the business. So long as these core skills can be demonstrated, developing good presentation and communication skills (essentially public speaking) can be taught as part of a continuous program of staff improvement.

## The Job Description

When you are recruiting for any of the five analyst roles described above, it is important that the job description focus on *one* specific role. Identify what roles you currently have and what roles you specifically require in order to meet the team's objectives by using the radar chart approach shown in Figure 8.2.

As shown in Figure 8.4, you may start with a junior analyst or with a part-time technical analyst. Wherever you start, use your job descriptions to establish three areas of importance:

**Educational background**   There is a strong overlap in the skills base for all roles within the digital analytics team—they are all data analysts. The base qualification you are looking for is someone who considers data part of their daily diet—the building blocks of facts used as a reference point on which to build a hypothesis or make a decision. The role involves a lot more than being numerate, being clever with Excel, or knowing web development and web architecture. Scientists, engineers, and economists are good candidates. Potential other degrees to consider are philosophy and linguistics. However, very few of these professionals are aware of their potential for the role of digital analyst—digital analytics is still a nascent industry and it may not sound particularly exciting. Hence a good job description needs to extol the influence and opportunities the digital analytics team has within the business.

Although there are lots of smart people around who do not have degrees, experience has taught me that a degree is a basic necessity for recruiting an analyst. Having a PhD is not a requirement, though of course it should be welcomed if you find such a candidate.

### What About Statisticians?

Tools such as Google Analytics take care of a great deal of the heavy lifting when it comes to statistical analysis. That means, very little raw data processing is required by the digital analytics team. Strong knowledge of statistical techniques is essential; this is why scientists, engineers, and economists are ideal candidates. However, unless you have a need to process raw data regularly, a dedicated statistician may easily be bored in the digital analyst role.

**Analytical thinking** The candidate should have a scientific approach to problem solving. That means either coming up with a hypothesis and then hunting down data to either prove or disprove the theory (deductive reasoning), or isolating data from the noise to discover a pattern or unusual value, then building a hypothesis to explain why it is so (inductive reasoning). This is the core of what analysis involves.

**Creative lateral thought** The candidate should be able to make a leap of imagination in order to attempt the solving of a problem. Often, analysis does not lead to any definitive outcome—results can be fuzzy or even counterintuitive. Data points can be contradictory. A digital analyst needs to be able to take a sideways look at the data, inspect its quality, and if necessary take a calculated, educated guess as to how to come to a conclusion.

The candidate profile does not lend itself toward people with a natural flare for presentation or communication skills. The difficulty is that as a data analyst, these skills are essential. Rather than overemphasizing this requirement in the job description, instead look for the demonstration of core pedagogical skills during your interviews.

### Example of a Good Job Description

This is a real-world example of a job advertisement taken from www.itjobswatch.co.uk.

> **Web analyst** The role is to be an expert web analytics practitioner able to confidently own, and proactively deliver high quality analysis and insight to the business to support the daily evolution of our sites' functionality.
>
> Design and carry out appropriate analysis in response to business questions. Derive accurate and actionable insight from analytics data and deliver conclusions to business stakeholders and senior managers via persuasive presentations and engaging reporting.
>
> Regularly review analytics implementation to ensure all interactions are tracked and measured accurately and ensure new functionality is robustly and accurately measurable.
>
> Support CRM and marketing teams through development of segmentation analysis and multi-channel attribution models.
>
> Champion a testing and measuring culture, utilizing all available data to help identify candidate areas of the sites where a customer's experience could be improved.

Lead regular workshops with business stakeholders to ensure analytics insight is being appropriately disseminated and understood within the business.

**Comments** I like this ad for many reasons. It emphasizes the need for insights, not reporting, and relates this to the business via stakeholders. In addition to the nice use of appealing analytical terms to attract the right audience, the advertisement uses phrases such as "confidently own," "persuasive presentations," and "engaging reporting," rather than harping on about communications skills (I think that is particularly skillful). If I were looking for a job, I would apply for this one.

### Examples of Poor Job Descriptions

These are real-world examples of job advertisements I have come across at www.itjobswatch.co.uk:

**Audit assistant** Have you got a flair for data—seeing trends, identifying and investigating unexpected results, solving problems? Do you have strong IT skills—particularly using Excel to manipulate data? Are you also good at admin—keeping on top of tasks that need to be completed, ensuring work is completed accurately? This role does involve lots of data, so you need to have a real interest in data, and the ability to analyze this and to solve problems.

**Comments** The title is immediately off-putting as it highlights a junior position, exacerbated by the reference to admin duties. However, there is confusion, as "seeing trends, identifying and investigating unexpected results, solving problems" are skills acquired by more experienced and senior practitioners. It is a confused message that does not know what type of person it is looking for, other than someone working for admin assistant wages.

**Web service analyst (university)** We are on the lookout for a talented analyst to join our Digital Development Services team. With outstanding communication skills and an approachable demeanor, you'll act as a bridge between students, staff and the technology we provide.

Working as part of a team you'll be responsible for the support, configuration and maintenance of a number of our key services. As such, you'll be customer-focused and a natural problem solver. You'll be comfortable administering services through web interfaces and powershell scripts, and happy to occasionally delve into the command line.

### What's the Going Rate for a Good Analyst?

With a scarcity of skilled individuals, expect to pay a premium for a knowledgeable and experienced analyst. My tip is to not overly focus on tool expertise itself, rather the expertise of the person. Tool knowledge is of course a bonus. However, a good analyst will use the right tool for the job and will be adaptable.

The website IT Jobs Watch provides some useful salary data for the UK market:

www.itjobswatch.co.uk/jobs/uk/web%20analyst.do
www.itjobswatch.co.uk/jobs/uk/data%20analyst.do

**Comments**   This is a common mistake of combining multiple roles into one catchall superhuman. The use of "outstanding communication skills"…acting "as a bridge" does not match with "responsible for the support, configuration and maintenance…administering powershell scripts…delve into the command line." This ad mixes the role of an analyst with the role of a programmer/IT administrator.

### Sample Interview Questions

As you may have guessed, there is no killer question to ask your candidates to determine if they are suitable for the role of digital analyst in your organization. A good analyst is a combination of all the five roles I describe, to a greater or lesser extent. It is the ability of a candidate to combine all those roles into a mix that suits their strengths that creates a great analyst.

From a hiring manager's point of view, you need to focus on the specific role. For example, are you looking for a reporting and data analysis type of person, or an implementation and data architecture type? Although there is a skills overlap for these, it should be clear to the candidate what you are looking for.

Sample questions:

**Describe an example of when you have worked with stakeholders to define key performance indicators.**   For this question I look for evidence of a structured process being used, such as details of who the stakeholders were; how or why they were selected; how expectations were managed; how KPIs were delivered; the timeline; and what action was taken by the business as a result of the delivered KPI.

**What metrics do you use to determine success?**   This is really a trick question. It is the business that determines success and it's the analyst's job to figure out how to measure it. Essentially, a whole process needs to be put in place to define what exactly is online success to the business. This requires a lot more thought if the business concerned does not have an e-commerce website.

Avoid anyone (whether a candidate, consultancy, or agency) who tells you how to measure success without a good understanding of your business model, your website, your marketing strategy, your product, your service, your staff, and your competitors.

**Talk through an advanced accomplishment you have achieved with data.** This question helps you understand the technical ability of a candidate (*advanced* in this context correlates with *complex*, *difficult*) and assesses their storytelling ability. An important aspect to look out for when assessing storytelling is how well the accomplishment is defined in the first place. In analytics, the definition of the question, problem, or issue to be investigated is a key part of being able to go on to answer and solve it. Look for role clarity, analytical capability, and critical thinking. As a follow-up, if the candidate were to do the process again, how would they do it differently?

## SPEAKING OF BUILDING YOUR TEAM...

| When I hear this... | I reply with... |
| --- | --- |
| Our IT team's budget pays for Google Analytics Premium and therefore they wish to establish the digital analytics team within IT. Can this work? | In this situation I find it best to develop core digital analytics responsibilities for the IT team. Focus on implementation, data quality, and core metrics that provide context and overview, such as total traffic volumes, mobile versus computer usage, page speed, e-commerce conversion rate, and visitor engagement rate (if IT is also responsible for web design). I then devolve other metric responsibilities—campaign analysis, attribution analysis, social sharing performance, and so forth—to stakeholders.<br><br>It's a difficult balancing act, but it is critical that other stakeholders play their parts in the analytics process and are not just *served* reports on a plate by the IT team. |
| We have a junior marketer who wishes to change roles and be trained in digital analytics. What is the best role for them? | Unless this person has a degree-level background in science, engineering, math, economics, or linguistics (potentially philosophy), training such a person is unlikely to prove successful—unless you send them off to gain such a degree first. A scientific approach to problem solving with data is not something that can be taught in a few workshops. It's a personality trait that those interested in science develop throughout their education.<br><br>A junior marketer can still play an important role in the digital analytics team. However, this should be as a power user—a bridging role for marketing. |

| When I hear this... | I reply with... |
| --- | --- |
| We have been unable to recruit and keep a good full-time digital analyst. What can we do? | First, check your job description—does it follow the best practice I describe, or is it a mishmash of roles that targets no one? Also ensure you are offering a competitive salary ($20,000 per year in the US or Europe is not going to be taken seriously—I have seen this offered!). If these have been optimized and you are still struggling, then hire the services of a good GACP to conduct the work for you.[6] |

## CHAPTER 8 REFERENCES

1 The figure of approximately 3% is based on the number of visitors leaving PII from my own clients' experiences and from the e-tailing group's 12th Annual Merchant Survey of 2013. US merchants report the most common purchase conversion rate as between 1.0% and 2.9%: www.e-tailing.com/content/wp-content/uploads/2013/04/pressrelease_merchantsurvey2013.pdf.

2 Population information for London: http://en.wikipedia.org/wiki/London

3 For visitors who come to your website multiple times before converting, the multi-channel funnel reports allow you to see the paths and order taken over a 90-day look-back window: https://support.google.com/analytics/answer/1191180.

4 I have written a detailed white paper specifically about tracking offline marketing. Download from http://brianclifton.com/track-offline.

5 Google's social data hub is a powerful feature whereby social networks can share relevant activity happening within their platform—such as discussions that mention your organization's name or products—with website owners. However, it does not include Twitter, Facebook, or LinkedIn. https://developers.google.com/analytics/devguides/socialdata/

6 You can view the list of global GACPs at www.google.com/analytics/partners.

7 Brand architecture is described at http://en.wikipedia.org/wiki/Brand_architecture.

8 If you wish to read further about the differing roles of analytics professionals, I highly recommend the research study "Four Functional Clusters of Analytics Professionals" by Greta Roberts and Pasha Roberts: http://www.talentanalytics.com/talent-analytics-corp/research-study/.

9 http://sloanreview.mit.edu/article/predicted-to-perform-how-to-hire-analytic-talent

# Using
# Key Performance Indicators
# and Dashboards

**Three main challenges face every** digital analytics team:

1 Keeping on top of data quality—maintaining trust in the data
2 Avoiding data overload—staying focused and not swamped with the endless possibilities
3 Communicating data insights effectively—telling the story to the rest of the organization in order to drive change

Chapter 4 discusses data quality and how to introduce a quality control process. This chapter focuses on points 2 and 3 by using KPIs. Of course, all data is important to understanding what is happening on your website, and during the course of its investigations the digital analytics team will probably touch on all of the data points. However, with over 100 reports available in Google Analytics by default, it is not possible (or desirable, if you wish to keep your team's sanity) to analyze all of the data all of the time. In addition, the business outside of your team is not interested in every single data point and cannot absorb the information it provides. Therefore, you simplify the process for everyone involved by focusing on a subset of your data—the most important data points, also known as KPIs.

## WHAT KPIs ARE AND WHY THEY ARE IMPORTANT

KPIs are not unique to digital analytics—they are a management technique used to help an organization define and measure progress toward organizational goals. Hence there are a number of definitions to suit different purposes.[1] For digital analytics, I define a KPI as

*a measurement used to evaluate success*

Think of KPIs as a set of temperature gauges to measure the health of various parts of the business. Two types of KPIs should be considered by your organization:

**Progress KPIs** For these, success is defined in terms of making *progress toward* strategic goals—how far a visitor to your website has gone toward completing your aim, purpose, or objective for them. For example, an e-commerce website will wish to describe the percentage of visitors browsing the site that flow to product search ⇨ add to cart ⇨ checkout ⇨ purchase complete. This is your sales funnel, shown schematically in Figure 9.1. Each step in the funnel can be defined as a KPI—for example, the proportion of visitors that go from step 1 to step 2 (48.0%) and so forth.

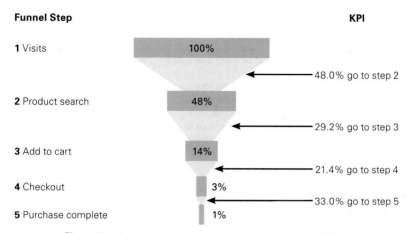

**Figure 9.1** *An example sales funnel showing progress KPIs*

For a non-transactional site, a progress KPI could be the flow of visitors from one section to another (assuming this is your website's objective and it has been designed to facilitate this). Alternatively, it could be the number of visitor engagements achieved, such as number of visitors with one engagement, number of visitors with two engagements, and so forth. This is based on the hypothesis that the more engagements a visitor has with your brand, the stronger the relationship with you and the more likely they will go on to become a customer.

**Achievement KPIs** These are *repeated, periodic achievements* of an operational goal, such as the number of new visitors you have gained this month or the percentage of visitors who do not bounce away (viewed more than one page). If you sell directly online, important achievement KPIs are amount of revenue generated, average order value, and return on investment. If you do not sell online, corresponding KPIs include number of new leads generated, level of visitor engagement with your site, and per visitor value.

Examples of both types of KPIs are shown in Table 9.1.

Choosing the right KPIs depends on a good understanding of what is important to the organization. This will vary by department (your stake-holders) and their level of metrics understanding. For example, the KPIs useful to the strategy and operations team will be different from the KPIs required by the sales team, and different again from those needed by the marketing and communications team. Similarly, the ability of your

**Table 9.1** *Progress versus Achievement KPIs*

| | Progress KPI | Achievement KPI |
|---|---|---|
| Transaction-specific | • Proportion of visits that add to cart<br>• Proportion of visits that progress to step X of Y in the purchase funnel<br>• Propensity to purchase (a combination of the above)<br>• The value of a customer (low, medium, high) | • Number of new customers gained<br>• Number of transactions<br>• Revenue generated<br>• Average order value<br>• Return on investment<br>• Value per visitor |
| Non-transaction-specific | • Proportion of visitors that made one or more engagements, two or more engagements, and so forth<br>• Proportion of visitors that complete form page X of Y of a multi-form process (for example, completing a loan application)<br>• The value of a visitor (low, medium, high) | • Number of new leads generated<br>• Percent of engaged visitors (visitors performing an action beyond viewing a page of content*)<br>• Proportion of visits showing intent to purchase, such as clicking your store finder widget<br>• Proportion of visits that click on an ad (content publisher websites) |

\* Engagement can be further subdivided by specific engagement type—downloading a product catalog PDF, sharing your content via a social network, and so forth.

stakeholder to absorb, understand, and act on the data will determine which KPIs are most suitable for them.

It is therefore critically important that your stakeholders—the people that know their part of the business very well—be involved with defining KPIs from very early on in the project. Your stakeholders' role in the process is to define and communicate what constitutes *success* to

## Be SMART with Your KPIs

Choose KPIs that follow the SMART criteria.[2] Each KPI should have a **S**pecific purpose for the business and be **M**easurable, **A**ctionable (for example, if it changes ±10% a senior manager picks up the phone to ask why), **R**elevant to the success of the organization, and **T**ime phased—quoted for a specific period (for example today, last week, last 90 days).

To be consistent with my own advice, Table 9.1 should therefore be time bound, as in the "proportion of visits that add to cart over the last 30 days." I omitted a time frame for clarity of purpose at this stage.

them. The digital analytics team's role is to identify what KPIs to use to measure this.

## SELECTING AND PREPARING KPIs

With a well-defined set of KPIs in place, your team will remain focused on what is important to the business and have a clear set of relevant success metrics that can be communicated throughout the organization without difficulty. This clarity means that intuitively everyone in the organization is able to understand the KPIs and their importance.

Developing KPIs is a collaborative process; your stakeholders should be involved from the beginning, rather than the digital analytics team delivering their version of what data is important after everything has been set up.

Working with stakeholders is my approach throughout this book—it's a fundamental requirement for the success of the digital analytics team (Chapter 8). Your stakeholders were first identified in Chapter 1 (see Figure 1.3). They are key players in the implementation of Google Analytics, helping the digital analytics team gain a good understanding of what metrics are required by the business (Chapter 3). Your team's production of KPIs for them, and the building of the concomitant story behind the numbers, is the reward for your stakeholders' labors and investment.

### Who Should View KPIs?

Your stakeholders are your KPI audience—they help define them! Hold regular KPI review meetings (monthly or quarterly) with your stakeholder teams. At first, these are usually single stakeholder meetings where the discussion is focused on their specific needs and understanding. These meetings should consist of a three-point agenda:

1 **Describe the story**
   The digital analytics team describes the story behind the numbers, such as this month's marketing campaign performance. What have we learned?
2 **Build an action plan**
   The group assesses the options as a result of the story. The objective is to build a list of required action items that define what to do next. For example: run the campaign again with a modified message; test alternative landing pages; cull the campaign. If the data is inconclusive, how can it be improved for next time?

### 3 Implement the plan

Perhaps there are changes to the marketing approach or landing page layout required. Who performs the work? What is required to ensure the subsequent data is consistent and comparable with before so progress can be shown?

Once a strong level of understanding and trust in the data is built within each stakeholder department, bring all your stakeholders together for your KPI meetings. That way knowledge is shared. After all, the overall business aim is the same for all stakeholders, and there will be a strong overlap in KPI requirements between them.

Apart from your stakeholders, anyone within your organization should be proactively encouraged to view KPIs. They are a great way to focus the minds of all staff if your digital activities are an important part of the business strategy. I have seen KPI dashboards built within an intranet's home page, displayed on large TV screens on office walls, and printed as posters displayed around the workplace. I encourage you to explore all of these.

## Key Considerations for Defining KPIs

The following are the general rules I apply when working through what KPIs should be defined for an organization. All of them are of equal importance.

### Avoiding the Silo

Often I find that after data insights are delivered (step 1 of the process), the digital analytics team is not a part of the subsequent change meetings—the meetings where the action items are discussed and decisions are made about what to change in order to improve. Perhaps in a siloed organization it is felt that the digital analytics team is not sufficiently a part of the day-to-day operations to require involvement. However, it is important that the digital analytics team be a part of any subsequent change discussions to ensure these can be quantified, their impact measured and benchmarked to determine the before-and-after effect.

Case study 1 of Chapter 10 shows what happens when the digital analytics team is not involved in change discussions—a dramatic loss of revenue that was not recognized for months.

**KPIs are built separately for each stakeholder** KPIs are not one-size-fits-all. That is, one set of KPIs will not be applicable to the entire organization. For example, the marketing department will have a different set of requirements from the PR and communications team. Likewise, sales, IT, consumer insights, customer support, senior executives, product managers, and brand managers, all have data needs—the only difference is they use it to make different decisions. Therefore, KPIs need to be tailored to your individual stakeholders. That said, there will be overlap. Overlaps are important so that each stakeholder can see they are a part of a bigger whole.

**KPIs must be essential for success** Intuitively this makes sense. However, I have found most stakeholders stumble at this point. The confusion relates to what information is interesting to know versus what information indicates success. I use the following question to keep the stakeholder focused on only *essential* data:

> If the value changes by ±10%, who will you call to find out what happened?

If there is no answer to this question, the proposed KPI is not essential to the business.

**KPIs must be actionable and accountable** By *actionable* I mean that if a KPI value changes significantly for better or worse, there is a plan of action that can be taken to increase or decrease the effect. For example, if an ad campaign has resulted in an improvement, you can run the ad campaign again, or if a change tested well on a single product page, you can copy the change to the site-wide template. Conversely, if the KPI has changed for the worse, you can stop or pause the campaign, or roll back the design change to the previous version. *Accountable* means there is a person responsible who understands what the change signifies (can sanity-check to verify it) and can put into motion the action plan.

**Not just Google Analytics data** Although Google Analytics is the main data source for the digital analytics team, I encourage you to think creatively. What other data should be brought to the table to augment the story? This could be your call center performance data, store sales from your Main Street stores, stock-keeping data, your media plan and media spend, and so forth. This is first-party data—it is data produced by your organization and usually belongs to you.

In addition, third-party data can be of interest. For example, if you own a YouTube channel, your videos will be watched on YouTube.com as well as other sites where your video has been embedded. That is, *away* from your website and therefore away from your Google Analytics data collection. You can access YouTube statistics for your videos via the YouTube.com user interface, or programmatically import it into a spreadsheet or database via the YouTube Analytics API.[3] Either way, if relevant, such third-party data must be accessed, aligned, and integrated with your Google Analytics data. Other examples of third-party data include Facebook, Twitter, LinkedIn, Pinterest, and weather.com (useful if your business is sensitive to weather patterns).

**Always use $$$ where possible**   Using a monetary value is always the best way to hold your audience's attention and have them remember the KPI. For example, the following statement gets immediate attention: "Because our website does not work properly when viewed on Android devices, we are losing $170,000 to $230,000 per month." The amount may be a relatively small percentage for the organization as a whole, but it quickly gathers a response: "How much will it cost to fix it?" You just added an immediate action item to the next meeting.

Even if you have a non-transactional website, it is important to monetize it by adding goal values to your Google Analytics setup. This allows you to differentiate and investigate your high-value visitors. For example, visitors submitting their personal details are much more valuable to you than those anonymously downloading your PDF catalog or brochure. Without monetization, all goals are shown as equally important in your reports.

**Use percentages, ratios, or averages rather than raw numbers** Raw numbers tend to become meaningless to an audience when more than a handful are shown. It is too many digits to remember, and in itself a pile of numbers contains little or no story. On the other hand, a ratio—for example, "Half of our marketing budget is going down the drain as these visitors are bouncing off our website"—contains a story that is easy to remember and conveys a sense of urgency. No one likes to waste money!

There are three exceptions to this rule:

- In discussions of monetary amounts, revenue data always carries a greater impact when the raw number is used.
- When the percentage being reported is very small, raw numbers are better. For example, it is much clearer to say "the campaign only

## Not All Visitors Are Equal

The value of a visitor to your site (the per visit value) and the value of a page of content (page value) are important KPIs for any business. To obtain these you need to track monetary values. This is a one-time setup that can be achieved in two ways:

- You have an e-commerce website tracking your transactions.
- You have a non-ecommerce website with defined monetary values for each engagement goal.

If you have a transactional site, both of these methods can be applicable, as transactional sites often have non-transactional goals (subscribe, sign up, and so forth).

When you provide a transactional or goal value in your Google Analytics setup, Google Analytics will *automatically* assign a value to all of your visitors and the pages they view. The value depends on which pages and what goals your visitors complete. Top-performing pages (in terms of value) bubble to the top of your reports. As with monetizing visitors, you can highlight where your most valuable visitors are coming from.

Monetizing goals is discussed in detail in Chapter 3. Understanding page and visitor value is discussed in Chapter 5.

produced 10 new customers" than to quote a percentage increase of 0.01%.

- To understand changes in new visitor acquisition, I prefer raw numbers rather than quoting the default percentages from Google Analytics. For example, an increase in the "percent new visitors" to your website sounds like your visitor acquisition strategy is doing great. However, the change in percentage could equally have resulted with the number of new visitors remaining static—due to a decrease in the number of returning visitors. It is very easy to convey the wrong message for your KPI in this case.

**Time-based context**  Always put your KPIs into context by making them relative to time. "We have 1,000 new customers" lacks any context. "We generated 1,000 new customers over the past 30 days" provides meaningful context.

**Limit KPIs to 10 per stakeholder**  Stakeholders are your main KPI audience. They do not work with Google Analytics on a day-to-day basis, yet they have to make strategic decisions based on many pieces of information. Avoid overwhelming your stakeholders by consolidating your KPIs where possible. Even for experienced analysts, absorbing more than a handful of key metrics is difficult.

**Hierarchical KPIs via segmentation**   When stakeholders are asking for more than 10 KPIs, it is usually due to the requirement for segmentation. For example, a stakeholder wishes to take action on the growth of mobile visitors to their site (a defined KPI). Their team however needs finer-grained information to understand the growth and to plan what should be done. Consider these as hierarchical KPIs—that is, a subset of the main KPI. In this way, your stakeholder's focus is not diluted, while their team has more detail to work with.

Hierarchical KPIs can be classed as primary, secondary, and tertiary—indicating their level of importance or detail. Secondary and tertiary KPIs may be temporary—that is, removed when an investigation is complete. However, the main KPI remains in place, as it is fundamental to the business. See the section "Sample Advanced KPI Dashboards" later in this chapter.

## Defining Your Visitor Goals

*Goals* is the word used by Google Analytics to highlight anything of value that visitors do on your website beyond viewing standard content pages. These are actions that strengthen the relationship with your otherwise anonymous visitors. An obvious important goal is the completion of a transaction. However, even without an e-commerce facility, goal completion is important.

Defining and measuring your website's visitor goals are the building blocks for your KPIs. Therefore, it is important that you do this early on in the process—they are a major part of defining your Google Analytics implementation. Goal setup and their monetization are described in detail in Chapter 3. The goal examples from that chapter are reproduced in Table 9.2.

All of the goals in Table 9.2 highlight visitor engagement with your content. Apart from the first item, these goals are applicable whether you have a transactional site or not.

☞   *There is a Google Analytics report set dedicated to showing the performance of your goals.*

## Translating Goals into KPIs

Some goals can be translated directly into KPIs (the terms are often used interchangeably): the KPI is obtained directly from your Google Analytics goal reports. Examples of direct goal-to-KPI translations include

**Table 9.2** *Goal Examples*

| Goal Type | Visitor's Action Defining the Goal |
|---|---|
| E-commerce | • Purchase confirmation<br>• Add-to-cart action (e-commerce site)<br>• Got to step 3 of 4 in the purchase funnel (came very close to becoming a customer)<br>• Transaction failed—a negative goal (one you would rather see less of) |
| Lead generation | Any action where personally identifiable information is passed on:<br>• Completed a contact request form<br>• Clicked a mailto link<br>• Subscribed to your newsletter |
| Purchase intent | • Logged in to your site<br>• Visited your store finder page<br>• Clicked an outbound link to a reseller |
| Brand engagement | • Logged in to your site<br>• Downloaded a file—such as your product brochure or price list<br>• Viewed a specific page, such as a special offer<br>• Watched a video clip<br>• Watched a video clip to completion (or passed a threshold of $x$%)<br>• Shared or commented on your content on Facebook, Twitter, Google+, LinkedIn, your blog, and so forth (social sharing)<br>• Used a widget (such as a loan calculator)<br>• Viewed $n$ or more product pages during a long visit (where you have set a threshold, such as $n > 10$ and time > 5 minutes)<br>• Used advanced features of your internal site search facility (examples: more than one related search; using filters)<br>• Used any content feedback or rating mechanism |
| Other revenue | • Clicked on a third-party advertisement |

**Site engagement rate**   percent of visits where *any* goal is completed (obtained from your Goal Conversion Rate report)

**Bounce rate**   percent of visits that only viewed one page and did nothing else (obtained from your Audience Overview report)

**New customers**   the number of new customers gained (obtained from your Goal Conversion Rate report)

**Per visit value**   the average value of a visitor to your website—what a visitor is worth to your business (obtained from your Conversions reports)

**Page value**   the average value of a page on your website (obtained from your Site Content reports)

### Negative Goals and KPIs

In the vast majority of cases, you will wish to increase the number of people that complete your defined goals and KPIs. But there are circumstances where you may wish to reduce the number of goal completions and thus the KPIs. Examples include self-help support websites, where minimizing the number of engagements the visitor requires in order to obtain their answer is the desired outcome; reducing the number of zero results returned to the visitor from your onsite search tool; and reducing the number of visitors that close their account with you.

I recommend you start with these KPIs as overview indicators of success. You can then get specific by segmenting these KPIs. For example, the engagement rate KPIs for noncustomers versus customers clearly represent two quite different segments of visitors. Likewise, you can segment your overall *per visit value* by which source referred your visitors—comparing Google versus other search engines, for example; paid search versus free search versus email, banners, and other campaigns. For *page value*, you can segment your overall site-wide page value by section—allowing you to compare the relative values of each website section.

If you have a transactional site, add the following list of KPIs that can be plucked directly from your Google Analytics reports:

**E-commerce conversion rate**    the proportion of visits that transacted with you (obtained from your E-commerce Overview report)

**Revenue**    the amount of money your website made for this period

**Average order value**    the average value of a visitor's transaction

These can be further refined using segmentation, such as by product category, or new customer versus existing customer. If you operate in multiple markets, both transaction and non-transaction KPIs can be segmented by country or by language settings of your visitors.

### Calculated KPIs

Although the above examples are a great place to get started, the KPIs your stakeholders ask for may not be found directly in your Google Analytics reports. That is because every business is unique in its approach. Even within the same business sector, organizations have different staff, ideas, processes, customers, web content, and ambitions. You will need to

**Quote KPIs in Context**

Apart from quoting the value of the KPI itself, always quote the percentage change from the previous time period—for example, "The proportion of people that interact with our site (do more than just view pages) is 45% this month, up 13% compared to this time last year." This provides a comparable time period so your stakeholders can easily understand the context of how significant the 45% number is—and what the previous efforts have achieved.

manipulate your Google Analytics data (adjust the numbers) or combine it with other data that is not directly a part of Google Analytics, in order to calculate a KPI metric that is more in sync with your organization.

Here are some examples of advanced *calculated* KPIs:

**Average customer lifetime value (CLV)**  The value of a customer relationship to your organization. It is important if you have repeat customers. This is a bespoke calculation not available in your Google Analytics reports—see sidebar.

**ROI of your campaigns**  How much more money (as profit) you make back from your marketing spend. You will need to import your marketing costs and profit margins, and combine that information with your Google Analytics data in order to calculate this—see sidebar.

**Affiliate and partner performance**  The revenue generated from affiliates (or strategic partners) broken down by where they occur in the customer's journey. For example, if a click from an affiliate is the first, middle, or last click of a visitor's path to your website before they became a customer, then you may wish to credit your affiliates differently. This is the basis of attribution modeling, discussed in Chapter 6.

Understanding the monetary value of your affiliates and partners provides you with the opportunity to model and experiment with how you should reward them in order to achieve optimal performance. A KPI for this could be the *average affiliate payout*. Increasing this KPI is a good thing—it means the affiliate is bringing you more business!

**Mobile app conversion rate**  The number of visitors who install your app divided by the number who search for your app on an app store. App store searches and installs happen away from your website and therefore

## Examples of Advanced KPIs

### Customer Lifetime Value (CLV)

For an e-commerce site where the customer is expected to make regular purchases (or a subscription-based business model), *CLV* can be defined as follows[4]:

$$CLV = \frac{average\ revenue\ per\ customer \times gross\ margin\ per\ customer}{churn\ rate}$$

where *churn rate* is the percentage of customers who end their relationship with your organization in a given period.

Example:

$$CLV = \frac{\$100\ average\ monthly\ spend \times 25\%\ margin}{5\%\ monthly\ churn}$$

$$CLV = \$500$$

That is, on average, a customer is worth $500 to you.

For this example and with Google Analytics transactional tracking set up, only the *average monthly revenue per customer* is available directly from your reports. You need to add the other data. (This calculation can also be made using annual data.)

### Return on Investment (ROI)

*ROI* is defined as follows:

$$ROI = \frac{(revenue\ from\ campaign \times profit\ margin) - campaign\ cost}{campaign\ cost}$$

Example:

$$ROI = \frac{(\$100 \times 0.5) - \$35}{\$35}$$

$$ROI = 42.3\%$$

That is, for every $100 you spend acquiring customers, you make $42 in profit.

This is a simple yet powerful calculation for evaluating the performance of your marketing campaigns that Google Analytics cannot do for you—it has no idea what your campaign costs are or what profit margins you operate with. The exception is AdWords. However, for your AdWords ROI, Google Analytics uses only your gross revenue generated. Hence, its default calculation is quite blunt and can be misleading. I recommend you always take profit into account as per the above calculation.[5]

require the import of third-party data or the export of Google Analytics data into a spreadsheet to be combined with your app store data. (For Android apps, you can link the Google Play app store to your Google Analytics account and obtain this number directly.)

As you will have gleaned from the list of advanced calculated KPIs, if the KPI you wish to report on is not directly available in your Google Analytics reports, you have two options:

- Import the other required data points into Google Analytics and define a custom metric. Note that although this imports your external data into the reports, a custom calculation cannot then be performed. It is not possible to divide a set of Google Analytics reported numbers by a set of imported numbers.
- Export your Google Analytics data into a spreadsheet (or application) with other data, then perform your bespoke calculations. This is my preferred method as it provides much greater flexibility to experiment with your calculations.

## PRESENTING KPIs

"Above all else, show the data," the veteran visualization expert Edward Tufte[6] said in 1983. However, there are three important points to remember when communicating KPIs outside of the digital analytics team:

**Present KPIs, not a data dump**   Understanding how much your stakeholders know, how best to present information to them, and how much of it they can absorb is difficult to judge before presenting your initial KPI report. So keep it simple by presenting your story in slides. Make it a presentation and not a data dump.

Once your story and supporting data are understood by your stakeholders and there is a general agreement of what constitutes success (this often changes when stakeholders actually view their KPIs), consider automating the production of KPIs with a dashboard. This can be done within Google Analytics itself—by either logging in or using the built-in email scheduling service. For advanced dashboards, I advise using a separate dashboarding tool that can present a custom visualization without revealing the inner complexity of Google Analytics.

**Emphasize the story, not the data**   The story is what is compelling about the performance of a website and its marketing. The data is there to support the findings and the hypothesis behind the conclusions and recommendations. If you find there is no story to tell, revisit the definition of the KPI with your stakeholder. Always add your opinion to each chart and metric shown.

**Keep it simple; don't make me think** Because data is often considered bland, there is a tendency by analysts to pimp visualizations to create impact. Avoid this by keeping your visualizations as straightforward as possible. The more familiar an audience is with the data presentation, the more they will absorb.

All charts should be easy to understand at a glance. If the viewer needs to think for more than a few seconds or ask a question to understand it, then the visualization has failed. Well-presented line and bar charts are effective at conveying trends—change over time. For displaying data snapshots, use well-formatted tables of metrics and simple gauge charts. Sunburst charts and the like[7] look stunning, but should be avoided unless your audience is advanced and comfortable with their meaning.

---

"Complexity is your enemy. Any fool can make something complicated. It is hard to make something simple."

—*Richard Branson*

---

Example KPI visualizations are shown in Figures 9.2 and 9.3.

## Using Dashboards

A dashboard is a summary of information for your stakeholders. It provides an overview of success and status metrics in a user-friendly format, usually graphical. Its purpose is to quickly inform recipients *at a glance*—that is, without the need for a dedicated meeting, though that may follow. It is analogous to how a car dashboard informs the driver—you do not need to stop driving in order to get an overview of important information.

A well-built KPI dashboard serves a number of important purposes. It

- Provides a user interface—a customized report view of the data, tailored to the requirements and level of the audience (do not use a one-size-fits-all approach).
- Simplifies the data view—removes the congestion of features and options from Google Analytics that a stakeholder does not require.

| Role | Name | Year of the... | Debut | Number of Fans | Takedown Rate |
|------|------|---------------|-------|----------------|---------------|
| Face (The Hero) | The Ultimate Warrior | Tiger | May-2011 | 97320.00 | 86.2 |
| Face (The Hero) | Hulk Hogan | Oxen | Jan-2008 | 988551.00 | 61.978 |
| Face (The Hero) | Macho Man Randy Savage | Monkey | Feb-2008 | 157618.00 | 59.29 |
| Face (The Hero) | Hacksaw Jim Duggan | Pig | Mar-2008 | 30300.00 | 53.4332 |
| Face (The Hero) | Superfly Jimmy Snuka | Dragon | Mar-2008 | 12341.00 | 52.7 |
| Heel (The Bad Guy) | Rowdy Roddy Piper | Rooster | Jun-1968 | 71645.00 | 45.4 |
| Heel (The Bad Guy) | The Million Dollar Man Ted DiBiase | Rat | Apr-1975 | 449342.00 | 43.7689 |
| Heel (The Bad Guy) | Mr. Perfect Curt Henning | Rat | May-1980 | 13773.00 | 38 |
| Heel (The Bad Guy) | Jake the Snake Roberts | Snake | Jul-1975 | 5609.00 | 37.99 |
| Jobber (The Unknown) | Brad Smith | Sheep | Aug-2008 | 1103.00 | 36.316 |
| Jobber (The Unknown) | Ted Duncan | Sheep | Aug-2008 | 200.00 | 33.61 |
| Jobber (The Unknown) | Joey the Uber Nerd Cherdarchuk | Snake | Aug-2008 | 5.00 | 21.0196 |

a

| Role | Name | Year of the... | Debut | Thousands of Fans | Takedown Rate |
|------|------|---------------|-------|-------------------|---------------|
| Face (The Hero) | The Ultimate Warrior | Tiger | May-2011 | 97.3 | 86.2 |
| | Hulk Hogan | Oxen | Jan-2008 | 988.6 | 62.0 |
| | **Macho Man Randy Savage** | **Monkey** | **Feb-2008** | **157.6** | **59.3** |
| | Hacksaw Jim Duggan | Pig | Mar-2008 | 30.3 | 53.4 |
| | Superfly Jimmy Snuka | Dragon | Mar-2008 | 12.3 | 52.7 |
| Heel (The Bad Guy) | Rowdy Roddy Piper | Rooster | Jun-1968 | 71.6 | 45.4 |
| | The Million Dollar Man Ted DiBiase | Rat | Apr-1975 | 449.3 | 43.8 |
| | Mr. Perfect Curt Henning | Rat | May-1980 | 13.8 | 38.0 |
| | Jake the Snake Roberts | Snake | Jul-1975 | 5.6 | 38.0 |
| Jobber (The Unknown) | Brad Smith | Sheep | Aug-2008 | 1.1 | 36.3 |
| | Ted Duncan | Sheep | Aug-2008 | 0.2 | 33.6 |
| | Joey the Uber Nerd Cherdarchuk | Snake | Aug-2008 | 0.0 | 21.0 |

b

**Figure 9.2** *Visualizing the same data with a table: (a) poorly; (b) clearly*
These are general data examples taken with permission from www.darkhorseanalytics.com/blog/clear-off-the-table.

- Integrates the data—combines Google Analytics with other data sources such as offline sales, call center performance, video views that happen away from your website (YouTube, Vimeo), weather .com, social media activity (Facebook, Twitter), and so forth.
- Updates and adjusts automatically, without the user having to drill down or apply their specific segments or customization.

KPI dashboards are useful to all data users—whether analyst, marketer, stakeholder, employee, or investor—both within the digital analytics team and in the broader audience. Ensure you use a separate dashboard to accommodate the specific needs of each.

**Figure 9.3** *Good and bad KPI visualization techniques*
*(a) Gauges can be a powerful conveyer of success when your stakeholder defines the boundaries.*
*(b) Simple bar charts are effective at highlighting differences.*
*(c) Geographic variations are best viewed with a map.*
*(d) Avoid using advanced visualizations for KPIs—save these for your analytics team.*
Figure 9.3d is from d3js.org.

Within the digital analytics team, most initial analysis takes place by viewing raw reports using Google Analytics. As this analysis matures and the meaning of the data is understood, it is often then migrated to a KPI dashboard—providing ease of use, automation, and the ability to combine Google Analytics data with other sources.

Outside of the digital analytics team, KPI dashboards are an essential technique for organizations. This is because of the widening gap between the technology of data analysis and the business needs of senior managers. Dashboards bridge this gap by providing a simplified user interface—a way for both sides of the business to communicate and make informed decisions together. Hence, dashboards are critical to the success of the digital analytics team. This is illustrated schematically in Figure 9.4.

Google Analytics is an analysts' tool, one that requires both expertise and experience to use properly; analysis is a full-time job. I recommend you avoid providing stakeholders direct access to your Google Analytics

### Save Automation Until Last

With such vast volumes of data available, it is tempting to prioritize automation of your dashboards to demonstrate efficiency. However, save this until last. In the first instance, show KPI reports using slides, presented as a story your team describes, not a data dump.

This allows your stakeholders to absorb and understand the impact of the data presented to them and begin to formulate their thoughts on how to act on it. Acting on the data may not be a simple process for them. It can take several iterations for your dashboards to be accepted and solidified by your various stakeholders.

At that point, you are ready to invest in automation.

reports. The product is complex with many caveats that can catch out inexperienced users. In addition, all Google Analytics users should be familiar with the implementation and configuration deployed, so that the scope and limitation of the reports are appreciated. For your stakeholders and other non-analyst users, custom dashboards, rather than Google Analytics access, are the best method of communicating data.

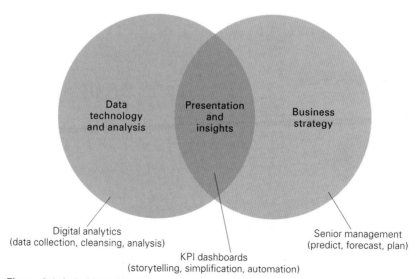

**Figure 9.4** *A dashboard is the intersection between the team that generates the analysis and the stakeholders that use it.*

### Which Dashboard Tool to Use

There are a number of tools available for you to experiment with building dashboards. Google Analytics itself has a dashboard report area, allowing you to extract specific data from a report and display it alongside other specific data. An example is shown in Figure 9.5. These dashboards can be scheduled as emails to your stakeholders each day, week, month, or quarter.

In the first instance, I recommend you experiment with Google Analytics dashboards to familiarize yourself with the technique and what works for your organization—every organization is different. Although powerful, the visualization and customization options are limited, and of course you only have the one data source, Google Analytics, to work with.

If your organization is ready to go beyond what Google Analytics dashboards have to offer, there are numerous enterprise-level commercial dashboard tools available.[8] You can also build your own in Excel by importing Google Analytics and other data into a spreadsheet; there are Excel plugins to simplify the process.[9] In a similar vein, I am a particular fan of Google Docs add-ons for importing Google Analytics data into a spreadsheet, shown in Figure 9.6. With your data embedded in Google Docs, it is then straightforward to build your own dashboard by placing charts and data on a restricted web page.[10]

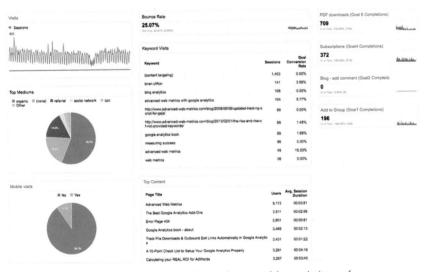

**Figure 9.5** *A Google Analytics dashboard summarizing website performance*

## Sharing the Love

I am a big fan of democratizing data—sharing information throughout an organization and therefore not working in a silo. After all, the wisdom of the crowd can be significant when compared to a small dedicated team.

However, Google Analytics processes raw hit data sent to it into raw reports for *analysts* to use. The reports need to be validated—checked for correctness, filtered, segmented, and interpreted correctly to build a story. A simple example to illustrate this point is a chart showing the average visitor time onsite. If this increases, it is not necessarily a good thing for you—visitors may be getting lost and confused rather than more engaged.

Therefore, use a dashboard to share the love of data rather than providing carte blanche access to your Google Analytics reports.

## Sample Advanced KPI Dashboards

A good dashboard conveys the information the recipients want, in a format they understand, is clear to read at a glance, and does not raise the question, "What does that mean?" Whether it is successful or not at achieving these is very much in the eyes of the beholder (your stakeholder), not you!

Dashboards are tactical by nature; therefore, ensure these are tailored to each stakeholder's needs. Hence it is critically important the person or team building the dashboard visualization know the stakeholder well at a professional level—how they consume data, how much of it can be absorbed, what analytical level of understanding they are at, and what they will actually do with the information (what decisions will be made).

**Figure 9.6** *Three Google Docs add-ons for importing Google Analytics data into a spreadsheet*

With a team of experienced analysts, it should always be the digital analytics team that determines the best way to convey data. However, this is a two-way process of working with your stakeholders.

☞ *I generally advise against presenting dashboards to board-level management (VP and CxO). Dashboards are aimed at people making tactical decisions. For the boardroom, a more long-term strategic data approach is required, one where the business story is more important than seeing the underlying data—assuming the storyteller has the confidence of the board.*

### A Non-transactional Website
The vast majority of commercial websites remain non-transactional (I estimate this to be 80% for advanced markets such as the EU and US). At first glance, determining a list of KPIs may appear difficult. However, any engagement signifies a potential customer and is a good prerequisite to be a KPI. The following is a real dashboard example.

**The website**  A global brand; business-to-consumer website, non-transactional; focused mainly on brand awareness and promotion of specific events; decentralized marketing (country-level marketers manage this); social media activity perceived as important. There are four key areas for the visitor to choose from. These are schematically shown in Figure 9.7.

**The business requirement**  With a digital budget in excess of $100 million per year, the senior management wants to understand the traffic distribution and engagement of their website—which parts of the site are popular and what engagements happen (beyond the pageview). With this information the management team's intent is to make informed decisions on how to distribute the digital budget for maximum impact and efficiency.

**The dashboard audience**  The site has four sections for the visitor to choose from: Blog, Help, Product, Service. Each has its respective stakeholder (head of department). In addition, section-agnostic stakeholders are included: head of PR and communication, head of marketing, all members of the board of directors. The dashboard shown in Figure 9.8 is the overview all stakeholders review every month.

At first glance, the dashboard presented in Figure 9.8 appears complicated—there is a lot of information to absorb. But this has been built in collaboration with the stakeholders, so the structure is familiar to them

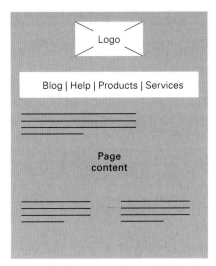

**Figure 9.7** *Schematic website structure for the KPI dashboard of Figure 9.8*

(an important point!). To guide you, I describe the three areas of interest—labels A, B, and C in Figure 9.8.

**Label A** The data table is a key focal point for information. Using a table for displaying data requires careful consideration. Tables are great for displaying a large amount of detailed information—the real numbers. However, that is also their problem—lots of data will rapidly make your audience's eyes glaze over. Absorbing the meaning of a lot of numbers on a page is difficult even for experienced analysts. Therefore, the design and layout of the table, as well as restricting the content to the key facts, are critically important.

In this example, the stakeholders are familiar with the website sections and each section stakeholder shares the same Primary KPIs (the most important information):

- The proportion of visitors their section receives
- The proportion of those visitors that engage with the section's content (do more than just view a page)
- The proportion of visitors that bounce away from the site—view one page only and have no engagements—the hypothesis being that such a visitor experience is a very poor one (see sidebar "Bounce Rate—An Important Engagement KPI").

| | Blog section | Help section | Product section | Service section |
|---|---|---|---|---|
| **Primary** | | | | |
| % visitors | 50% **+20%** | 25% **+11%** | 30% **−80%** | 18% **−50%** |
| % engaged | 2% **−50%** | 12% **−22%** | 7% – | 5% − 5% |
| bounce rate | 57% **+ 3%** | 25% **−30%** | 27% – | 17% − 8% |
| **Secondary** | 99 article click-throughs | 338 video starts | 29% used widget | 8% submitted contact form |
| | 9 social shares | 201 video completions | 8% purchase intent (click store finder) | 2% completed survey form |
| | 45 read only 1 article | 59% completions / starts | 31% download PDF | 4% emailed us |
| | 6 read > 1 article | 15% rated support | | |
| | | 22% zero search results | | |

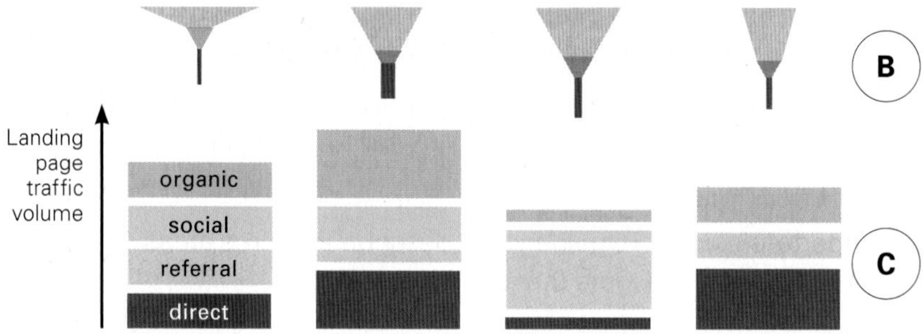

Figure 9.8 *KPI dashboard for a non-transactional brand awareness website*

All of the above metrics are shown as percentages, with a comparison to the previous month color-coded to highlight any significant change (anything greater than ±5%)—green indicating a change for the good, red a change for the worse.

The row of secondary KPIs is stakeholder-specific. In the Blog section, I break one of my own guidelines by showing raw numbers rather than percentages or ratios. The rationale for this is the extremely low values. That is, using 0.001% instead of the raw number becomes meaningless. I also wanted to emphasize the reality. For example, showing 9 social shares (Like, Tweet, Google+, and so forth) really does highlight how underperforming this section is compared to the spend on social promotion.

Note that with tables and dashboards in general, it is important you assign a priority to the information displayed. This can be visually—by the order it is placed, or using a label such as *primary, secondary, tertiary*, and so on.

### Snapshots versus Trends

Figure 9.8 is an example of a *snapshot* dashboard—it tells the audience what is happening now (or within the last time period). There is very little information as to the trends that are occurring—that is, what is happening over time. For example, is the 20% growth of visitors to the Blog section a one-off blip or part of a long-term trend? The dashboard does not show this. This was a deliberate decision and was planned for. For this particular high-level overview report, trends were not considered important. However, it is clearly a potential for the next dashboard iteration and straightforward to add.

**Label B**　Not a KPI in itself, this is a schematic visual representation of the engagement funnel for each section. It shows the natural decrease in visitor numbers as they become more engaged with your brand, as explained in Figure 9.9. The width of each step is proportional to the volume of visitors. The whole process is analogous to a checkout funnel for a transactional site. For this website, the rate and size of the decrease vary by section, and the stakeholders wish to compare these.

**Label C**　The chart shows which channels visitors are coming from for each section. It is aimed at those stakeholders with responsibilities for marketing and communications. For example, do the volume of traffic and channel match the marketing spend and effort?

### A Transactional Website

Dashboards for transactional sites tend to be easier to build than for non-transactional sites for the simple reason that headline KPIs are better defined when money is changing hands. All website stakeholders in this type of organization have a keen interest in revenue, order volume, visit-to-sale conversion rate, and average order value. These KPIs are the fundamentals of how you make a living with e-commerce. The following is a real dashboard example.

**Website description**　European brand; business-to-business website, transactional with standard shopping cart–like functionality; 30,000+ products available to buy online; focused on generating new customers and online sales from new and existing customers; online sales account for approximately 40% of total business revenue; centralized marketing team with significant investment in search engine marketing—both paid advertising and free organic search.

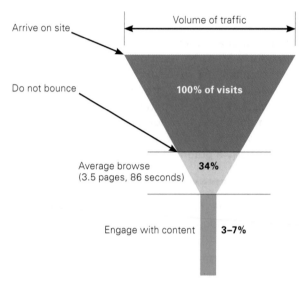

**Figure 9.9** *Website engagement funnel*

**The business requirement** A high-level overview of the performance of the online business that is comparable to how the performance of the offline business is reported, to be able to model the impact of different profit margins on existing-revenue and return-on-investment calculations.

**Dashboard audience** The board of directors requires an understanding of the potential for the online business in order to determine future investment levels. For example, what is the optimal split of online/offline sales for the business? This is currently at 40%. Is 100% achievable or desirable? The data will allow for informed discussions to take place. The dashboard shown in Figure 9.10 is reviewed each month by the director of e-commerce, with key takeaways reported to the board.

As with the non-transactional dashboard of Figure 9.8, at first glance the dashboard presented in Figure 9.10 appears complicated if you are not a stakeholder involved with building it. The following labels will help you familiarize yourself.

**Label A** This row of the dashboard provides a view of how well the site is converting visitors into customers. The funnel visualization is a breakdown on the headline figure to its left. That is, 85 visitors enter the top of the sales funnel for each sale generated.

**Bounce Rate—An Important Engagement KPI**

A bounced visitor is one that only views one page on your site and has no other engagement. Hence the bounce rate is the proportion of visitors that do this. The hypothesis is that such a visitor experience is a poor one.

The hypothesis is valid so long as you do not deliberately design your site to cater for a bounced experience. Why would you? For example, if you create a great one-page article, your visitors will likely wish to do one of the following:

- Rate it
- Share it socially on networks such as Facebook, Twitter or Google+
- Click to read more, because the article is spread over multiple pages
- Click to enlarge an image
- Click to start a video
- Add a comment
- Click to print or download the PDF version
- Connect with the author (read the author's bio, contact the author via email, connect via a social network)
- Read related articles
- Subscribe to updates
- Click on an ad

All of these are reliable ways to track that a visitor has engaged with your content. The use of any of them will mark the visitor as non-bounced. Cherry-pick the best for your situation so that the hypothesis is valid.

**Label B**    The revenue and customer conversion rate are key metrics indicating the health of the business. Hence, they are given prominence in the center of the dashboard. Year-on-year comparisons are made because for this business sales are seasonal. Comparing to the previous month would be misleading.

**Label C**    By knowing the revenue generated and the costs to acquire sales, the ROI can be calculated by the simple formula (revenue − cost) / cost.

These metrics are shown side by side over time in the dashboard. For this Google Analytics installation, the revenue captured is the total amount paid by the customer. To obtain the real ROI, I substitute profit for revenue in the above formula. The amount of profit made is determined by the profit margin (50% shown). This can be adjusted at label C1. This allows the business to forecast the impact of varying prices and profit margins.

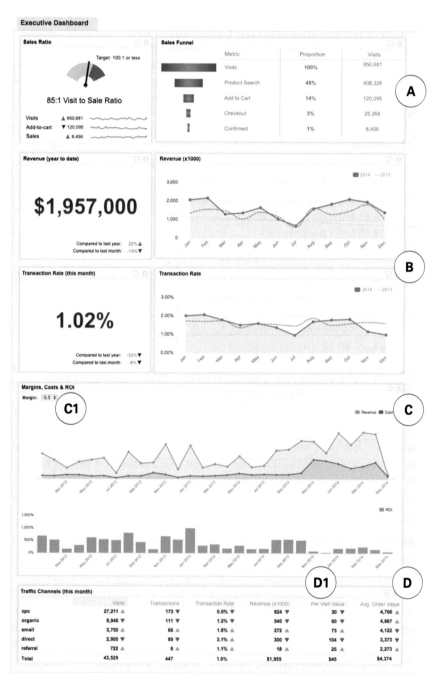

**Figure 9.10** *KPI dashboard for a transactional website*

## Dashboard Templates

Data visualization and storytelling are the creative side of the digital analytics team and are critical to the team's success. Therefore, avoid using dashboard templates for this. Although data-over-time charts are standard visualization tools and will be used regularly, consider ways of adding more context and relevance to those points.

Every story can be presented in a different way, and every stakeholder has a different knowledge level and approach to working with data. The guiding principle is to always keep it simple and clear to understand. Don't make me think.[11]

**Label D**  The table summarizes which marketing channels are driving sales and how cost-effective they are. A key calculated metric available directly within Google Analytics is the *per visit value* (label D1). This determines the value of every visit to your website whether visitors purchase or not. For example, from the table each paid search visit (from AdWords) is worth $30, yet each organic visit (free search) is worth $60. The *per visit value* is calculated by dividing the total revenue for a marketing channel by the total number of visits from that channel. It is available directly from Google Analytics reports. Understanding value is explained in Chapter 5.

## SPEAKING OF KEY PERFORMANCE INDICATORS...

| When I hear this... | I reply with... |
| --- | --- |
| What is the priority when building a KPI dashboard? | Get to know your stakeholders well. Delivering a KPI report or dashboard will fail without understanding who your audience is, what their data requirements are, their level of metrics understanding, and what they will do with the data—what decisions they will make. |
| I need a real-time dashboard with 50 KPIs built. | Working with real-time dashboards inevitably leads to making real-time mistakes. Unless you have a clear cause-and-effect correlation, spend time considering the implications of any KPI changes. Hence real-time is best served as daily updates. If 50 KPIs really are essential to your business's success, ensure you classify your KPIs into primary, secondary, and tertiary hierarchies. |
| What KPIs do you recommend in order to understand how visitors flow around our website? | Changes in visitor flow are not necessarily a good or a bad thing. Hence, I do not consider this a KPI. Rather, it is a visualization to help you understand visitor behavior.<br><br>If you have a well-defined path for your visitors, use a funnel visualization with KPIs to indicate the conversion rate of one step in the funnel to the next. |

| When I hear this... | I reply with... |
| --- | --- |
| We have a non-transactional website that is used to promote our brand. Therefore, it is not possible to monetize it. | All websites have goals—otherwise you would not have built it in the first place. If the goal of your website is only to raise brand awareness, you still wish your visitors to engage with it—and engagement has a value.<br><br>For example, asking your visitors to comment on your content is a way to engage and this activity can be monetized. Other examples include completing a short questionnaire, sharing your content on a social network, and commenting on a blog post. |

## CHAPTER 9 REFERENCES

1    Key performance indicators have been around as a management technique for some time: http://en.wikipedia.org/wiki/Performance_indicator.

2    I have changed the definition of the SMART acronym slightly. For my purposes I use *actionable* to replace the original *achievable*: http://en.wikipedia.org/wiki/SMART_criteria.

3    YouTube Analytics API: https://developers.google.com/youtube/analytics/

4    Taken from Wikipedia: http://en.wikipedia.org/wiki /Customer_lifetime_value#Methodology

5    My blog article explaining how to calculate your real ROI: http://brianclifton.com/real-roi

6    http://en.wikipedia.org/wiki/Edward_Tufte

7    D3.js is a JavaScript library for manipulating documents based on data. It can be used to produce stunning data visualization, such as a sunburst chart: www.d3js.org.

8    Tableau (www.tableausoftware.com) and Klipfolio (www.klipfolio.com) are two well-respected data dashboard tools that integrate with Google Analytics as well as other data sources.

9    Excel plugins for importing Google Analytics data can be found on the Google Analytics App Gallery web page: www.google.com/analytics/apps/results?category=Reporting%20Tools.

10   With your data imported into Google Docs, it is straightforward to build your dashboard as a Google Site. Watch the video from Google engineer Nick Mihailovski: http://youtu.be/rL4N3qFyycg.

11   A phrase I often use when discussing data visualization with analysts is "Don't make me think." It comes from the title of the groundbreaking 2003 book from Steve Krug, *Don't Make Me Think: A Common Sense Approach to Web Usability.*

# Insights
# and Success Stories

**The real-world success stories in** this chapter will whet your appetite for the types of insights (knowledge) your digital analytics team can produce. These are short stories—intended to exemplify what investment in digital analytics can achieve and illustrate how providing *insight snippets* for quick wins allows an organization to improve their business. These snippets provide the basis for making rapid, incremental progress—the "release early, release often" approach I learned at Google and that has been adopted by many other agile organizations.

> "We can't assume they will learn anything from mere statistics. Let's show them one or two representative cases to influence their [thinking]."
>
> *—Daniel Kahneman, Nobel laureate*
> *and author of* Thinking, Fast and Slow

The case studies in this chapter are based on my (or my company's) direct involvement as an independent digital advisor for clients throughout Europe and the United States. Some are straightforward insights gleaned from diligent observations and analysis. Others required more deep-dive analysis, lateral thought, and correlation. None of the work is magic or rocket science, and *all* cases had a significant impact on the bottom line

## Release Early, Release Often

The "release early, release often" approach means that rather than building a long, complicated plan for your website and its marketing activities, it's wiser to set your ship in the right direction (with a clear vision and purpose), apply best practices at all junctures, then adjust with regular incremental changes to account for the current market and technology trends.

The reasoning is that the digital ecosystem, and the concomitant user behavior, is evolving rapidly—in many cases unpredictably. For example, who knew we needed an iPhone until we saw one, or that the explosion of the mobile web—using a conventional browser on a mobile device—would actually shrink in usage as people moved to dedicated mobile apps instead?[1]

Adapting your business to constant rapid change requires an agile digital strategy. This means placing many small bets on potential winners, reducing risk.

of the businesses involved—real dollars were either saved, made, or real-located as a result of the insights. Often with such knowledge gained (and trust in the process), the consequence was further digital investment.

I group the insight and success stories into four key disciplines, though in reality these all overlap:

**Marketing insights**  Help you target, manage, and optimize your visitor acquisition strategy—spotting opportunities to get the most qualified visitors to your site, in the maximum volume, at the most efficient cost.

**Visitor insights**  Help you understand what visitors are doing on your site—where they go, when, what actions they take, and how these correlate to your business. This helps you build up a picture of what the visitor journey is on your site, and therefore what your visitors' expectations are.

**Conversion insights**  Help you understand how visitors drop out of a process you wish them to complete such as completing your multi-step checkout process all the way to payment confirmation, completing a request for information or contact form (becoming a new lead), or applying for a job or university enrollment (becoming a new employee or student). Such conversions are typically the objective of your website—why it exists. Understanding where, when, and how people who have started

### The Cost of a Poor User Experience

Poor user experience is a pain for all of us. Nobody likes to be kept waiting for slow service, arrive on a page only to find it doesn't match our expectations, arrive on a page that doesn't contain the content we want, or be told there are no results that match our search query when we know the information is there, somewhere.

Whatever the reason, a poor digital service is no different to your customers from a poor face-to-face or phone experience. However, it is much easier to count the cost of a poor digital experience to your organization. In the following two articles I discuss estimating the business costs of a poor digital user experience:

http://brianclifton.com/easyjet
http://brianclifton.com/electrolux

On the same theme, these humorous YouTube videos from Google capture the frustration perfectly:

Checkout: http://bit.ly/video-checkout
Site search: http://bit.ly/video-sitesearch

such processes bail out can have make-or-break implications for your business.[2]

**User experience insights** Help you understand whether your website visitors have a good or bad experience. Do they find what they are looking for, and is that a quick and simple process? Or do they bounce away? Are there pain points? Do visitors provide feedback—either directly via a survey or indirectly by rating an article, sharing your content on social networks, or commenting on or reviewing your products and services?

## CASE 1: MARKETING INSIGHT

| | |
|---|---|
| **Website description** | Online sales of eyewear, contact lenses, and accessories. |
| **Category** | Consumer e-tailer, active throughout northern Europe. |
| **Client request** | Our much-anticipated website redesign is having little impact. There is no improvement to the previous version. Please investigate. |

### Something That Often Happens When a Website Is Redesigned

**Insight gained** After a review of where visitors were coming from, the focus turned to organic search engine traffic. It was ascertained that following their website redesign, traffic from organic sources, such as Google search, dropped by nearly half (Figure 10.1). This resulted in a severe loss of revenue. However, the loss was masked by the launch of a new marketing campaign promoting the redesigned brand. The overall revenue remained constant, and because of this it took several months before the organic issue was spotted.

**The investigation** To a business, any loss in traffic is a concern. However, the loss of organic visitors was a particular concern for two reasons:

- Organic traffic is earned media, meaning it cannot be bought. It not only takes a great deal of time and effort to build your organic reputation, it also implies a source of credibility in the eyes of your visitors (being top ranked on Google counts a lot!). In other words, organic traffic is highly valued by users and website owners alike.
- High credibility in the eyes of organic visitors is reflected in the data for this website—new visitors from organic sources have the highest purchase rate of all referrals (3.6% monthly average).

The reason for the loss of traffic was that the new website used different URLs in its architecture. However, search engine results contained

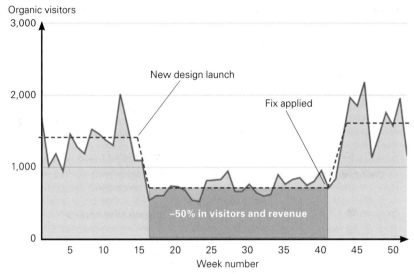

**Figure 10.1** *Organic traffic levels following a website redesign*

the old historical URLs. If a visitor followed these links (just as search engine crawlers do), they produced error pages—the historical URLs no longer existed. Google would have noticed the error pages during its automatic crawl and therefore demoted the ranking of previously high-ranking pages. The demotion was significant, and rightly so—no one wants to visit error pages.

Once identified, the fix was relatively straightforward—applying redirects to the new content so that anyone arriving via a historical URL (including search engine robots) was automatically redirected to the new URL where the content was hosted. As a result, pages are now ranked in similar positions to before the redesign, and organic traffic levels have returned to normal.

**What happened next?** The issue was identified and fixed relatively quickly, with organic visits and revenue returning to normal levels. However, the loss spanned four months in total and represented a significant amount of lost income. The lesson learned is to keep the digital analytics team in the loop *before* changing your website—both incrementally and for extensive redesigns. In addition to ensuring a consistency of tracking, the analytics team will place more emphasis on tracking errors (as per the audit document shown in Figure 4.1, row 9). For example, by configuring custom alerts for error pages, the drop in organic traffic and revenue could have been spotted automatically within a matter of days—saving the company millions in lost revenue.

## CASE 2: CONVERSION AND VISITOR INSIGHTS

| | |
|---|---|
| **Website description** | Brand awareness and engagement site for alcoholic drinks manufacture. Requires the visitor to submit their date of birth details before they can enter the site (their age must be above the minimum drinking age for the country they access from). |
| **Category** | Global brand awareness and engagement. |
| **Client requests** | • To what extent do visitors engage with our brand?<br>• Do our visitors match the demographic age group our marketing targets?<br>• Which sections of our site are most popular?<br>• Is our site siloed? |

### Do Visitors Engage with Our Brand?

There are four key sections of the website where virtually all content to be engaged with is hosted. This is shown schematically in Figure 10.2.

**Insight gained**  A common analyst question is, What proportion of our visitors convert from an anonymous visitor with an unmeasured interest level to one who demonstrates *engagement* with our brand? In this case, it was found that only 3% to 7% of all visitors engaged with the brand and that there were two significant pain points—the age verification process and the lack of engaging content in some sections.

**The investigation**  Firstly, the organization needed to define what constitutes a successful engagement. This required a KPI workshop with all stakeholders, to brainstorm a visitor's objective once on the site. These discussions resulted in the following six KPI definitions of engagement:

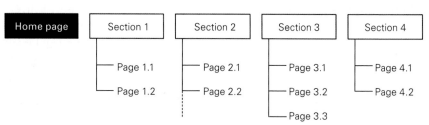

**Figure 10.2** *Schematic website structure for Case 2*

- Visitors who do not bounce—that is, who go beyond the age verification page (being forced to submit your age is an obvious barrier to any visitor)
- Visitors who read more than one blog article
- Visitors who share content on a social network
- Visitors who show purchase intent (view the store finder widget)
- Visitors who start to watch a video
- Visitors who watch at least $x$% of a video

The necessary tracking was implemented so that these visitor engagements could be understood. To know the total number of *unique* engagements (*unique* means that a visitor can only become engaged once, despite being able to trigger multiple KPIs), an engagement funnel was built (Figure 10.3).

**Funnel Step 1** Visitors arrive on the website and either bounce away or stay to view content. For this site, a bounced visitor is one that does not proceed past the age verification page—whether or not they try and fail. If age verification is successful, the visitor is logged in funnel Step 2.

**Funnel Step 2** Visitors browse around the website, including the use of site search and the viewing of any page content. No engagement

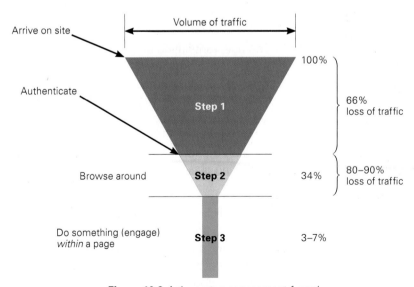

**Figure 10.3** *A three-step engagement funnel*

happens—as defined by the KPI list. If the visitor does engage, they are logged in funnel Step 3.

**Funnel Step 3** A visitor is logged in Step 3 only if they engage with the website—for example, share content on a social network or click to start an embedded video (as per the KPI list). Engagements are only logged once per session, even if multiple engagements occur.

With the hard work of establishing what defines engagement and then ensuring the data for these is being collected, the insight is fairly straight-forward. In Figure 10.3, there are two distinct (and substantial) drop-offs.

The first drop-off is the high loss of visitors due to the requirement of age verification—66% of visitors bounce here and go no further. No content is viewed, and so this is a significant pain point. For every $100 spent on acquiring visitors, $66 is wasted! Note that the annual marketing budget for this site is a multiple of $100,000 per year.

The second drop-off shown in Figure 10.3 reflects the lack of content engagement. Although the stakeholder group identified six engagement KPIs, the vast majority of site content relied on one—the use of social media "Love" buttons to entice visitor engagement. The funnel drop-off shows that between 80% and 90% of visitors who view content do not engage in any way. Unless content has a clear benefit for the visitor or there's a reason to share it, that content may even damage engagement: visitors may subconsciously train themselves to ignore areas of your pages that are superfluous. The phenomenon is called *content blindness*.

**What happened next?** The age verification of Step 1 is a legal require-ment for alcoholic drinks content in all markets this business operates in. The high drop-off (bounce rate) from this step stresses how critical getting this right is to the business—a small improvement here will have a much larger impact further down the funnel. The obvious decision is to perform testing—that is, the testing of different age verification page designs to see which one creates the least friction (drives more verified visitors through it). A/B split testing is currently being deployed to exper-iment with

- Simplification—adding one-click social media buttons to ease the verification process, such as "verify via Facebook," rather than hav-ing to manually select your day, month, and year of birth.
- Using humor—using a light-hearted approach to overcome the obvi-ous pain of requesting user information, when apart from access, there is little given back in return for the visitor's effort.

For improving the drop-off from Step 2, the design and content teams are now focused on optimizing content for engagement. Rather than producing a smörgåsbord of random content in hopes of catching a visitor's attention, the new process focuses on content with a call to action. For all content, both teams now ask the questions, What is the purpose of this page? and What do we expect the visitor to do once it is consumed?

Answers are allowed to be loosely defined. For example, we expect visitors who enjoy the content to give feedback with our one-click star ratings; we expect engaged visitors to click the "read more" link. If there is no answer to these questions, the content is rejected during the review process—it has no purpose and is a dead-end journey for the visitor.

In addition, this investigation provided two KPIs that are now reported to the senior management board on a quarterly basis—the *site bounce rate* and *visitor engagement rate*. Previously only total traffic levels were reported.

### Do Our Visitors Match Who We Target?

**Insight gained** This site is proactively targeting a specific age range—young millennials—a generation of people who are currently in their mid 20s to early 30s.[3] Figure 10.4 shows the age distribution of visitors, with the weighted average calculated at 33.4 years old. The key takeaway from

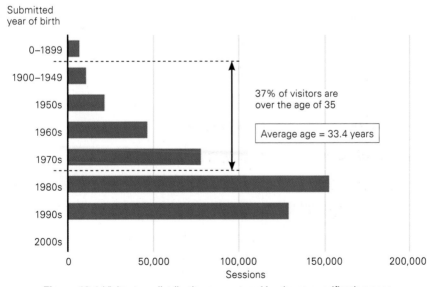

**Figure 10.4** *Visitor age distribution as captured by the age verification page*

this is that the site is attracting an audience at the higher end of the young millennial age range. The distribution shows a significant proportion (37%) of visitors over the age of 35—outside target, in other words.

**The investigation** As viewing content requires the visitor to submit their date of birth, tracking code was implemented to capture this detail as an event. Ages are an interesting demographic for marketers. Usually, though, marketing and consumer insights teams must rely on aggregate estimates, extrapolated from small (because they are expensive to conduct) focus group studies. Having large numbers of visitors submitting this information themselves, from various countries and cultures, is a gold mine of information.

To provide additional insight to the Google Analytics collected data of Figure 10.4, the client's YouTube.com account was also compared. YouTube collects demographic data from subscribers and anyone with a Google account that is logged in when accessing the client's video content on YouTube.com. Both sets of data showed good age alignment.

**What happened next?** Capturing the date of birth of visitors also allowed the segmentation by country. Figure 10.5 shows the difference in age ranges for Germany and the US The organization had no access to this type of information before—only anecdotal evidence from country marketing managers. Obviously, understanding the ages of your visitors

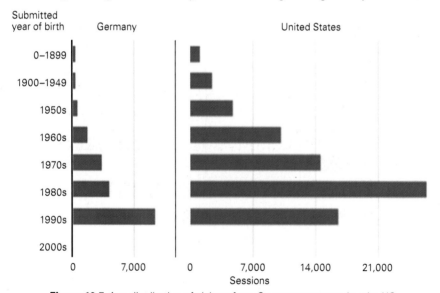

**Figure 10.5** *Age distribution of visitors from Germany compared to the US*

## Do People Lie about Their Age?

Quite possibly, but we wanted to put a figure on that. Two assumptions were made about people's reasoning for not wishing to enter their correct date of birth:

- Underage—the visitor is under the legal age and therefore lies about their date of birth in order to gain access.
- Laziness—annoyed at being requested to enter this information, the visitor takes the easiest option and simply enters 01-01-1900 as a quick fix.

Although the first reason cannot be accounted for, the laziness factor is easier to identify. The assumption is that people looking for a quick fix will use a simple number combination for the year, such as 1111, 1000, 1234, 1900, or 1919, which are easy to type (compared to finding your real birth year) and will all verify successfully on the site.

In the first two columns of Figure 10.5, the number of potential liars is around 5% of total visits. In my view, that is surprisingly low.

(and in near real-time) allows you to better target your content and marketing efforts. Powerful information when your organization operates in multiple markets.

## Which Content Sections Are Most Popular?

**Insight gained** As shown in the schematic diagram of Figure 10.2, there are four sections for this case study website. Sections 1 and 2 were receiving the lion's share of investment—both in terms of website development and marketing spend. However, the investment was not reflected in the traffic distribution received. Figure 10.6 shows the vast majority of visits are for sections 3 and 4—with a combined total of more than 90% of the total visits (89% of visitors).

Cross-referencing this with which section drives engagement revealed a similar picture. That is, sections 1 and 2 are vastly underperforming compared to the resources being spent on them.

**The investigation** On the surface, defining section interest appears straightforward—a page viewed within a section defines the visitor as interested in that section, right? However, what if visitors view more than one section during their visit?

The overlap of visitors viewing multiple sections makes it difficult to account for the interest in each section—you end up counting the same

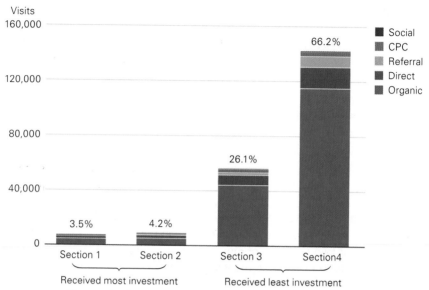

**Figure 10.6** *The website visit distribution around four sections*

visitor multiple times. If for example all visitors view all four sections of the site, summing the number of visitors to each section gives four times the total number of visitors to the site! Hence, a different definition of a section interest is required.

In the case of Figure 10.6, section interest is defined as a visitor who has either *arrived* OR *exited* from the section in question. The hypothesis for this is threefold:

1 A visitor arriving on a specific section page knew what they were looking for and found the right section online (usually via a Google search). This should be true if the section in question is visible and optimized to rank highly in the search engines.

2 A visitor exiting the site on a specific section page found what they were looking for and then exited at that point of satisfaction.

3 An alternative reason for the exit is that the visitor did not find what they were looking for and exited at the section that was potentially the closest match.

Any pages viewed in other sections within the visit are ignored for the purpose of segmenting. That is, only the start and end points define what constitutes section interest.

**What happened next?** The result of this analysis was a reevaluation of the digital strategy: what do visitors want from our website? A recent "be more digital" initiative from the CEO had in fact caused a loss of focus on core visitor needs. Further analysis revealed that significant engagement was happening away from the website on other channels, such as You-Tube. So a new direction of expanding the digital mix was adopted (rather than only expanding website content).

As you can imagine, redirecting a digital strategy is an enormous change for an organization—requiring strong leadership and a conviction in the data and its analysis.

## Is Our Site Siloed?

**Insight gained** A site operating as a silo means that visitors stay within a single section of your website—they do not branch out and explore content in other sections. I cannot think of a business that would want to intentionally silo its visitors and limit its potential to cross-sell, but many websites operate this way. Measuring the extent of *siloization*, or its inverse, *visitor spread*, is a way to understand if you have this problem.

For this case study website, the amount of siloization is 70%. That is, 70% of visitors who land in a section remain there for the duration of their visit and do not visit any other section.

**The investigation** Similar to defining section interest, determining if your visitors are viewing in a silo is not as straightforward as you may initially think. A siloed visit is defined as a visitor journey that meets all the following conditions. The visitor

- I Enters a section—for example, section 1.
- II Stays *within* section 1 while continuing to browse other content pages.
- III Exits the site from section 1.

Segment conditions I and III are prebuilt into Google Analytics. However, condition II is not available by default and therefore requires the subtraction of two segments as follows:

First, use conditions I and III to define a single segment. What visitor journeys will this contain? Consider the schematic in Figure 10.7 for two scenarios—both of the journeys match conditions I and III. However, only a segment for visitors that match journey A is desired. To obtain this, we need to create a second segment to account for journey B visitors, then subtract it from the total.

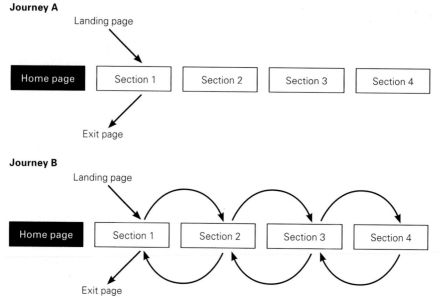

**Figure 10.7** *Examples of visitor journeys that cannot be separated with a single segment*

By repeating the process for each website section, you can build your siloed section chart as shown in Figure 10.8.

The percentage siloization shown in column F of Figure 10.8 shows how siloed the visitors are for each section. If this equals 100%, the section is operating as a perfect silo—all your visitors stay within the section. Anything less than 100% shows the degree to which your site is a silo, with 0% representing a perfect spread—all your visitors moving between sections. For example, section 4 shows that 83% of visitors land in and exit from this section, and do not visit any other section.

An overall figure for how siloed the site is can be obtained from the total number of siloed visitors (sum of column D) divided by the total number of visitors applicable to this segment—see sidebar "Scaling the Silo Calculation." For this case study website, the overall amount of siloization is 70% (151,761 / 217,000).

☞ *For the soundness of the calculation, it's important to exclude from all segments the following:*

- Any bounced visitors—those who view only a single page (visitors may have arrived by mistake, or for the wrong reasons)
- Visits that land on the home page—as this is a natural moving-on page

| A | B | C | D | E | F |
|---|---|---|---|---|---|
| Section name | Number of visitors who land in and exit the same section* | Number of visitors who land in and exit the same section but also view other sections** | Number of siloed visitors (B – C) | Number of visitors with section interest*** | % siloization (D / E) |
| Section 1 | 2,544 | 455 | 2,089 | 7,578 | 27.57% |
| Section 2 | 2,607 | 360 | 2,247 | 9,084 | 24.74% |
| Section 3 | 34,605 | 5,878 | 28,727 | 56,212 | 51.10% |
| Section 4 | 123,757 | 5,059 | 118,698 | 142,516 | 83.29% |
| Total | | | 151,761 | | |

\* As per Figure 10.8a and b
\*\* As per Figure 10.8b
\*\*\* Data taken from Figure 10.6
Total visitors applicable for this period = 217,000

**Figure 10.8** *Calculating the siloization of your website*

**What happened next?**   I use a traffic light system as a guide for understanding the levels of siloization:

⬤**Red: >50%**

For a silo level above 50%, you should prioritize working on integrating your content to encourage cross-section visitors. For this case study example, the website contained a section dedicated to product news articles (section 1). These were listed separately from the product sections (sections 3 and 4). Therefore, the plan of action was to integrate relevant news articles *within* the product pages themselves. That way, visitors viewing products get to see related news articles at the same time and point of interest.

⬤**Yellow: 25%–50%**

A silo level within the amber range may indicate the section is in the Goldilocks zone, where visitors browse broadly enough to view your many different offerings, but not so broadly as to lose focus. Use the techniques described below for the green zone to investigate if this range is indeed the optimal level.

## Scaling the Silo Calculation

As there is no default silo segment available within Google Analytics, calculating your degree of siloization requires the setup of two segments and a subtraction of these for each section. This makes it challenging to scale. If you have numerous sections, consider grouping them into super-category sections, or using the API to automate the process.

### ● Green: <25%

A silo level less than 25% indicates your visitors are moving around your website sections—a good sign. However, I consider this the beginning of further analysis. Perhaps visitors are lost on the site and therefore jumping between sections to find what they are looking for. To investigate further, create a segment just for visitors who move between multiple sections, then examine the site search terms used (from the internal search engine) and what engagements are completed.

A red level of siloization is clearly defined as actionable. However, yellow and green are not so clear-cut and require further analysis to establish if these are the right levels for your site. Understanding siloization requires a deep understanding of your website visitor journeys. This probably explains why such a report is not available by default within Google Analytics—it's too unique for each user.

## CASE 3: CONVERSION INSIGHT

| | |
|---|---|
| **Website description** | A global leader in higher education.[4] As for most universities, this website provides information to all interested parties, including students, staff, and prospects (potential new students). The university has over 1,000 semiautonomous websites specific to schools, marketing, events, societies, sports, and its leadership team. |
| **Category** | Education; major US university. |
| **Client request** | We need to understand the value of our website so we can plan the appropriate budgets for marketing. |

## Monetizing a Non-ecommerce Website

**Insight gained** The discovery that a university website, though not selling anything directly online, has a value of tens of millions of dollars per month. Although the university considered the site a valuable resource, they had no idea what monetary value their website was to their organization.

The initial internal guesstimate as to what proportion of traffic constituted prospects was 50%. The remaining 50% was thought to be from existing staff and students. Analysis found the prospects group to be much higher than expected—approximately 75% of all website visits are from potential new students.

**The investigation**   There are two key website engagement goals for the university prospects (potential new students):

- The completion of a request for information form—"RFI submission." This is a one-page form that registers the visitor's interest and results in the university mailing (via regular post) a printed information pack about the university, specific schools, the location, environment, fees, and scholarships.
- The completion of an enrollment application—"enrollment form submission." This is a multi-step form process for a specific degree program enrollment. Detailed personal information is requested, including the applicant's school grades, ethnicity, next of kin information, and so forth. Partial form completions can be saved and submitted at a later date. To complete the process, a fee of $50 is required. This is used to qualify the applicant as being of genuine interest. However, it is not used as part of the e-commerce value because of its relatively small amount.

Both of these engagement goals were monetized as e-commerce transactions—capturing the course name, course ID, and school name of interest as product name, product ID, and category fields, respectively—and sent to Google Analytics as a transaction with a monetary value. The assigned monetary values were $1,000 for an RFI submission and $4,000 for an enrollment form submission.

Applying this pseudo e-commerce technique to the key engagement points, allows the entire e-commerce section of Google Analytics to become available for detailed reporting. The result, shown in Figure 10.9, is an e-commerce report showing the revenue generated per course.

The e-commerce reports bubble up popular courses, provide side-by-side comparison, and show what marketing campaigns are driving the RFI and enrollment submissions. With the new Enhanced Ecommerce reporting feature of Google Analytics, these reports can be very detailed.[5]

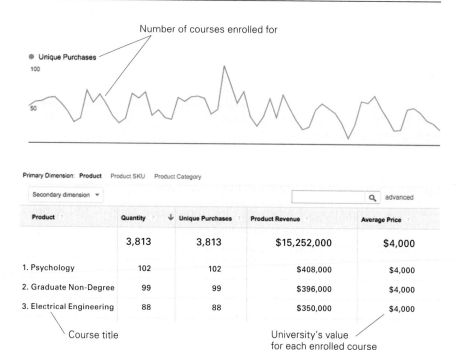

**Figure 10.9** *Monetizing a university website*

For the university, they have become a rich source of information for identifying and understanding the multiple levels of value throughout their website.

As part of the investigation, the crucial prospects segment from the myriad of other visitor types was identified. This was achieved by applying a visitor label (cookie) when such visitors logged in to the private MyUniversity section of the site. The cookie was persistent, meaning that once set it remained in place on the visitor's browser when they returned to the website. This was the case even if the visitor did not log in again. Hence, subsequent visits from staff, interns, and students could be identified whether they logged in or not. Note that all new staff, interns, and students were required to log in at least once while at the university to confirm their account.

Identifying all staff, interns, and student visits allowed the prospects segment to be obtained by a process of elimination (approximately 75% of all visits were from prospects). This enabled the building of reports containing only visit data from prospects—the target group of potential new students—for all marketing activities.

## How Monetary Values Were Calculated

A full econometric study[6] to accurately determine the monetary value of a new student would be based on the course selected, level (graduate or postgraduate), its duration, probability of being completed, additional lifetime revenue, probability of receiving a scholarship, and so forth. Such a study was not feasible for the university at this stage. Therefore, we took a simpler approach to arrive at an approximate value of a new student.

It was generally established in the organization that a student's value was between $10,000 and $30,000 per year—the exact value dependent on all of the above factors. We knew that on average 25% of students who enrolled went on to be accepted and that RFI submissions are four times higher than enrollment submissions. That is, to obtain one new student, the simplified process is

| Anonymous prospects (visitors) | ⇨ | Strong interest shown (RFI form submitted) | ⇨ | Application made (enrollment form submitted) | ⇨ | Student accepted and enrolled |
|---|---|---|---|---|---|---|

and, on average, the numbers for each step are

| 21,000 | ⇨ | 16 | ⇨ | 4 | ⇨ | 1 |
|---|---|---|---|---|---|---|

To ensure the assigned monetary values would be taken seriously throughout the organization, the following method of approximation was agreed upon by the senior leadership team:

- Take the midpoint of the student value ($20,000 per year).
- A prospective student completes *both* an RFI form and the enrollment application process. Although this is not a requirement in the process, intuitively it was agreed this makes sense, as it is unlikely such a major life decision is made without the additional information pack the RFI provides.
- A submitted enrollment and its concomitant RFI request therefore have a combined value of $5,000 (as there is a 1 in 4 chance of being accepted).
- An enrollment submission has four times the value of an RFI submission (as there are four RFI submissions to one enrollment submission). Therefore, a submitted enrollment is valued at $4,000 and a submitted RFI is valued at $1,000.

**What happened next?** Providing a solid reference mark for the number of prospects visiting the website allowed for greater credibility to be achieved throughout the organization for web metrics data. Such data could no longer be dismissed because of a large unknown factor ("The website data is mostly generated from internal staff and students—we can't use this for marketing budgets").

Being able to specifically identify the prospect segment opened up significant budgets for further marketing investment—for example, applying remarketing techniques.[7] Remarketing, also known as behavioral retargeting, allows you to target digital advertising at visitors who have previously visited your website but not yet converted. This works by displaying a targeted ad to such visitors as they browse *other* websites containing Google advertising—for example, a gentle reminder to the visitor that they should revisit the university website to complete an RFI or enrollment submission before the closing date.

Once the visitor converts—or the advertising time or frequency cap is reached—the ad is no longer displayed. Studies have shown that remarketing is very effective at generating repeat visitors compared to standard display banners.[8]

Understanding the monetary value of the university's website had a dramatic effect on the investment for web measurement and the approach to digital marketing in general. For example, because a monetary value was assigned, Google Analytics was able to automatically calculate the value of every page and visit—as described in Chapter 5. Being able to target high-value visitors using specific high-value pages is gold to a digital marketer. This was instantly recognized by leadership and a new centralized team, reporting to the president's office, was formed specifically to understand and take advantage of these insights.

## CASE 4: CONVERSION INSIGHT

| | |
|---|---|
| **Website description** | Europe-based flight comparison engine covering over 700 airlines—also expanding into hotels and car rentals. Travel arrangements can be booked and paid for directly online. |
| **Category** | Travel aggregator; e-commerce. |
| **Client request** | Our AdWords ROI is so low that we cannot justify the overhead of managing the account. Should we close it and focus our efforts on more valuable channels to our business? |

## Who Should Get Credit for a Conversion

**Insight gained** It was discovered that AdWords made a significant yet previously unrecognized contribution to the business bottom line. AdWords visits were being undervalued by as much as 41%.

**The investigation** Senior management considered AdWords advertising (paid search advertising) to be ineffective. In their view, although it drove significant traffic to their website, AdWords was ineffective at driving sales. The AdWords account was about to be closed.

On the surface, AdWords did appear to be underperforming in terms of sales generated and its ROI. On inspection we discovered that was because the business was using a last-click attribution model, where only the last marketing channel in a visitor's path was given credit for generating the sale.

Figure 10.10 represents a person making four visits to the same website and converting (making a purchase in this example) on their final visit. For each visit they arrived via a different referral source. Let's say these are

Visit 1: AdWords click-through, followed by
Visit 2: An organic search, followed by
Visit 3: An affiliate link, followed finally by
Visit 4: An email link from your special offer newsletter that they subscribed to on visit 3.

For this specific referrer path, a last-click model attributes *all* revenue to the email newsletter. The other three referral sources that indirectly contributed to the sale process receive zero credit. For the above scenario, AdWords is not recognized as being a part of the sale—despite the

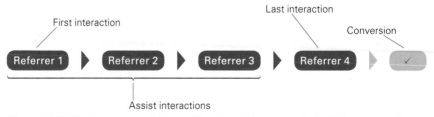

**Figure 10.10** *Visitor path—a visitor making four visits to a website before converting on their last visit*

fact that without it, the visitor might never have arrived at your site in the first place!

All visitor paths were examined to see to what extent this might be a problem for the business—AdWords being a part of the visitor path, but not the last click. Figure 10.11 shows the corresponding report (the multi-channel funnel report). The top of the report (label A) shows that 1,186 sales came from visitors who had AdWords in their path. However, only 785 (66%) had AdWords as their last click. The remaining 401 sales came from visitors who clicked through via an AdWords ad elsewhere in their path.

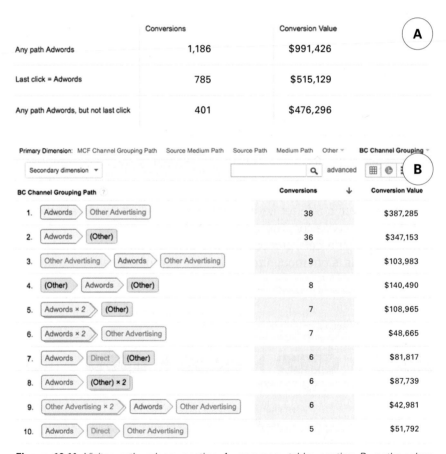

|  | Conversions | Conversion Value |
|---|---|---|
| Any path Adwords | 1,186 | $991,426 |
| Last click = Adwords | 785 | $515,129 |
| Any path Adwords, but not last click | 401 | $476,296 |

Primary Dimension: MCF Channel Grouping Path · Source Medium Path · Source Path · Medium Path · Other ▾ · BC Channel Grouping ▾

| BC Channel Grouping Path | Conversions ↓ | Conversion Value |
|---|---|---|
| 1. Adwords › Other Advertising | 38 | $387,285 |
| 2. Adwords › (Other) | 36 | $347,153 |
| 3. Other Advertising › Adwords › Other Advertising | 9 | $103,983 |
| 4. (Other) › Adwords › (Other) | 8 | $140,490 |
| 5. Adwords × 2 › (Other) | 7 | $108,965 |
| 6. Adwords × 2 › Other Advertising | 7 | $48,665 |
| 7. Adwords › Direct › (Other) | 6 | $81,817 |
| 8. Adwords › (Other) × 2 | 6 | $87,739 |
| 9. Other Advertising × 2 › Adwords › Other Advertising | 6 | $42,981 |
| 10. Adwords › Direct › Other Advertising | 5 | $51,792 |

**Figure 10.11** *Visitor path values: section A, summary table; section B, paths where AdWords is a referral source but not the last click*

In effect, a third of sales were being ignored in evaluating the success of AdWords campaigns. The numbers are significant—almost as much revenue came from this group as from those visitors whose last click was AdWords. If all revenue generated by visitors who had AdWords anywhere in their path (assists + last click) was assigned to AdWords, its ROI would be double. However, this is the opposite extreme to assigning zero credit. The true value will lie somewhere between attributing no value to assisted AdWords visits that convert and attributing the full value for the assist. This is the basis of attribution modeling, discussed in Chapter 6.

Applying some scientific thinking and using attribution modeling, the attributed revenue for *all* referrers in a customer's path was reweighted. The result was a 70% uplift in revenue attributed to AdWords (Figure 10.12).

**What happened next?** As a result of this investigation, the use of the last-click model for assigning credit for a conversion was dropped. Instead, a custom attribution model was applied to all channels based on allocating more credit to the referrer that generated the initial lead. The theory is, in an industry with so many competitors, the initial lead has the highest value; subsequent follow-up visits cement the relationship; by the time of the last click, the decision has already been made.

AdWords advertising not only continued but also received significant investment as a good source of high-value (likely to purchase) traffic. Furthermore, the performance of other channels was analyzed and showed

| | | Last Interaction | | BC Custom | | % change in Conversion Value ▼ (from Last Interaction) |
|---|---|---|---|---|---|---|
| BC Channel Grouping | | Conversions ↓ | Conversion Value | Conversions | Conversion Value | BC Custom |
| 1. | (Other) | 2,164.00 | $19,943,712 | 2,022.64 | $18,609,438 | -6.69% |
| 2. | Direct | 2,007.00 | $14,866,323 | 1,910.31 | $14,285,605 | -3.91% |
| 3. | Other Advertising | 1,691.00 | $15,627,056 | 1,557.70 | $13,636,349 | -12.74% |
| 4. | Adwords | 335.00 | $2,190,567 | 474.03 | $3,714,335 | 69.56% |
| 5. | Organic Search | 208.00 | $1,306,549 | 384.24 | $3,109,262 | 137.98% |
| 6. | Referral | 84.00 | $539,312 | 134.82 | $1,073,150 | 98.99% |
| 7. | Social Network | 6.00 | $29,912 | 11.26 | $75,287 | 151.70% |

**Figure 10.12** *Comparison of two attribution models showing an AdWords uplift of 70%*

similar improvements in ROI when the new attribution model was applied. As a result, new opportunities were identified for YouTube, display advertising (banners), and organic search—see row 5 of Figure 10.12.

☞ *Attribution modeling s discussed in detail in Chapter 6.*

## CASE 5: MARKETING INSIGHT

| | |
|---|---|
| **Website description** | European mail-order company for B2B office, shop, and industrial equipment. There are 40,000 products available online that range from office interiors and warehouse storage equipment to workshop cabinets and personal safety equipment. |
| **Category** | B2B industrial; e-commerce via registered account and invoice. |
| **Client request** | We have maxed out on our AdWords account and are unable to expand its reach further. Can you help? |

### Advertising (AdWords) Optimization

**Insight gained** The AdWords channel was discovered to be underperforming and not well optimized. Optimization improved the click-through rates and conversion rates from these visitors three- and fourfold, respectively. As a result the cost per transaction was halved. This led to a renewed interest in the channel by the company, growing revenue by over 300% (over $600,000 per month in additional revenue).

**The investigation** With AdWords accounting for 60% of traffic and 40% of revenue, AdWords was already established as the largest online revenue generator for this business. However, with an average order value from AdWords visitors in the range $80 to $100, the client had reached its maximum investment capability in the channel. That is, the amount they were prepared to pay AdWords for a visitor to transact—their *cost per transaction*—had grown to the same level. In effect, if they tried to gain more AdWords visitors by broadening their reach (attracting slightly less qualified visitors), the cost per transaction would be higher than the average order value. They would take a loss!

The challenge was, "Can we lower our customer acquisition costs so that we can expand our AdWords reach and gain more customers?"

An optimizing process for the AdWords account was embarked upon to see what potential was available. This consisted of revising the targeted keywords, employing remarketing techniques,[6] and revisiting the bidding

## Cost per Transaction

The *cost per transaction* (CPT) is a metric not directly available within the Google Analytics reports interface. It has to be obtained via a custom report or an API call. The calculated metric is

$$CPT = \frac{AdWords\ cost}{number\ of\ transactions\ from\ AdWords\ visitors}$$

strategy. Figure 10.13 shows the three phases of the AdWords account performance over time for the CPT.

Phase 1: Previous position before any account optimization
Phase 2: AdWords account optimization—reducing the CPT
Phase 3: AdWords growth—broadening targeted keywords to acquire more visitors

Before the beginning of the project (phase 1), the CPT was between $80 and $90. Once optimizing began (phase 2), this value started to drop dramatically and after three months was below half of its original cost. That is, the AdWords advertising budget was halved while maintaining approximately the same number of transactions and revenue—a dramatic improvement for the business.

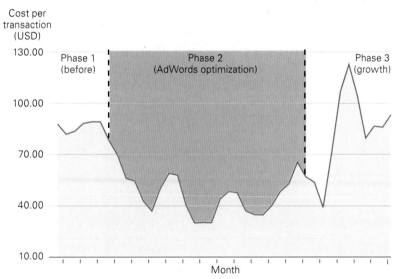

**Figure 10.13** *Cost per transaction—how much it costs to gain a transaction from an AdWords visitor*

This considerable advance was achieved by improving the ad click-through rate and subsequent conversion rate. Figure 10.14a shows the improvement in click-through rate for visitors clicking on ad impressions. Figure 10.14b shows the concurrent improvement in the e-commerce conversion rate—the percentage of AdWords visitors who purchase. These

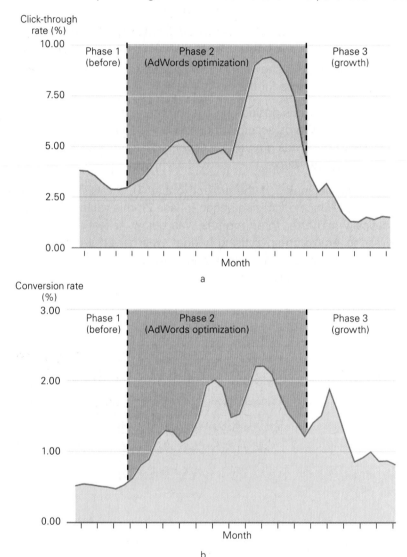

**Figure 10.14** *Better-qualified visitors have (a) a higher click-through rate; (b) a higher conversion rate.*

## Why Optimization Results Vary

The charts shown in Figures 10.13 through 10.15 display undulating patterns—not a smooth S-shaped curve of continuous optimization. This is due to the experimental nature of the optimization process. There is no guaranteed fix for improvement. It requires an iterative process of incremental change, data analysis, learning, and readjustment.

are dramatic results—the click-through rate increased threefold while the conversion rate increased fourfold!

**What happened next?** Creating three- and fourfold efficiencies in marketing campaigns gained the attention of the senior management board. With their confidence in the data and an optimized AdWords account, phase 3 involved a large investment in the channel. By broadening the list of targeted keywords that advertisements were placed on, the business was able to reach a much larger audience.

By definition, a broader audience equals a less qualified audience. Hence during phase 3 you see the CPT rising again in Figure 10.13 due to a drop in click-through rate and conversion rate. This is to be expected. The difference now, however, is that the audience and customer base are much larger. Hence the revenue generated is greater. Figure 10.15 shows this happening over time—the growth in revenue is three times higher

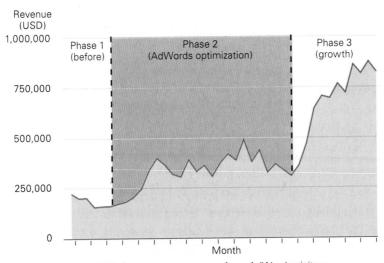

**Figure 10.15** E-commerce revenue from AdWords visitors

than at the beginning ($600,000 per month greater). This could not have been achieved during phase 1, as the CPT of the unoptimized account would have exceeded any profit made.

## CASE 6: MARKETING INSIGHT

| | |
|---|---|
| **Website description** | European finance company for businesses and consumers. Website contains content for branding purposes and an online banking section for customers. |
| **Category** | Finance—both personal and business. |
| **Client request** | Our senior executives are struggling to understand the marketing performance of our website. We need to report website insights to the board for our annual review. Can you help? |

### Understanding Channel Performance

**Insight gained**  For the company's annual review, a detailed breakdown of visitor acquisition costs (the *cost per visit*) was produced. The summary chart is shown in Figure 10.16. Prior to this analysis, only rudimentary visitor numbers had been reported.

**The investigation**  In the first instance, campaign tracking was implemented to ensure all marketing campaigns were tracked correctly. Following this, the cost per visit KPI was calculated by dividing the channel costs by the number of channel visits—with one alteration: adjusting for bounced visitors. That is:

$$\text{cost per visit} = \frac{\text{channel marketing cost}}{\text{number of non-bounced channel visits}}$$

For this case study website, a bounced visitor was considered a mistake, or a failure. That is, the organization defined a well-targeted visitor (a non-bounced visitor) as one that wished to do more than view a single page or—for a single page containing a loan calculator widget—wished to use and interact with that widget. To obtain the number of non-bounced visits, the prebuilt segment within Google Analytics was used.

Channel marketing costs were obtained from the organization's marketing department. As we wanted to compare the effectiveness of the

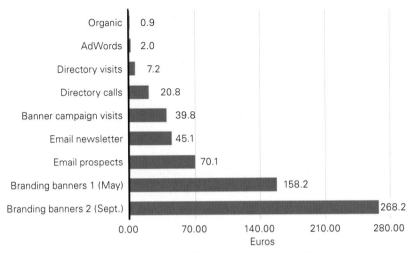

**Figure 10.16** *Breakdown of website visitor acquisition costs*

marketing channels, any associated setup costs were excluded by specifying the following criteria:

- Organic—because of the long incubation period required for SEO, the total SEO agency fee for a 12-month period was divided by the total organic traffic received for the same period.
- AdWords—only media spend was included. All agency management fees were excluded.
- Directory listing—only the listing fee was included. All agency design and management fees were excluded.
- Banners—only media spend was included. All agency design and management fees were excluded.
- Email—only the cost for sending the emails was included. Mailing list purchase fees were excluded.

☛ *Implementing campaign tracking is a key requirement of a best-practice Google Analytics setup. It ensures all marketing campaigns and channels are tracked correctly. See Chapter 6 for more details.*

In addition to the marketing cost breakdown, the proportion of traffic coming from existing customers versus prospects was investigated. Clearly the marketing team wished to target prospects (customer development and retention was managed elsewhere in the organization), and there was a suspicion that AdWords money was being wasted on attracting click-throughs from existing customers—see sidebar.

To examine this scenario, a segment for existing customers was defined as those who log in to their online banking service. This was achieved by setting a custom label as a persistent cookie when such visitors logged in (see the section "Understanding Segmentation and Its Importance" in Chapter 5"). If these visitors returned to the website yet did not log in, they could still be identified by the existence of the customer cookie. Customers were known to be active within a 30-day period. Therefore, 60 days was allowed for before beginning analysis, to ensure all customers were tracked.

The results are shown in Figure 10.17 and reveal that over half of all traffic to the website is from existing customers. Figure 10.16 was therefore revisited and the "customers only" segment applied. This indeed revealed that a consistent one-third of AdWords visitors were existing customers. This pushes the *cost per visit* up to €2.7 per non-bounced visit—a significant change, though still extremely small compared to the cost of other channels.

**What happened next?** Figure 10.16 shows the very broad range of visitor acquisition costs the organization was paying. Organic and AdWords search engine marketing are the clear winners—being the cheapest by far to acquire (less than 1% of the cost of banner branding advertising!). As

### Why Would Existing Customers Click an Ad?

It can be common for existing customers to click on your AdWords ad rather than type your web address directly into their browser. This is due to modern browsers employing an *omnibar* as the address bar. The omnibar combines the URL address box with a search box. That way, visitors can type in a web address or something they want to search for in the same place.

Within Firefox and Chrome,[9] the default search engine used for the onmibar is google.com. Hence if a visitor types your company name in the omnibar, rather than your web address, a search is performed, with the top-placed result likely to be your AdWords ad. The visitor clicks your well-targeted ad to go to your website.

The same process can happen if there is a typo in the URL the visitor entered: the browser conducts a Google search to find a match.

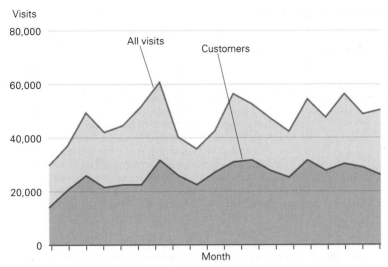

**Figure 10.17** *Customers account for more than half of all website visits.*

a result of this investigation, the branding banners were dropped and the savings invested in further SEO (organic traffic) and increased AdWords spend. This was a significant sum of money—on the order of hundreds of thousands of dollars for the year.

In addition, more resource was provided for email marketing, to experiment with improved newsletter design (A/B and multivariate testing) as well as different email database lists.

For the issue of 33% of AdWords visitors being existing customers, not prospects as initially intended, the increased expense was understood and accepted by the management board. The reasoning was that competitors were also bidding on the company's brand terms. Hence, if their ad was not visible to customers following this path, there was a strong chance of the customer visiting a competitor's website.

## SPEAKING OF INSIGHTS...

| When I hear this... | I reply with... |
| --- | --- |
| If you were to analyze our website for the first time, what is the first thing you would do? | The first requirement for *any* third party to be able to help you is for them to understand your organization's business model, online objectives, knowledge level, and available resources. Spend time with that person or team so that they become an extended yet integrated arm of the business—not an outsider whose input ends when they leave the room.<br><br>Assuming that relationship is in place and that your data quality is being monitored and is good, I focus on a handful of quick wins that make a difference to the organization—even if it is a small difference.<br><br>Small, incremental steps are easier to achieve, communicate, absorb, and act upon. Summed together, their impact is often significant.<br><br>For example, knowing that half your web traffic is from existing customers, or that two-thirds of all visitors are bouncing away with no interaction, is a key insight the marketing team can use immediately for assessing campaign performance. |
| Which insights get the biggest buy-in from senior executives? | Anything with a monetary value gets immediate attention from senior executives. However, avoid quoting metrics in isolation—for example, "We generated $X million last month in online sales." That fact will already be known from other sources and often results in a "so what?" response from your audience.<br><br>Instead, tie that number to information *unknown* to the business—ror example, "$X million (45%) comes from visitors whose first language is not English, when we only have English content."<br><br>Even for non-ecommerce websites, per visit and per page values are very powerful. Knowing each visitor to your site is worth on average $5 but some are more valuable than others gets attention. "Who are more valuable and how do we get more?" is usually the next question. So be prepared for suggested next steps. |
| What is the hardest thing to analyze and gain insights from? | A non-ecommerce website poses an insights challenge because there is no direct monetary value involved. Therefore, the first step is to monetize it.<br><br>Case study 3 of this chapter is a great example of the impact doing this can have. Adding well thought through (though still approximate) monetary values to two key processes brought huge credibility to the measurement project. As a result, six-figure sums were invested in digital marketing—where previously there was little investment—and a new team was hired to take the organization's digital strategy to the next level. |

## CHAPTER 10 REFERENCES

1    According to Nielsen's research for Q4 2013, 89% of consumer media time on mobile is spent within mobile apps, 11% on mobile web: www.nielsen.com/us /en/reports/2014/an-era-of-growth-the-cross-platform-report.html.
     However, this metric is a little misleading considering the three main usages of mobile content consumption (email, social, news) are better suited to apps rather than browsing. A better metric would be to filter this data by excluding those activities. I suspect the split would then not be as great as 90:10.

2    The vast majority of websites have very low conversion rates—typically 3%. However, many more visitors than this will start the process: www.e-tailing.com/content/wp-content/uploads/2013/04/pressrelease _merchantsurvey2013.pdf.

3    There are no precise dates when the millennial generation starts and ends. Researchers and commentators use birth years ranging from the early 1980s to the early 2000s: http://en.wikipedia.org/wiki/Millennials.

4    *Times Higher Education* produces global university performance tables to judge universities across core missions—teaching, research, knowledge transfer, and international outlook: www.timeshighereducation.co.uk /world-university-rankings/2013-14/world-ranking.

5    Google Analytics Enhanced Ecommerce reporting feature: https://support.google.com/analytics/answer/6014841

6    "Econometrics is the intersection of economics, mathematics, and statistics. Econometrics adds empirical content to economic theory allowing theories to be tested and used for forecasting and policy evaluation." Taken from http://en.wikipedia.org/wiki/Econometrics.

7    Remarketing lets you show ads to users who've previously visited your website as they browse the web: https://en.wikipedia.org/wiki/Behavioral_targeting and https://support.google.com/adwords/answer/2453998.

8    Research from Criteo found that the average click-through rate (CTR) for retargeted ads to be ten times that for normal display ads (0.7% CTR compared to 0.07%).
     A comScore study comparing the different placement strategies of display advertising found that retargeting generated the highest lift in search queries, at 1,046%. Site visitation within four weeks of ad exposure was up 726%.
     Taken from https://econsultancy.com/reports/display-retargeting-buyers-guide.

9    Browser usage statistics: http://gs.statcounter.com/#desktop+mobile -browser-ww-monthly-201405-201405-bar

# Appendix:
# Terminology Explained

**The definitions presented here are** specifically in relation to their usage with Google Analytics and digital analytics in general.

## A

### A/B split testing

The science of experimenting with the display of different versions of content to different sets of visitors—one version (A) shown to one set of visitors and another version (B) shown to others. The purpose is to statistically determine which version is favored over another by your *customers* and *potential customers*, rather than guessing.

Version preference is determined by measuring the difference in subsequent goal conversions. The version that drives more visitors to a call to action—such as a click on an "add to cart," "contact us," or "read more" button—is the preferred version. This is a statistical method that utilizes sampling techniques (Which visitors see which version?) and significance tests (Is the measured preference real or by chance?). It can be applied to content on your website, app, or advertising campaign.

Although the technique is often called A/B testing (or just split testing), more than two versions (A/B/C/D . . .) can be tested in the experiment.

## AdWords, AdSense, and DoubleClick

These are advertising platforms from Google.

AdWords is an auction system for text ads where advertisers bid to have their ad displayed based on a user's search term. It is a type of *contextual* advertising. The advertiser only pays if their ad is clicked on—there is no charge for display. Hence, the format is also often referred to as pay-per-click or cost-per-click advertising. AdWords ads are served alongside organic Google search results and other Google properties, such as YouTube and Google Maps. They can also be displayed on Google partner sites such as AOL and other portals.

AdSense is a tool for Google partners (for example, portal sites) to manage how Google AdWords ads are displayed on their site. Partner sites that display AdWords ads receive a share of the revenue generated by any visitor click-throughs.

DoubleClick is a tool for advertisers to manage display (banner) advertising. As with AdWords, DoubleClick uses the technique of contextual advertising for displaying banners relevant to a visitor's query or preference.

## API

Abbreviation for *application programming interface*. An API is a standardized protocol to share data between applications—for example, between Google Analytics and an Excel worksheet. Google is a stalwart of the API method and virtually all of its products provide one on a free-to-use basis (within limits). For Google Analytics there are developer libraries available for the end user to experiment with API calls, and there are third-party vendors with prebuilt applications to achieve certain tasks.

A common use of Google Analytics APIs is the extraction of data into a simplified dashboard format.

## attribution modeling

*Attribution* is the term used to describe who gets the credit for a conversion. That is, for a visitor that comes to your website multiple times via different referral sources, which referrer should get the credit when that visitor becomes a customer? Historically, the last referral source has been assigned the credit, as it was the easiest to determine.

Attribution modeling allows the credit to be *shared* among some or all of the referral sources. For a visitor who converts on their third visit, you can attribute 33% to each referral, split as 40%, 20%, 40%, or use some other model. Attribution is discussed in detail in Chapter 6.

## B

### bounce rate
The percentage of visitors that bounce away from your site—that is, view only a single page with no other *in-page* interaction.

Generally, a bounced visit is considered a poor user experience, and therefore the bounce rate is often a KPI that organizations wish to minimize. The hypothesis is that a visitor, even with a low interest level, would at least click onto a second page or interact with something within a page, such as a loan calculator widget.

The reasoning is valid so long as you do not deliberately design your site to cater for a bounced experience. Even if you create the perfect one-page article, your visitors will likely wish to tell you this (rate or comment on it), read related articles, connect with the author, share it with others, subscribe, click a related ad, and so forth. Any such action results in a visitor's not bouncing.

## C

### campaign tracking
Required to track specific marketing campaigns. The method consists of appending parameters to landing page URLs. This can become very precise—for example, a visitor click-through from a text link in an email campaign that is sent to your California customers only.

Up to five campaign parameters can be specified: *source* (where you place your ad); *medium* (the digital channel used); *campaign* (the campaign name); *content* (type or version of content used); *term* (keywords targeted) if the ad is related to search marketing.

These parameters are not required for AdWords if your account is linked to Google Analytics. Campaign tracking is described in detail in Chapter 6.

### channel
A high-level grouping of campaign information. For example, the mediums "cpc," "ppc," and "paidsearch" are all classified into the "Paid Search" channel by Google Analytics.

Often the terms *channel* and *medium* are used interchangeably. However, they are subtly different within Google Analytics reports. See also *campaign tracking* and *medium*.

## conversion (synonymous with goal)

Any action that is considered a successful visitor engagement. These are pageview or event specific. Examples: a completed transaction (becoming a customer); a submitted contact request form (becoming a lead); the sharing of your content on a social network (becoming an brand advocate).

Up to 20 goals can be defined for each report set in Google Analytics, and each can be monetized by adding a goal value. The *conversion rate* is the number of completed goals divided by the number of visits, expressed as a percentage.

## cookie

All the main web analytics tools use cookies as the basis for their tracking methodology. A cookie is a small text file that a web server transmits to a web browser so that it can keep track of the user's activity on a specific website. The visitor's browser stores the cookie information on the local hard drive as name–value pairs. The latest version of Google Analytics uses a single cookie to anonymously identify a visitor—using an anonymous visitor ID.

## cost-per-click advertising (CPC)

A method of paying for advertising based on the number of click-throughs received (not the display of the ad). Almost all search engines use an auction bidding system to sell advertising alongside organic search results.

Also referred to as a pay-per-click (PPC) ad model, this technique is common for selling advertising space on sites in general—for example, news portals. Google dominates the market with its systems AdWords, AdSense, and DoubleClick, though the originator of the method was GoTo.com (acquired by Yahoo! in 2003). See also *AdWords, AdSense, and DoubleClick*.

## cross-domain tracking

The tracking of a visitor that traverses your subdomains or third-party domains, such as the following path:

www.example.com ⇨ shop.example.com ⇨ www.paymentsite.com ⇨

thankyou.example.com

If cross-domain tracking is not correctly set up, you can double-count your visits and lose valuable referral information. This is because the tracking method employed (cookies) is specific to the exact hostname of the website setting them.

### custom dimensions and metrics (*see also* visitor labeling)

All Google Analytics reports consist of showing dimensions. By default, there are over 200 available. You can extend this list by defining your own—typically by uploading data to populate your reports, or applying a label to differentiate and segment your visitors. Examples include defining a customer lifetime value; adding author and subject categories for publishing sites; and labeling your high-value customers.

The free version of Google Analytics allows you to define 20 custom dimensions and 20 custom metrics. For Premium, these limits are 200 and 200, respectively.

### D

### dimensions and metrics

Google Analytics reports display two types of information—metrics and dimensions. A metric is a number—for example, the number of visitors to your website, the number of conversions from a campaign, the amount of revenue gained, or the number of new leads generated. A dimension is textual information—for example, the countries your visitors come from, the list of top-performing pages, the most effective campaign names, your best selling products, and so on.

See also *custom dimensions and metrics*.

### E

### event tracking

Events are *in-page* visitor actions, as opposed to pageviews—for example, interacting with a loan calculator, scrolling through an image carousel, or zooming or panning around a map. Events are not tracked by default in Google Analytics and therefore must be defined and set up by you. An event can be classified with a category, action, label, and value.

### F

### funnel visualization

Directly analogous to a traditional sales funnel. In Google Analytics you can visualize the steps visitors take in order to convert (become a new lead or customer). For example, you can examine the drop-off rate of a shopping cart purchase.

## G

### GATC

The Google Analytics tracking code (GATC) is the snippet of code that is required to track visitors and users. For web pages, this is JavaScript code. Mobile apps use their own programming environment (Objective-C, Java, and so forth).

### goal (*see* conversion)

## K

### key performance indicator (KPI)

Key performance indicators are a set of metrics (defined by senior leadership) to measure progress toward organizational goals. For digital analytics, I define a KPI as *a measurement used to evaluate success.*

This is similar to defining a goal for Google Analytics reporting. The difference is that a goal is the language of your analysts. KPIs are the language of your business. KPIs are the success metrics for the business overall and often combine data that is outside of the Google Analytics realm, such as staffing levels or call center volume.

## L

### landing page

The first page a visitor views during their visit. Also referred to as the entrance page.

## M

### medium

When you define a marketing campaign, you can specify up to five parameters for Google Analytics reporting (see *campaign tracking*). The *medium* parameter refers to the category, or type, of content that contains a link to your site, such as "email," "paid search," or "organic search."

*Medium* is a precise value that may be set by the Google Analytics tracking code or defined explicitly by the user. It should not be confused with *channel*, which is a higher-level grouping of campaigns. Campaign tracking is discussed in Chapter 6.

# O

## organic search engine

The main search engines (Google, Bing, Yahoo, and so forth) return two types of results for a visitor's search query—organic results and paid results. Paid results are just that, advertisements (see *cost-per-click advertising*). Organic results, on the other hand, are earned results. That is, you cannot pay for placement; they are provided free.

Your web page ranking in the organic results—whether your page appears at the number 1, 10, or 1,000 position—is determined by multiple factors. The key ones are *relevancy*—does your page contain content relevant to the search term used?—and *authority*—how authoritative is your page compared to the plethora of other web pages of similar content (often determined by seeing how many other web sites link to your page or mention your content)?

My description is a huge simplification of a complex subject in computer science, one that employs the latest artificial intelligence techniques so that a computer network, such as Google, can emulate what a human's intent is when they type in a search query. An industry has grown up around improving a site's search engine visibility, known as search engine optimization (SEO).

## outbound link

A link, placed on your website, that points to a third-party domain. The third-party domain can be another web property you own or completely separate, such as a reseller or partner website. A visitor who clicks on an outbound link leaves your website. Hence, outbound links are not tracked in Google Analytics by default—you need to make a modification to your tracking code.

# P

## pageview (*see also* virtual pageview)

This is the default Google Analytics tracking method (hit type) for websites and is the fundamental measurement dimension. Reports also show *unique pageviews*. This aggregates pageviews that are generated by the same user during the same session. A unique pageview therefore represents the number of sessions during which that page was viewed one or more times.

Note that if a visitor returns to the same page URL, but the page title has subsequently changed, this is treated as a new unique pageview. That is, the combination of URL and page title defines if a page is unique in your Google Analytics reports.

# R

### referrer and referral

A referrer is a source of traffic to your website. Generally, this means any traffic source that is not a direct visit (where the visitor typed in your web address directly—either from memory or using a browser bookmark). A referrer can be from a specific campaign email, organic search engine, advertising campaign, another website, app link, and so forth.

However, Google Analytics automatically classifies referrer visits from organic search engines and AdWords (if linked). Therefore, the term *referral* is used specifically to identify those visits that have come via *another* website linking to you.

For Google Analytics to work effectively at identifying your traffic sources and referrers, campaign tracking must be set up. Campaign tracking is discussed in Chapter 6.

# S

### site search

The term used to describe your internal search engine, if you have such a facility on your website.

### STAG

The acronym I use for the site tracking assessment and guidelines document. It is an installation document that guides the web development team on what needs to be done in order to provide a best-practice setup (a data quality score of above 50). It sets out the required tracking methodology and the reasoning for the requirement. Building a STAG document is describe in Chapter 3.

# U

## Universal Analytics

The new name for the Google Analytics tracking code (as of May 2014). The term refers to the fact that Google Analytics is no longer simply a web measurement tool; it can be used to collect data from any Internet-connected device, such as mobile apps, barcode scanners, event turnstiles, parking lots, door sensors, and so forth. The potential for Universal Analytics is discussed in Chapter 6.

## URL

Uniform resource locator—this is the address as written in your browser address bar. It consists of multiple parts. The default tracking behavior for Google Analytics is to report on everything after the domain name, with the exception of the fragment (anchor). The domain can also be included in reports with the use of an include filter.

http://www.oursite.com/products/page1.php?size=large#marker

| protocol | host-name | domain name | path name (path and filename) | query string (name–value pairs) | fragment or anchor |

# V

## virtual pageview

The substitution of an alternative pageview URL for the default URL captured. Virtual pageviews can be used if a real URL is not generated by a visitor's behavior, or to construct more meaningful URLs than would otherwise be reported.

A typical example is when submitting a form, such as a subscription request. If the form URL does not change when a visitor submits their information, Google Analytics cannot differentiate between a form view and a form submission. This is overcome by sending a virtual pageview on the form submission.

## visitor labeling (*see also* custom dimensions and metrics)

This is the application of a label used as a form of classification. The purpose is to allow you to segment your reports based on your own classification names. For example, a label named Visitor Type can have the values Customer, Prospect, Staff, Student, and so forth.

Visitor labels can be applied at four levels:

- Visitor—the label is associated with the visitor on the current and any return visits (applied via a cookie). For example, Visitor Type = "customer."
- Session—the label is associated with all data hits of the visit for which it has been set. For example, Logged-In = "yes."
- Hit—the label is associated with the single hit (a page or an event) for which it has been set. For example, Page Interaction = "none."
- Product—the label is associated with the product for which it has been set (Enhanced Ecommerce only). For example, Product Meta = "discounted item."

Up to 20 different labels can be set in the free version of Google Analytics (200 for Premium). Each label can have unlimited names. The method to apply labels is via setting a custom dimension.

# Index

Note: Page numbers followed by *f* refer to a figure. Page numbers followed by *t* refer to a table.

## A

A/B testing
  in building the process, 72, 73
  terminology explained, 299
  tracking methods and testing, 169–170
access control, and data responsibilities, 196–197
account administrators, recommendation on people and access, 96
account setup, 95–98
accountable KPIs, 241
accuracy considerations, 192–195
achievement KPIs, 237–239, 238*t*
acquisition reports, 121
action insights, 23
actionable KPIs, 241
ad management software, Premium compared to free, 32–33
AddThis, 189
AdSense, 189, 300

AdWords
  advertising optimization, marketing insight, 288–292
  conversion insight, 284–288
  data and assessment of scorecard, 100–101
  and explicit values campaign tracking, 161
  integration of Google Analytics data, 134–135
  Premium compared to free, 33
  and return on investment, 248
  terminology explained, 300
affiliate and partner performance, calculated KPI, 247
agency visits, removal of, for data protection, 198
aggregate, non-personal data, privacy color-coding, 182
analysts
  conversion optimization analysts, 219, 221